BOOKS BY SELDEN RODMAN

History and Travel
THE CARIBBEAN
THE GUATEMALA TRAVELER
HAITI: THE BLACK REPUBLIC
MEXICAN JOURNAL
THE MEXICO TRAVELER
THE PERU TRAVELER
QUISQUEYA: A HISTORY OF THE DOMINICAN REPUBLIC
THE ROAD TO PANAMA
SOUTH AMERICA OF THE POETS

Art
CONVERSATIONS WITH ARTISTS
THE EYE OF MAN
THE FRESCOES OF OROZCO
HORACE PIPPIN: A NEGRO PAINTER IN AMERICA
THE INSIDERS
PORTRAIT OF THE ARTIST AS AN AMERICAN
RENAISSANCE IN HAITI

Verse
THE AIRMEN
THE AMAZING YEAR
DEATH OF THE HERO
LAWRENCE: THE LAST CRUSADE
MORTAL TRIUMPH AND OTHER POEMS
THE REVOLUTIONISTS

Music
THE HEART OF BEETHOVEN

Anthologies
A NEW ANTHOLOGY OF MODERN POETRY
ONE HUNDRED AMERICAN POEMS
ONE HUNDRED MODERN POEMS
THE POETRY OF FLIGHT
WAR AND THE POET (WITH RICHARD EBERHART)

SOUTH AMERICA OF THE POETS

by Selden Rodman

Illustrated by Bill Negron

Southern Illinois University Press

Carbondale and Edwardsville

Feffer & Simons, Inc.

London and Amsterdam

ARCT
URUS
BOOKS ®

To
Jorge Edwards in Chile,
Bill and Roz Brister in Bolivia,
Norman Thomas di Giovanni in Argentina,
John Davis in Peru,
Virgilio Nova in Brazil,
and Nena Ossa, wherever you are

NOTE OF ACKNOWLEDGMENT

It would be impossible to mention by name and thank adequately all the individuals and organizations who helped us during our two-month swing through the twelve countries discussed in this book, or on our previous visits to Chile, Peru, and Bolivia. Without the help of Miss Lida Livingston and Braniff International, which flew us without a hitch in time and with every possible courtesy through the various countries on their route, our trip would not have been possible; and the same applies to Luis Zalamea, whose South American Travel Organization assisted us with hotels and other facilities along the way. Among the many officials of government tourist bureaus, Jorge Ortiz in Colombia, César Cenzlar in Argentina, and Jorge Cariaga Rada in Bolivia were outstanding in their helpfulness. And we owe a special debt of thanks as well to Avianca Airlines in Colombia, Alberto Farias, U.S. General Manager, and Gray Wilson in New York, and to the management of the Tororica Hotel in Surinam.

CONTENTS

FOREWORD

South America of the Poets? A continent exploding with poets? Hardly —though there are so many in the chambers of government, and in the law and learned professions, that it sometimes seems so.

Then do these poets write superior poems? Only a handful do. Pablo Neruda of Chile may be the most widely read and admired poet alive in the world today. Jorge Luis Borges of Argentina, Carlos Drummond de Andrade of Brazil, Nicanor Parra of Chile, the late César Vallejo of Peru, are esteemed beyond their borders by other poets and intellectuals. But most are no better and no worse than the mediocre poets in other lands, and less of a force in their homelands than such masters of fiction as Gabriel García Márquez, of Colombia, Julio Cortázar, of Argentina, and Jorge Amado, of Brazil, who describe their societies with poetic imagination.

The fact is, however, that poetry, in the broad sense of the word, is woven more deeply into the fabric of these "technologically backward" societies, is more respected by the public, than with us. Moreover, as we begin to suspect the value of technology and its capacity to make us happy or fulfilled, the more we want to know—or need to know—about poetry, and about countries where poets are friends of ministers, and sometimes ministers themselves.

In the South American context (military dictatorships excepted) it is unusual to find a political figure who has *not* written poetry, or does not number poets among his friends. That Chile's Foreign Minister turns out to be a friend of Pablo Neruda, and that Gabriela Mistral once lived with the family of the same Minister, is part of the context. Neruda himself was once a Consul General abroad, and later a Senator. The great Brazilian novelist, João Guimarães Rosa, spent the better part of his life in the diplomatic corps and at the time of his death headed the Frontiers Service in the Ministry of Foreign Affairs. Rómulo Gallegos, Venezuela's foremost novelist, became that country's first freely elected President. Former President Fernando Belaúnde Terry of Peru is more likely to be remembered for the visionary poetry of the book in which he sought to revive Bolívar's continental dream than for the little he was permitted to accomplish while in office.

To understand what the poets and other artists of South America are up to, without talking about the social and political context, is impossible. And by the same token, where the artist is repressed, or underground, or in exile, it is vital to appreciate why this is so. In fact, it is more important, culturally speaking, to understand the politics of tumultuous countries like Bolivia and Paraguay, than of countries like Chile and Venezuela where artists move about freely and write as they please. But another reason for devoting considerable space to the way the countries are governed is this: A book written about American culture for Americans assumes a basic knowledge of American institutions; in the case of a book for North Americans about South America, the contrary assumption, unfortunately, must be made—total ignorance of what makes each of the dozen southern nations different from one another. Apart from John Gunther's *Inside South America*, written five years ago and with little reference to the national cultures, there is no available survey of the continent's politics.

To a somewhat slighter degree, the intelligent reader's unfamiliarity with the tangible properties of South American culture must be assumed. In this department there is no John Gunther to fall back on. There are old guidebooks, to be sure, that tick off the mountain peaks and churches; the best of them, Earl Parker Hansen's three-volume *New World Guide*, is more than thirty years out of date and doesn't include the Guianas. So it seemed worthwhile to explore the physical attractions of these countries and their folk arts—as further referents to their cultural identities. The poets and poet-novelists identify, naturally, as much with this background as with the sociopolitical foreground—in many cases more so.

Finally, it seemed important both to me and to Bill Negron (who made most of the trips with me) to accept frankly the fact that we were Americans—North Americans—and tourists, at least in the sense that our mobility was limited by a short supply of time and money. We determined to make virtues of those circumstances in so far as possible. As tourists we could at least help readers familiar with the major sites of interest to relate that knowledge to the cultural scene; and then we could go as far beyond the famous places as possible. As Americans, we would be in a good position to eavesdrop on those compatriots professionally involved in protecting American economic, political, and cultural interests. Their prejudices (good and bad), their provincialisms, their hang-ups, inevitably coincided with some of our own. Their shortcomings might provide some explanation for our glaring failure to project the nonmaterialistic side of American civilization in Latin America. And their virtues might throw some light on Latin America's failure to solve its economic and political problems or project its cultural image beyond the confines of the Hispanic world.

S. R.

These Spaniards are all an odd set; the very word "Spaniard" has a curious, conspiratory, Guy-Fawkish twang to it. And yet, I dare say, Spaniards in the main are as good folks as any in Duxbury, Massachusetts.

—HERMAN MELVILLE, *Benito Cereno*

During one of my lectures a Latin American student, Caesare Innocente, said, "Professor Peter, I'm afraid that what I want to know is not answered by all my studying. I don't know whether the world is run by smart men who are, how you Americans say, putting us on, or by imbeciles who really mean it."

—LAURENCE J. PETER, *The Peter Principle*

Seven fat years, and the people will thank God; seven lean years, and they will blame the United States.

—JOHN MANDER, *The Unrevolutionary Society: The Power of Latin American Conservatism in a Changing World*

I

JORGE LUIS BORGES' ARGENTINA

I arrived in Buenos Aires with as many prejudices as the next man. On the occasions when I thought of Argentina at all, I visualized it in these stereotypes: Gauchos on the pampas riding herd with rope and knife on other gauchos—the *Martín Fierro* syndrome. Mobs of hysterical unemployed beating up mobs of unionized workers, and vice versa, with bemedaled colonels and admirals watching the fun from balconies—the Juan Perón syndrome. A blind poet in a library, oblivious to the rest of the world, writing enigmatic stories about time—the Jorge Luis Borges syndrome.

I loved Borges' stories, even though many of them mystified me. Behind the intricacy of their plots, behind their philosophical implications— that time is circular, that everything that happens has happened before and will happen again—I sensed a human warmth transcending Borges' passion for literature, an affection for Argentina transcending (if indeed it wasn't dictated by) this writer's despair over the country's tawdry politics and its capital's dreary outskirts. In Chile I had talked with Pablo Neruda about Borges, and I could sympathize with that earthy poet's comment that "Literature should be like a good beefsteak, not a stew of other literatures," yet I found Borges' vision no less poetic, no less humorous, no less tragic.

1

Buenos Aires and Carcassonne

Since I wanted above all else in Argentina to meet Borges and talk with him, I asked a taxi driver at the airport to drive Bill Negron and me directly to the National Library. The taxi driver was our first pleasant surprise. During the two weeks we were to be in Argentina (in and out of it, for we were to make short visits from Buenos Aires to Paraguay and Uruguay before leaving) he left us only at night, arranged all our trips, and even talked the Tourist Ministry finally into paying for his own fares. He spoke excellent English and he wasted no time in intro-ducing himself: "My name is Hector Carcassonne." He was of English not French extraction, he added, and proud of it. And he was currently engaged in paying for the seven-thousand-dollar Dodge Valiant he was driving. He didn't waste any time, either, in telling us that the current authoritarian government of General Onganía was wholly to his liking— "the best thing that has happened to Argentina in a long time."

"You don't regret losing your vote?" Bill asked him.

"How could I regret it," he said scornfully, "when voting in Argentina meant nothing but choosing among three hundred do-nothing parties and confirming a corrupt Congress?"

"Isn't it Perón's pitch?" I said.

"Perón," he answered, "built things, but he was just as corrupt as the congressmen, and he used the public funds for display and self-glorifica-tion. Those who followed him were weaklings or idiots or both. This man [Carcassonne always referred to Onganía that way] gets things done with no fuss and no kickbacks. He saw that the deputies and senators, with their inflated salaries, were drones, wasting our taxes on projects in-tended only to perpetuate themselves in office. So this man opened the doors, marched them out, locked the doors, and removed them from the payroll—permanently. Then he paid off the public debt for the first time in history and started Argentina living on what it actually earns. No more waste, no more debates, no more strikes. Everybody goes about his business, and the government is where it should be, in the background, assuring stability and order only when it has to."

"By repressing—?"

"No repression!"

"Carcassonne, you couldn't be a government agent, could you?"

"If this man offered me anything," he snorted, "I'd go underground. But the press is free. When the students went out on strike, this man just let them go—until they got tired of the vacation and came back. They had no real grievances, of course."

We were driving by one of those vast shantytowns which cluster around all South American capitals. The Chileans call them *callampas* (mushrooms), the Peruvians *barriadas* (districts), the Brazilians *favelas* (little bean flowers), and so on; but the Argentinians call them what they are—*villas miserias*. Rising straight out of the middle of this particular *miseria* was a towering stainless steel apartment block.

"To rehouse the slum dwellers?" I asked Carcassonne.

"That was the idea," he said, "but they hadn't been in twenty-four hours before the plumbing fixtures were taken out and sold, the light bulbs and sockets disappeared, and finally even the aluminum window frames and doors were beginning to be ripped off. The police had to come in and drive them out. Now the buildings are rented to the middle class who know how to take care of them, and pay the rent."

The immense city, which we were now beginning to penetrate, seems more like New York, Chicago, or Philadelphia than any Latin-American city—even Mexico. Poverty, except for that introductory glimpse near the airport, is well concealed; as in Los Angeles, it gets shunted so far away horizontally that most visitors never see it, and, as in Los Angeles, the sheer volume of middle-class affluence is staggering to behold. Everybody, at least in the streets, seems to be young and swinging. The girls with their wild flowing hair and miniskirts, the men open-shirted with sideburns, flow from block to block like a torrent. Toward the center of the city the buildings are uniformly six stories high, brick faced with cement to look like cut stone. With their balconies and sidewalk cafés they give much the appearance of Paris or Madrid. There is no dearth of parks, ornamental fountains, heroic bronze monuments. The boulevards are immense. One of them, Avenida 9 de Julio, is said to be the world's broadest, with lanes for sixteen cars abreast. Pedestrians are wholly at the mercy of motorists, who indeed gun their cars when they see one of the helpless creatures trying to scurry across an avenue that has no traffic island. The policemen, unlike the kindly *carabinieri* in Santiago de Chile, are not the pedestrians' allies; they look like uniformed bullies and their only mission seems to be to keep the vehicles moving—fast.

Norman Thomas di Giovanni

Arriving at the Library we were informed that Borges was "being taped" by some French radio-TV crew; his aide would speak to us. This turned out to be our second happy encounter in Buenos Aires. The young American who emerged to greet us introduced himself as Norman Thomas di Giovanni. When we introduced ourselves, he turned to me and said: "You wouldn't remember it, but I visited your house in New Jersey ten years ago with Mark Strand and Rico Lebrun. But long before that your *100 Modern Poems* changed my life. I doubt whether I'd be here in Argentina were it not for that anthology. Borges will be happy to see you, I know; but while he's tied up in there let's go out and have a drink."

Over *chopps* (Argentine for beers) the story of Norman Thomas di Giovanni began to unfold. It threw a good light on Borges' personality, and on Argentina. In New Hampshire where he had been working on a novel, Norman had heard that Borges was lecturing at Harvard and had gone to see him. Soon after Borges left he decided to chuck everything and fly to Buenos Aires. He had majored in Spanish in school, he loved Borges' work, and he saw no reason why the poems, on which Borges' early fame in Argentina rested, shouldn't receive as much recognition in the English-speaking world as the stories. He would try to convince Borges of this, and then he would organize the best poet-translators from all over the world to prepare a book, under his and Borges' supervision.

He succeeded beyond his wildest expectations. Borges was delighted with the idea. So delighted, in fact, that he soon began concentrating on writing poems again at Norman's instigation. The result of this was Borges' first new book in nine years, *In Praise of Darkness*. Translators from England and the United States began sending in their versions which Borges and Norman would scrutinize minutely, mailing them back for improvement whenever necessary. Most happily for both men, the younger quickly became indispensable to the older, as go-between with the increasingly unwieldy flow of visitors, promoters, publishers, and lecture agents; and as friend, for the Argentine writer has always felt closer in spirit to the Anglo-American literary world than to the French-oriented one traditional in Argentina.

But Norman's sudden eminence baffled the intellectual community of Buenos Aires. Who was this upstart—from North America of all places. It made them feel better about it to invent all kinds of academic credentials for Norman. He began to be referred to in the press as "Dr. di Giovanni" and as "the well-known scholar from Harvard," and Norman, with a typically American contempt for titles, would have none of it, though Borges said, "Can't you see it makes them happy to call you Doctor, Norman? Go along with them. Play their little game." One day when they were sitting next to each other at a TV panel interview, Norman had lunged forward to protest his Harvard identification; Borges seized him by the elbow and whispered in his ear: "Norman! . . . Avoid veracity!"

A friend in Chile, Nena Ossa, had already told me something about Borges' humility. She had met him in Santiago and taken him to a television studio where he was to be interviewed. "I was trying to guide him across the streets, but he insisted on guiding me. I was with him when the girl was putting pancake makeup on his face. I'll never forget the way he apologized to her for 'this indignity—having to touch this old and ugly visage.' The girl, thrilled by the privilege of so intimate a contact with such a great man, was speechless."

Norman confirmed the genuineness of Borges' reaction by telling us of the time he had accompanied Borges and his wife on a speaking engagement to a town in the south of Argentina that involved an exhausting six-hour journey by rail. They arrived only to discover that a mistake had been made in the invitation: the lecture was to have taken place the day before. The college officials were furious. "We'll get to the bottom of this terrible insult, Dr. Borges. The clerk responsible for the error will be fired!" Borges looked at them open-mouthed. "But why?" he said. "Can't you understand that I'm delighted? I won't have to lecture now!" But their outrage—and Señora Borges'—persisted. "At least the young man must be exposed—" "Please, no, no," Borges insisted. "Can't you see that I'm grateful to the young man? He's my benefactor. If you punish him, I'll never come back."

Borges in the Library

Walking to the Library, we reentered the gloomy structure that was once the National Lottery, its brass balustrades on the grand staircase having as their motif the spherical baskets in which the tickets are shuffled. The director's office, with twenty-foot ceilings and ornately carved wooden walls, has a curved desk especially designed for Borges' predecessor, Paul Groussac, who was also blind. (Is there something symbolic about these blind librarians in a Latin-American institution devoted more to reverence than use?) Borges, who never uses the desk, was seated at a large conference table staring into space. He looks at first sight more like a harassed, tired executive than a poet. It is only when he leans on his cane, grabs you just above the elbow, and starts pouring over you (at very close range) his passion for literature that you catch the gleam in those piercing blue eyes under their drooping lids, the dedicated, almost Gothic bony structure of that long, slightly pouchy aristocratic face with its sparse gray hairs and unruly eyebrows. He talks fluently in English but with an accent, almost a Scotch burr, rolling his r's. It's not easy to stop him once he starts, because he has a disconcerting way of looking you straight in the eye, holding you close to him, and occasionally laughing at his sallies with a flash of white teeth; you can never be sure that he doesn't see you.

He asked me some question about Neruda, whom he had met in Buenos Aires about 1946 and hadn't seen since. Though acknowledging, perfunctorily I thought, that Neruda was a great poet, he was quick to express his distaste for the Nerudian personality and politics. Neruda had once written a series of poems denouncing the South American dictators, he said, without including Perón. "That was while Perón was in power," he added. "It seemed Neruda had a law suit pending in Buenos Aires at the time."

I questioned the accuracy of this observation, its implications at any rate; perhaps only outsiders can have ambivalent feelings about the aging dictator, I thought. I reviewed what little I knew myself. In Chile I'd heard about the time when Perón was a young military attaché there and had been caught red-handed stealing strategic plans. President Arturo

Jorge Luis Borges
BUENOS AIRES ARGENTINA - 1969

6

Alessandri, before putting him aboard a plane for B.A., had taken him to a window in Santiago, pointed to the snowcapped Andes, and said: "Why do you bother, *amigo?* There are our defenses against Argentina." That was in 1938. The next year Perón was assigned to Italy where Mussolini's performance made an indelible impression on him. In 1943 Perón had a job in the War Ministry which he used cleverly to build a cadre of bureaucrats dependent on him for their jobs. The following year as Labor Minister he may have pondered the lines from *Martín Fierro:*

> The gaucho just has to grin and bear it
> until death comes to swallow him up
> or we get a Criollo chap to rule
> this land in the gaucho way.[1]

At any rate Perón now became a champion, not only of the gaucho against the big landowner who had ruled Argentina in the past, but of unorganized labor against the elite of the unions. He sponsored a rival labor federation, wholly subservient to him and soon strong enough to back him into the presidency.

Inevitably I thought too of Evita, the radio actress who was Perón's mistress and wife and collaborator, until she died, leaving him helpless: Evita inflaming the *descamisados* (shirtless ones); Evita with her Foundation which gave handouts to everyone in need but made no accounting of its millions in government funds; Evita with the guts Perón lacked but quite lacking in the sense of the absurd which characterizes Argentines—who nevertheless idolized her. I thought, too, of Borges' little essay about the mourning general who set up a tiny shrine in the Chaco one day in 1952 and accepted contributions, candles, and flowers from the poor who came to worship the blond doll inside:

What kind of a man, I ask myself, conceived and executed that funeral farce? a fanatic, a pitiful wretch, or an imposter and a cynic? Did he believe he was Perón as he played his suffering role as the macabre widower? The story is incredible but it happened, and perhaps not once but many times, with different actors in different locales. It contains the perfect cipher of an unreal epoch, it is like the reflection of a dream or like that drama-within-drama we see in *Hamlet.* The mourner was not Perón and the blond doll was not the woman Eva Duarte but, neither was Perón Perón, nor was Eva Eva. They were, rather, unknown individuals—or anonymous ones whose secret names and true faces we do not know—who acted out,

[1] José Hernández, *Martín Fierro.* A bilingual edition, translated by C. E. Ward. Albany, State University of New York Press, 1967.

for the credulous love of the lower middle classes, a crass mythology.[2]

I asked Borges if the tale was true. He said it was; he had had it from two men in the Chaco who didn't know each other. He gave us a long account he had had from a friend here of torture by electric wires in one of Perón's prisons. He described the various parts of the body shocked, almost clinically. He also told the old joke about Perón's wish to have the name of the city of La Plata changed to Evita and how they finally compromised on La Pluta (with its suggestion of La Puta, "whore")—a joke, he said, that was invented by Peronistas and invariably told, with much guffawing, by them. Perón himself enjoyed it. Perón's influence, he added, was far from dead. "In fact," he said, "Perón is more respected now that he is in romantic exile than when he was among us and almost anyone could see how small and venal he was." He was gently derisive of Onganía's predecessor, Ilia. "They marched a squad in," Borges said, "and he asked for time to go in the next room to think it over. Everybody waited for the pistol shot, but then Ilia walked back in and surrendered. He had only been to the bathroom."

I asked him what he thought of Onganía. "Onganía? . . . It is too early to say, but he is a gentleman. I have met him once or twice. He does not raise his voice or strike poses. He may speak commonplaces but his actions so far seem dictated by good sense."

Borges' conservatism is moral. He is offended by Perón's morality—his lack of morals. There are overtones of snobbism in the description of the religious Peronista—the use of the words "the woman" and "credulous." Borges may or may not have been offended by Perón's radicalism, but he certainly does not recognize that that radicalism brought fundamental, necessary changes to Argentina, breaking the back of the old oligarchy, forcing all future governments to think in terms of social welfare, labor benefits, public works. Borges is concerned only about the means—which is a tenable philosophical position, of course.

We went to pay a call on Borges' mother who lives nearby and is astonishingly spry at ninety-three. She moves, in fact, more nimbly than her son. Borges' sister Norah, who paints, was leaving as we entered the eighth-floor apartment. Señora Borges told us that she was reading English again—"lest I forget." ("Mother often called me a quadroon," Borges confided behind his hand, "for being a fourth part English.") He had always lived with her until, two years ago, his marriage to a widowed boyhood sweetheart in her fifties surprised his friends. It is said that he and his wife are antithetical—she loves to go shopping for dresses and furniture and take in the movies; and we were told that she was not

<hr />

[2] Jorge Luis Borges, "The Sham" in *Dreamtigers*. Translated by Mildred Boyer. University of Texas Press, 1968.

having dinner with us because she is jealous of Borges' intellectual friends, especially the foreign ones, whose company and conversation he prefers.

I asked Borges on the way down in the crowded elevator if my favorite among his stories, "El Sur" ("The South") was autobiographical. Did it reflect a physical accident that had turned him from poetry to prose? "Yes, yes! of course, and it is one of my favorites too, because it is on so many levels—the autobiographical, the man who kills the thing he loves, the—"

The elevator came to a jerking stop and we were spilled out into the inner lobby without my finding out what the other levels were.

Borges at Large

The restaurant to which Borges invited us to dine with him is one of his favorites. It is a homely establishment called the Caserio, cheap but with excellent food. On the way to it, he never stopped talking. Bill and Norman would get a block or more ahead of us and then stop to let us catch up. Borges tugged at my elbow so hard it was difficult to avoid lampposts and keep out of the gutter. (Norman told me that he had a sore arm for a week after arriving in Buenos Aires and that he still walks like a crab.) Once when we were agreeing how overrated Goethe was as a poet, and I delighted him by quoting the passage from *Faust*, Part Two, beginning *Wenn im unendlichen dasselbe* to prove that Goethe was best in philosophical nuggets like that, he pulled me off the curb and with taxis barreling by intoned a dozen lines from *Beowulf* to indicate the bridge between Teuton and English tongues. At an intersection he stopped me in the middle of the street to quote José Hernández—the idea being that *Martín Fierro* was somewhat cheapened by its propaganda content—"The poem was written, you know, to stop the killing of the Indians by the gauchos. Hernández' gaucho complains too much. Real gauchos are not so self-pitying."

"Is the gaucho character revealed in *The Purple Land* more accurate?" I asked.

"No. Less accurate. Hudson was a first-rate naturalist but not a first-rate novelist. His memory of the Banda Orientál played him tricks. I could give you a dozen instances of inaccuracy. He romanticized the Uruguayan back country hopelessly, all those silly loves, and so on."

By the time we were seated for our dinner we were quoting and counter-quoting. He'd quote Tennyson; I'd quote "a better poet of the same time, Hopkins." He'd quote a war poem by Browning; I'd quote "a better war poet, Owen." He'd cite Kipling or Chesterton or Stevenson; I'd cite Stephen Crane. I asked him whether he admired César Vallejo's poetry.[3] "Vallejo? Never heard of him." I couldn't believe my ears. "García Márquez' fiction?" I ventured. "Never heard of him either." I came back to safer ground: "Leopoldo Lugones?"

"Of course. Lugones was our greatest poet. But very limited, very Paris-oriented, by way of Rubén Darío who worked for years in Buenos Aires as a journalist."

"Drunk or sober?" I asked.

"Drunk, mostly," he said. "But Lugones showed his basic insecurity by frequently prefacing a sententious remark with 'As Rubén Darío, my master and friend, and I agree. . . .' Ah, he was a very distasteful person, Lugones, very negative. His mouth seemed shaped by nature to pronounce the word 'No.' Later on he would invent reasons to justify this word that his soul and facial muscles so automatically shaped."

Borges had, of course, read some Cortázar, but he didn't like the expatriate Argentine modernist. "He is trying so hard on every page of his novels and stories to be original that it becomes a tiresome battle of wits, no?"

When discussing English or American literature, Borges' whole personality changes. He beams, he expands, he glows. "You know I was brought up on English in my father's library. I was quite old when it occurred to me that poetry could be written in a language other than English!"

He ordered a plate of rice, butter, and cheese, while our mouths watered at the thought of the steaks we were about to be served. "I hate steaks," Borges said. "They are so common in this country. I can't eat but one or two a year."

Norman said: "Borges, I heard you mention Eliot a while back. . . ."

"Eliot is a little dry, don't you think? I prefer Frost. You like Frost, Rodman?" He was glad that I preferred Frost to Eliot. He asked me how Frost looked and talked. Did I think Frost's reserved Americanism had any kinship with Whitman's boisterous brand?

"I think Frost was a direct descendant of Emerson," I said.

"And Whitman was influenced by Emerson more than by anyone! That essay about the ideal American democrat, pioneer, yea-sayer, truth-teller —with a bit of Indian-Asiatic philosophy thrown in, no?"

"'I greet you at the beginning of a great career,'" I quoted.

He laughed. "And how distressed Emerson was that Whitman made big publicity out of that. Yet why not? If Emerson didn't expect it, why did he write it? Whitman was right . . . but don't you think Whitman tries too hard? That he is really a quite unspontaneous writer?"

"Not in *Song of Myself*," I said. "That's the most spontaneous poem in

---

[3] With the possible exception of Neruda, Vallejo is generally regarded as South America's greatest poet. His work is discussed in the chapter on Peru, as is García Márquez' in the chapter on Colombia.

the language. Even some of the later lines are pure magic, impossible to will."

"For instance?"

" 'I repose by the sills of the exquisite flexible doors.' "

Borges said it over to himself several times. "I don't get it. What's so wonderful about it?"

"You've revealed to me at last that English is only your adopted language," I said.

He laughed. "They didn't find me out at Harvard, or in Texas either." The lectures he had delivered at Austin had been a great experience, he added. "Every South American should visit the United States to see how completely perverted by lying communist propaganda the image of America is. The students, compared with ours, are so alert. I'll not forget the one who pointed out in class that 'The Golem' was a reworking of 'The Circular Ruins.' I was amazed! 'My God,' I said, 'you're right! I never thought of it, but it's true. Well, I only wrote it—once. You've probably read both stories many times.' "

He leaned toward Bill to answer a question and Norman said to me: "He says things like that all the time. He really means them. He thinks his present fame is a matter of good luck, not necessarily deserved and that any day the bubble may pop and he'll be forgotten, or relegated to a very minor role. Of course he's enjoying it while it lasts, rather astonished by the adulation, the translators all over the world haggling over the meaning of this or that arcane phrase—but not at all taken in by it, or spoiled, as you can see."

"Here," said Borges turning back to me, "examinations are like lottery tickets. In Texas a student wanted me to give a course all over again, unsure that he'd profited by it thoroughly, unconcerned about quick credits . . . that could never happen here."

"Can I ask you a Johnsonian question?" I asked.

"You mean like: What would I do if locked up in a tower with a baby?"

"Exactly. What does Argentina need most?"

He pondered. "More curious minds, perhaps—like yours. You saw that girl at the library this afternoon? Can you believe it? Her mother burned her books one day. She said to her: 'We're simple folk. We don't need books.' That's what we're up against."

Back to the Library

One day we had a date to meet di Giovanni and Borges at the Library at 10:30, but by the time we had fought our way into Braniff to get our tickets to Asunción confirmed, and then queued up for a taxi—a quaint custom in this bulging megalopolis—they had gone.

We walked to Borges' apartment on Belgrano, easy to find because it is diagonally across from a sign reading AMERICAN BAR: PRETTY GIRLS. He wasn't in, and as usual the maid looked as though she'd been interrupted at an embalming. Yes, Señora Borges was in but she was not to be disturbed. We could wait in the parlor if we wanted to, said the maid, still barring the door. Bill escaped, but I settled down, passing the time making a *catalogue raisonné* of the premises: Two potted rubber plants, two green-cushioned Morris chairs, a spindly dining-room set, two glass-shelved bookcases, two etchings in the style of Whistler, two eighteenth century engravings (Arch of Titus, Pyramid of Caius Cestius), a Dürer etching, a painting of angels by Borges' sister, a student exercise by Silvina Ocampo of a woman's back from the waist up, a cabinet containing Borges' medals and other literary awards, a wall rack with brandy decanters and glasses of red glass in brass holders, a Harvard shield, a glass coffee table containing an ashtray, Joyce's *Ulysses* (Borges thinks Joyce filled it with catalogs rather than character studies), Apollinaire in Spanish (*El Heresiarca y Cia*), and the complete works of Dürer in folio.

Presently Borges came in, and we made a date to meet in his apartment at four in the afternoon and go to the library for photos and drawings. I told him I'd like to meet his wife. He went through one of the closed doors and came back, closing it after him.

"She excuses herself. She's just had a bath."

"I'm beginning to think you don't have a wife, Borges."

His eyes twinkled. "Maybe it's better if we keep up the mystery?"

He took me to the elevator and I had trouble closing the accordion gate which has to be shut before any Argentine elevator will start. "What is this?" I said. "Some diabolical Argentine invention?"

"Heavens, no," he said, as my head began to disappear below floor level, "the Argentinians could never invent something as complicated as an elevator—or for that matter anything at all."

At four o'clock I picked up Bill and drove back to Belgrano. This time La Señora emerged, in her dressing gown, and greeted me cordially. She is a buxom, rather handsome woman in her fifties, with a nice smile. She surrendered her husband graciously. Bill was waiting across the street in the taxi, lest we lose it and have to queue up again. Even to get Borges across a street is a tug of war. This time he was talking about his story "Funes the Memorious" and about what a terrible thing it was to have insomnia.

At the library we rang the bell but no one answered. Borges had no key. Finally a character came up to us from across the street, concerned to see the old man with a cane standing hatless under the fierce sun, and asked us if we'd like to have a whiskey or a coke. Borges said we'd like to have a coke but that was the last we saw of our presumptive benefactor. Borges, by now engaged in quoting Longfellow's translation of an Old English poem, "The Grave," showed very little interest when the watchman, who should have been on duty, finally arrived with the key. To get the natural light for photography and drawing, we took three chairs out onto the narrow balcony that runs around the top of the huge, glass-domed main reading room.

I told Borges Carcassonne's version of how the Casa Rosada, Argentina's White House, had acquired its rosy hue. It seems that Sarmiento, the great liberal statesman of the nineteenth century, resolved a dispute between two painters with red and white paint by mixing the paints. Borges didn't confirm the truth of the anecdote but he was quick to appreciate the symbolism of resolving the two warring parties of the time. I asked him how important in shaping Argentine history was the fact that Argentina was a dependency of Peru from 1563 to 1776.

"Not at all," he said. "Communications were much too difficult in those times to give Argentina much sense of inferiority. We were pretty much on our own, with Spain giving us most of the trouble. In the War of the Pacific in 1879, everybody here sided with Peru against Chile. But the city of Buenos Aires has always been middle-class compared with aristocratic Lima. . . . Argentina has always been far too large, I've always thought. Our northwestern provinces, with their surviving Indians, would be better off as parts of Indian Paraguay or Bolivia."

I asked him whether he thought the nineteenth century domination of Argentina, by the British economically and the French culturally, had had a schizophrenic effect on his country.

"I don't think so," he said. "Both influences were accepted quite naturally, in my family at least. But we were not devoted to Spain. We thought of Spaniards as servants. I recall someone coming back from meeting the Infanta and reporting scornfully 'She talks like a *gallego*'— the equivalent of saying that a British princess talks like a limey."

He went on to say that Paris had had a bad influence on intellectuals and poets—"Like your Ezra Pound, for instance, who adopted his ridiculous pose there. Or was it in London that he first affected cowboy dress and talk? . . . Even Victor Hugo felt he had to strike an attitude, though he was a serious poet and a great one."

I reminded him of André Gide's famous remark—"Victor Hugo, alas"— when asked who he thought was France's greatest poet. "Do you think Baudelaire and Rimbaud were better poets?" I asked.

"Of course not," he said. "Baudelaire is overrated, and Rimbaud was a mere freak. . . . Do you know Hugo's splendid poem 'Boaz Endormi'?" I didn't, and he quoted it all, with its ending:

> . . . *L'herbe était noire;*
> *C'était l'heure tranquille quand les lions vont boire* . . .

I told Borges that I was haunted by his story "El Aleph," especially by the passage describing the magical appearance on the cellar step of the small iridescent sphere "whose center is everywhere and its circumference nowhere":

The Aleph was about two or three centimeters in diameter, but it contained cosmic space without diminution in size. Each object (the face of a mirror, let's say) was an infinite number of things for I saw it clearly from every point in the universe. I saw the populous sea, I saw dawn and dusk, I saw the multitudes of America, I saw a silver cobweb in the center of a black pyramid. I saw a broken labyrinth (it was London), I saw endless, contiguous eyes scrutinizing themselves in me as if in a mirror, I saw all the mirrors on earth and none reflected me. In the backyard of a house on Soler Street I saw the same flagstones which I had seen thirty years before at the entrance to a house on Fray Bentos Street. I saw clusters, snow, tobacco, veins of metal, water vapor; I saw convex equatorial deserts and each one of their grains of sand; I saw at Inverness a woman I shall not forget, I saw her violent head of hair, her proud body; I saw a breast cancer. I saw a round patch of dry earth on a path where before a tree stood; I saw in a country house in Androgue a copy of the first English version of Pliny, that of Philemon Holland; I saw at one and the same time every letter on every page (as a child I used to marvel at the fact that the letters of a closed book did not get mixed up and lost during the night), I saw a sunset in Querétaro that seemed to reflect the color of a rose in Bengal, I saw my bedroom without anyone in it; I saw in a closet at Alkmaar, a terrestrial globe between two mirrors, which multiplied it endlessly; I saw horses with whirling manes on the Caspian Sea at dawn; I saw the delicate bone structure of a hand, I saw the survivors of a battle sending postcards; in a show window in Mirzapur I saw a Spanish deck of cards, I saw the oblique shadows of some ferns on the floor of a greenhouse, I saw tigers, pistons, seaswells and armies. I saw all the ants on earth, I saw a Persian astrolabe; in a desk drawer (and the handwriting made me tremble), I saw obscene, incredible the very letters that Beatriz had addressed to Carlos Argentino, I saw an adored monument in the Chacarita, I saw the atrocious relic of what had deliciously been Beatriz Viterbo; I saw the circulation of my dark blood, I saw the gears of love and the modifications of death; I saw the Aleph from all points, I saw in the Aleph the earth, the Aleph again, and in the Aleph, the earth; I saw my face and I felt vertigo and I cried, because my eyes had seen the secret conjectured object whose name man usurps but which no man has looked upon: the inconceivable universe. . . .[4]

[4] Jorge Luis Borges, "The Aleph," translated by Zoila Nelken, *Short Stories of Latin America*. Edited by Arturo Torres-Rioseco. New York, Las Americas Publishing Company, 1963.

I asked Borges about the connection between the first part of this story and the last. "It's not clear to me." And I explained why.

"Now that you mention it, it's not clear to me either," he said. "I think I will change it and put in a much clearer relation between the buyer and the seller of the house, a hint at the very beginning that someone is going to buy the house. And I will put your name in, too, if you have no objection, as a tribute to you for improving it."

It was impossible to tell whether he was pulling my leg, mildly making fun of me—which he had every right to do. He told me about a reporter in Madrid who had come to him and asked him seriously whether the Aleph existed in fact. "Later on I wished I had encouraged him in this tomfoolery, but at the time I said, 'Of course not,' and he left quite crestfallen, and even disgusted with me for making such a deception! Tomfoolery should always be encouraged, don't you agree? But I let the poor man down and he left disconsolate." He added that the poet satirized at the beginning of the story was drawn from life, and that his mother had urged him not to make it so obvious. "But I said to her: 'He'll never recognize himself'—and he didn't!" I asked him where he found the title. "I took it from Bertrand Russell's Introduction to his *Philosophy of Mathematics* where it is used as the symbol for transfinite numbers."

"Why is the house in which the Aleph appears destroyed at the end?" I asked.

"It had to be destroyed," he said, "because you can't leave things like an Aleph lying around in this day and age, the way Aladdin left his lamp lying around, no? Not any more. The premises have to be tidied up, the supernatural suitably disposed of, the reader's mind set at rest."

Which, of course, is exactly what Borges doesn't do. For part of his genius is to leave the mysteries suspended, very disquietingly suspended, in these "real" settings which make the metaphysical content so alarmingly believable. Untypical in this respect is "La Intrusa," which I'd just read after being told that Borges regarded it as his best story. I told him that I liked it less than most of the others and he asked me why.

"The woman's reactions to what the two brothers are doing to her are never hinted at," I said, "with the result that I can't feel any involvement in her fate. I'm stunned by the conclusion, in other words, but emotionally indifferent to her fate. Why would it detract from the story if you presented her as a human being rather than as the animal they feel she is?"

"The more we are made to think of the woman as a kind of thing," Borges replied, "the easier it is for the reader to feel about her as the brothers did—and to understand that the essential subject of this story is friendship, not brutality. I wonder, by the way, if you noticed that the older brother is the only one whose words we are allowed to hear? It is he who dominates the story, finds the woman, invents the scheme of sharing her with his younger brother, sells her to the brothel, buys her back, and in the end knifes or strangles her."

While he was saying this, I had a close look at Borges' eyes. No wonder he looks just a little mad! The pupil of the right eye is so enlarged it almost fills the iris. The pupil of the left eye is very small and a little off center.

We didn't see Borges again for about a week. There were trips to Uruguay and Paraguay, with Carcassonne playing chess with us in the airport restaurants while the planes took their time arriving. Carcassonne was there to meet us when we returned from Paraguay and said: "I have a pleasant surprise for you." He had not only set up a trip for us to Bariloche over the weekend, but he'd switched us to a better hotel, courtesy of the Tourist Ministry (which he had visited on our behalf and unknown to us during our trips abroad). "We'll have to think up something very special for him before we leave," Bill said, after we'd been dropped at the new hotel. "I think what he might like most," I said, "would be to meet Borges."

On the way past the Casa Rosada on our way to the airport next morning, Carcassonne pointed out the adjoining Ministry of Hacienda, still pocked with bullet holes from the Perón ouster coup when the Army and Navy Ministries across the street opened fire. He also gave us a travel brochure with this frightening description of our destination:

> Bariloche's Hotel Llao-llao is feeling happy . . . completely renewed but still maintaining its traditional style of happy and breathing mountain air. Everything is ready. The Chef is there, the wonder barmen preparing your favorite cocktails, the gardeners putting the finishing touches to immense floral decorations, the Casino awaiting your good luck. You are cordially invited to expect in perfect harmony the reunion of Hoteles D'Onofrio and you, to participate in all this happiness. . . .

On the plane to the mountain resort, I was in a window seat and Bill was directly behind me. He could talk to me without being overheard by a middle-aged gringo couple on the way to all this happiness:

> SHE: "Is this your first trip to the Argentine? Where did you come from—Chile? Are things expensive there too? What do you do? . . . Oh, isn't that interesting! Henry does too, in a way. He's teaching Phys Ed on a fellowship. No, we don't know Spanish, but Henry knows five hundred words and when one of those words pops up he responds instantaneously. But he teaches in English."
>
> BILL (aside): "How many languages can you do a push-up in?"
>
> SHE (continuing): "He even gives them a little karate."
>
> BILL (aside): "Her specialty is oral karate. She's giving it to you right now."

SHE: "I can't resist photographing everything in this country. It's so photogenic! Can you resist writing about it?"

ME: "Well, it's not—ah—scriptogenic. I agree that it's photogenic. Would you excuse me if I move across the aisle to take a few shots of the Andes?"

Accompanied by Augusto Quatro, a public relations man who does caricatures of the guests at the Llao-llao (pronounced Yow-yow), we were taken to the hotel's Gift Shoppe and presented with two hideous little owl ashtrays. The hotel is a gigantic Swiss chalet of wooden gables and projecting dormers and balconies over white plaster and Tudor timber—a cozy Bayerischer-Gasthof-cuckoo-clock creation not at all out of harmony with the picture-postcard surroundings: piney hills tastefully capped with snow. The one really stunning spectacle, the glacier Tronador on the Chilean border, appears to be inaccessible either by land or water, though there is a tantalizing glimpse of it across a lake from the hotel's garbage-disposal unit in the rear. The Llao-llao is an ideal place for those Argentine and Brazilian hikers who can afford it, especially for the Germans among them with their rucksacks, knitted wool caps, and climbing boots. For Americans there is salmon fishing, deer hunting, and in winter (our summer), skiing.

We took a ride up the far side of Catedral mountain in the chair lift that runs all year round. Getting off and on this contraption at the top before it swings out over the abyss was an adventure, and so was eluding a bull which had taken over the shed at the top and threatened to charge as we entered. On the launch crossing Lake Nahuel Huapí, it was fun throwing bread to the gulls and getting them in camera range. The shores are very pretty with clumps of yellow-flowered *amancay*, purple lupin, and a wild rose (*mosqueta*) from the fruit of which they make marmalade.

At dinner I had a heated political argument with our guide, only a little cooled off at the billiard table afterward where he and his companion had a chance to commiserate with us over our poor showing. The gist of his position was that the United States rather than Russia menaces the peace of the world—and the very economic survival of Argentina and the other South American republics, as he called them. He advised us to pull in our horns all over the world (which we seem to be doing without his advice) and attend to our own *violencia* "which dwarfs that of all other nations." Hollywood films and the US-taped TV programs, he assured us, "are sent abroad in order to encourage gangsterism and immorality." When I suggested that they might only be made by people with bad taste to sell to people with the same taste, he threw up his arms derisively.

This time, on the fan jet back to Buenos Aires there were no interior distractions—save the maddening sound of cocktail music that never stops, even in flight. The landscape is one more proof that abstract artists can't compete with nature, or even with nature's patterns modified by man: squares within squares of different colors (Albers), free-floating biomorphic shapes (Baziotes), hard-edge plantation compounds with oblique angles (Kelly). No Goyas or Turners, of course. All the forests in Argentina appear to be square.

The travel brochures are square, too; this one, for instance, which we found on our seat, describing the country's major beach resort (I haven't altered the Madison Avenue Spanglish):

> Let us visit Mar del Plata. Let us peep into its beaches, let us live in it, and in this way let it become ours. The city will be recreated by our experience. The sea is refreshed by an iodic breeze . . . Topics of conversation are various: the weather, forgotten business matters, ondulating girls . . . Thus the name of Mar del Plata—"the happy city." In the fishing port work colors the zone, and summer tourists, carelessly cheerful, watch working fishermen, whose hard job has toughened their skin and sharpened their looks. The combination of both groups, that of people watching, commenting, taking photographs and preparing their appetite, and that of the men who return from their battle against the waves, is in itself an element of attraction to which we can add seagulls and seals, all of them anxious to get what is left over. . . .

The Man from *Sur*

Victoria Ocampo, we discovered on landing, was in Mar del Plata, and this alone made us sorry we wouldn't be going there. Our appointment to meet the grand old lady of Argentine letters had been canceled by our trip to Bariloche. She couldn't return in time for the rescheduled date, Monday, and sent Enrique Pezzoni, who has now taken over most of the burdens of editing *Sur*, as her deputy. Pezzoni, a young man of great charm, was waiting for us at the hotel when Carcassonne dropped us there. He knew that we had been seeing Borges.

"It's no longer fashionable among the intellectuals to hate Borges," he told us, "as it was even five years ago. He's become a sacred monument again, though more than ever the young don't go along with his political conservatism."

"Are they anti-Onganía?" I asked.

"The young students and intellectuals are. They don't like his puritanism, his censorship of the cinema, his contempt or indifference for culture. Oddly enough, he doesn't censor the most vulgar burlesque shows; but like a typical bourgeois he thinks art must be pure. *Sur* protested recently when they burned the whole edition of a novel—printed in Franco's Spain, of all places—because one of the characters had a Russian name. Yet, inconsistently, Onganía does not censor the periodical *Primera Plana*,[5] though it is well known to be Fidelista. There is political balancing involved. As in the case of the Interior Minister, Borda, who is a Peronista."

"Is Perón still popular?"

"The workers still idolize him. And for that reason the communists make no headway among the workers. The students despise Perón, of course."

I asked him about Cortázar's reputation. "How can he be so popular when he is so difficult?"

"Perhaps a lot of buyers just put the novels on the table as conversation pieces; as they do with a writer like John Barth in the United States. Cortázar's latest, *Sixty-Two*, sold an unprecedented 20,000 copies on publication day here."

I asked him who he thought Argentina's best poet was, after Borges and Lugones.

"Perhaps Alberto Girri. He is cold, abstruse, intellectual, a little like Eliot but without the lyrical rhythms. . . . Borges' verse, as you know, stresses the illusions of time and personality by way of historical types. His new poems are more low-keyed than the old ones. . . . Girri is forty-eight. I admire very much, too, Alejandra Pizarnik, who is only twenty-nine. Her poems are in the surrealist tradition. Juan Gelman is

[5] Onganía's crack-down on this publication came a few months later.

twenty-five; he writes a more socially-oriented verse with popular idioms and characters."

"Is there the kind of a division here," I asked him, "that we have currently between those who react explicitly to the world they live in, like Lowell, Dickey, Ginsberg, and those who are more obsessed with a language to express their malaise, like Olsen, Duncan, Creeley?"

"The big problem here," he said, "is and always has been the divorce between Buenos Aires where more than a third of us live, and the rest of the country. Should one be sophisticated, looking abroad, as Lugones in his early *modernismo* phase, or Cortázar today; or should one be self-consciously rustic in the tradition of *Martín Fierro?* The late Martínez Estrada analyzed this dilemma very well in his *Goliath's Head*, as Sarmiento had much earlier in *Civilization vs. Barbarism*. Sarmiento, of course, equated civilization with England and the United States. He hated Spain."

Borges the Iconoclast

Borges, who admires Sarmiento more than any other Argentine, and shares his Anglophilia, revealed something of this when we told him we'd been to Bariloche and Uruguay. He'd never been to Bariloche, and only once or twice to Mar del Plata, detesting it.

"What has Bariloche to do with Argentina?" he said. "In my childhood it didn't even exist. It is an invention of the Swiss and is populated with tourists and those who live off them. Of course it has mountains. But I spent the most impressionable years of my boyhood in Geneva where there are mountains just as good, and a civilized society as well.

"Uruguay is something else again," he continued. "It is a very small and poor country, so things like poetry and football are taken over-seriously. They say—as they never would here, or with you—'I want you to meet my friend the poet so-and-so.' You can't joke about the gauchos or their national heroes, either. But it's like that all over South America, no? In Peru they asked me seriously: 'Are you on the side of Pizarro or Atahualpa?' We don't think of such ethnic absurdities here. My best friend, the poet Carlos Mastronardi, comes of Italian stock on both sides. I'm all mixed up racially myself. It doesn't matter. We're all Argentines. So we never think of it. In Berlin, Miguel Angel Asturias made a speech beginning: 'I want to tell you I'm an Indian.' He'd be laughed off the stage if he said that here. I'd say to him: 'Then why do you speak Spanish and wear Western clothes? Why do you publish books and not *quipus?*' In Colombia, though there's an enormous gap between the rich and the poor—and that terrible *violencia*—they're more sensible. They say: 'The only hope for us is the American Marines.'" He smiled mischievously. "—And the only hope for South America as a whole is that you can conquer it. Nowadays you fight only small wars which you're not very good at, and which you wage half-heartedly, with a sense of guilt—like the

British in South Africa when they almost lost to the Boers. You both win the big wars, of course; and if you were to conquer South America in the same spirit, without any misgivings, you'd be universally admired for it, you can be sure!"

"You've got to be kidding, Borges," I said.

"Not so much as you might think," he said, with a smile. "But to come back to Uruguay, I've always rather liked Montevideo. Being partly Uruguayan myself must account for such a peculiar taste! But the countryside is lonelier and poorer than ours."

Bill told him about the drawing he had made of the Salvo Hotel and Artigas' monument.

"Artigas was a cruel man," Borges said. "He used to sew up his enemies in the hides of cows and leave them in the hot sun until the hides shrank. But he had his good points. Once when our.Rivadavia sent him one of his own enemies as emissary, Artigas saw through it and sent him back with the message: 'Don't expect me to be your executioner.' "

"The Salvo," I said, "is one of those buildings that's so ugly it's beautiful."

He laughed. "I knew a man once who said: 'I live at the Salvo because it's the only place in Montevideo from which the building can't be seen.' "

We were taken to dinner that night, our last in Argentina, by Señor Cenzlar of the Tourist Ministry. On the way, he asked us what had impressed us most in Argentina.

"After Borges," I said, "the streets of this city. Especially Florida and Lavalle. It's a wonderful idea to have denied them to automobiles at night; it's wonderful to be swept along with those couples, strolling arm in arm, or hand in hand, well dressed or in shirt sleeves and dungarees, at their own sensual pace, past the steak houses and rathskellers and bars without an empty seat, and the shopwindows offering at least as much variety of fine clothes, jewelry, perfumes, hi-fis, record albums, TV sets, curios, and modern art as any area in midtown Manhattan; it's fantastic the way this seems to stretch on every side to infinity. By comparison, the heart of Mexico City seems provincial. . . ."

"And Borges?"

"Not because he is a great artist—which he is, of course—but because unlike most great artists—and I've known quite a few—he is a great man: completely honest, utterly unpretentious, with such a great sense of humor about himself and such a great capacity for enjoying every person, place, and thing under the sun without regard for its importance in the hierarchies established by politicians, critics, and snobs. Perhaps he cherishes the past so much and has such an indifference to the future because he realizes that the present is all we have. With so little of it available, there is no time to waste, striking attitudes or expressing hate."

The Meson Español is a delightful restaurant in the southern suburbs,

built around the courtyard of a carriage house that must have graced a lordly *estancia* a century ago. On the stage, reels were being played by a *balician* consisting of bagpipes, clarinet, snare, and bass drums. Dressed in red vests, black pantaloons with a red sash, black boots, and buttoned leggings, and sporting black one-cornered *monteyas* over their wrinkled, sharp-featured faces, this quartet reminded us instantly of Brueghel's "The Blind Leading the Blind." The rest of the entertainment consisted of a band of Spanish singer-dancers, a three-piece orchestra (accordion, violin, contrabasso), and an Indian who did some incredible things with his *bollos* until one of the balls snapped off the rope and almost brained a woman in the audience. A lot of the verbal wit from the stage, between numbers, was at the expense of Carcassonne, who'd had an exhausting day; he slept in the front row from start to finish. "This man proves we must be doing *something* wrong! . . . The next number will be entirely for *him*. . . ." But it was all good-natured: obviously a family place, with plenty of three- and five-year-olds racing around the tables till past midnight.

"What makes Argentina unique in South America," said Cenzlar proudly (after we'd talked Carcassonne out of returning to challenge the Master of Ceremonies to a duel), "is that this is a country where many immigrants feel at home without ever losing their identities. We have in Buenos Aires four hundred thousand Jews, for instance, almost as many Italians, half as many Germans, thousands of Yugoslavs, English, Swiss, Poles, and so on. One million Argentines still carry Italian passports!"

Farewell to Borges

We had about an hour to say goodbye to Borges before catching the plane to Lima. We took Carcassonne with us to Borges' apartment and introduced him. I took along a copy of a book by Fernando Guiberts called *Compadrito* which I had picked up in San Carlos de Bariloche. I asked Borges whether the following description of the hoodlum of the Buenos Aires outskirts was accurate:

> . . . his betrayal and oblivion of the pampas, where this without-a-horse man was born . . . this dismounted peasant no longer riding his destiny . . . his mother out for hire by day, dragging her tasks along; the father only a forsaken portrait in the bureau drawer [whose] courage is at bottom, a passion servile and sticky, a craving to be the man he will never become . . . attending to the drama of his own vital impotence, his impatience and studied manliness . . . stabbed in the rear by his resentment, at once actor and public: always boasting about "facing the facts" and "speaking up," leaving labor to the poor foreigners, sissy-britches and women. . . .

I had seen enough of the deracinated slum dweller in Lima, Mexico, and Santiago to be sure that there was some truth in this description, but I knew Borges well enough by this time to know that he wouldn't recognize it as his truth. He said he had lived in those neighborhoods "in the time the writer pretends to describe," and that it was not like that. He had me read another bit about knife fights. He went to another room and came back with two wicked-looking silver-handled poniards. He demonstrated that instead of holding the point down, as Guiberts indicates, it should be held up—"to get up under the shield of the poncho wrapped around the left forearm. Of course there are instances of all these attitudes he describes, but to harp on them only produces caricature."

The knives reminded me anew of the fatal encounter at the end of his story, "El Sur."

"What were the other levels," I asked Borges, "on which that story was written—the levels you were starting to tell me about the other day?"

"Well," he said, "one is that it was all perhaps a dream. You remember there's a circumstance hinted at in the beginning—that the protagonist may have died under the surgeon's knife. Then, at the inn, the protagonist has the *Arabian Nights* with him again, and the storekeeper is like the interne at the hospital, and the store reminds him of an engraving. So couldn't it all be a dream at the moment of dying? . . . The autobiographic level is in the thinking of the violent death of his grandfather—as I did so often of mine. A student once asked me in Texas: 'When did the protagonist die?' I answered: 'You pays your money and you takes your choice!' . . . Still another level is the protagonist's love for the South—and its symbolic knife. He loves it, and it kills him."

Jorge Luis Borges
BUENOS AIRES ARGENTINA · 1969

I thought of the exaltation of courage in Borges' poems, not the physical courage he may have lacked, or thought he lacked, as a young man—
as some have conjectured—but courage as a spiritual legacy, as in the
poem about his great-grandfather, who turned the tide during the battle
at Junín:

> . . . *His great-grandson is writing these lines,*
> *and a silent voice comes to him out of the past,*
> *out of the blood:*
>
> *"What does my battle at Junín matter if it is only*
> *a glorious memory, or a date learned by rote*
> *for an examination, or a place in the atlas?*
> *The battle is everlasting and can do without*
> *the pomp of actual armies and of trumpets.*
> *Junín is two civilians cursing a tyrant*
> *on a street corner,*
> *or an unknown man somewhere dying in prison."* [6]

Or the poem about the dying thoughts of Doctor Francisco Laprida, set
upon and killed September 22, 1829, by a band of gaucho militia, which
Norman had translated from the same book: [7]

> . . . *I who longed to be someone else, to weigh*
> *judgments, to read books, to hand down the law,*
> *will lie in the open out in these swamps;*
> *but a secret joy somehow swells my breast.*
> *I see at last that I am face to face*
> *with my South American destiny.*
> *I was carried to this ruinous hour*
> *by the intricate labyrinth of steps*
> *woven by my days from a day that goes*
> *back to my birth . . .*

We told him we must leave, but he wanted us to stay and have tea. We
declined, thinking we'd stayed too long already and were tiring him. He
went out of the room to fetch a copy of Dr. Johnson's *Dictionary* to show
me. Carcassonne said, very perceptively: "He looks and talks like a drunk
or a madman, but everything he says makes sense." Borges came back
lugging the huge eighteenth century tome and remarked that the Preface
was a great piece of prose. "This book was sent to me by a man from
Sing Sing."

[6] Jorge Luis Borges, "A Page to Commemorate Colonel Suarez, Victor at Junín,"
Selected Poems 1923-1967, edited by Norman Thomas di Giovanni. Translated by
Alastair Reid. New York, Delacorte, 1970.
[7] *Ibid.*

"The prison?"

"No. The town."

"But there is no town by that name any more. They renamed it Ossining. It must have been a prisoner who sent it to you, Borges!"

He liked the idea. "Yes. A prisoner of the eighteenth century. What a good place to be imprisoned. With all those Latinisms!"

As we edged our way toward the elevator, I asked him whether he'd like to have a copy of the new biography of Byron's sister which I'd ordered for Neruda.

"Some poets, like Byron," he said, "are so much more interesting than their poetry, aren't they?"

"Hemingway, for instance," I said.

"Yes," he said. "A very uninteresting writer, really."

As we went through the door Carcassonne whispered to me: "This has got to be something I'll tell my grandchildren about."

"It was a great pleasure meeting you, Borges," I said lamely as we stepped into the cage and pulled the accordion doors shut.

"It was a pleasure and great honor meeting you," he replied graciously.

"We'll always remember it," said Bill in a louder voice as we started down.

"If you do forget," we heard his laughing voice say as we plunged out of sight, "write it down and remember the spelling—B—O—R—G—E—S—Borges!"

On the plane to Lima, quite possibly directly over Junín, I translated the last four lines from one of his poems:

> *I seem to hear a stirring in the dawn*
> *of multitudes departing; I perceive*
> *the loves and memories that now are gone;*
> *space, time, and Borges take their leave.*

2

URUGUAY AND PARAGUAY:
LANDS OF UNLIKENESS

Their names rhyme. They almost touch. They are small and poor in mineral resources. Their histories are swaybacked from trying to stand up to their giant neighbors, Argentina and Brazil. But there the similarities end.

Uruguay is racially the most homogeneous country in South America, with no Indians and very few Negroes. Paraguay, Indian-Spanish with the Indian strain dominant, is the only land where an aboriginal tongue is spoken by almost everybody. Uruguay is the best-governed country on the continent in terms of democracy, social services, freedom from militarism. Paraguay is the worst governed—a tradition of dictatorship, lack of social services, subservience to militarism. Yet, curiously, Paraguay appears to be moving forward, while Uruguay is in the doldrums of sloth, violence, and spiritual despair. Why?

Uruguay as Hudson Saw It

We left Argentina jet-bound for Peru, but must postpone that landing to report on the two earlier visits that interrupted our conversations with Borges. The critical things Borges had to say about Uruguay—and more specifically about W. H. Hudson's novel about Uruguay, *The Purple Land* —had aroused our curiosity. We not only reread the novel but we discovered an essay in which (twenty-eight years earlier) Borges had expressed the same enthusiasm for the book we were experiencing ourselves. He had found it "unexcelled by any work of Gaucho literature," including *Martín Fierro*. And he had linked it with *Huckleberry Finn* as "one of the very few happy books in the world."

Like Hudson himself, and like us, the hero of *The Purple Land*, Richard Lamb, had come to Uruguay from Argentina. Uruguay, or the Banda Orientál as it was then called, had just emerged as a nation following successive conquests by England, Portugal, Spain, Brazil, and Argentina. It was a small country, but not small enough to contain two hundred fifty thousand people who had just discovered the pleasures of warlike party politics. Already the city (Montevideo) was at odds with the country—Gauchos who sipped their bitter maté, smoked long cigars, engaged in friendly knife fights, and, when the spirit moved them, rode herd on the millions of beef cattle that were then, as now, Uruguay's only source of moveable wealth.

It doesn't take the pragmatic Lamb long to discover that nothing works in this kind of a country. He can't get a job. He is appalled by the casual cruelty practiced upon man and beast. He joins, without wanting to, the ill-planned war of the countrymen (Blancos) against the export-import crowd in the capital (Colorados). He sees through the egocentric ambitions and political childishness of both contestants. He is amazed by the gluttony of *estancia* owners who have to take powdered ostrich stomach to enjoy their siestas. ("The consumption and waste of meat was something frightful!") His heart goes out to the children with no childhood who have never had a story told to them. He imbibes the prevailing morality: "In the Banda Orientál you are not looked upon as an honest man unless you steal."

But the interesting thing, and the point of the novel, is that Richard Lamb (Hudson in retrospect) not only comes to love this life but to value its pleasures beyond anything Europe or civilization has to offer. The violence, since it is disorganized, leaves no scars. The country hospitality, with time no factor in shortening the yarns spun around the fireplace, seems infinitely preferable to the petty vices of urban society. The passionate women (though like a good Victorian, Lamb remains faithful in body if not in spirit to his distant wife) have no subterfuges or secrets. Nature's pastoral beauties seem all the more memorable following the brawls and skirmishes. The romantically lost love of the Blanco *caudillo*, General Santa Coloma, becomes a noble thing when sublimated in his futile quest to subvert his *patria*. So Lamb-Hudson concludes his narrative with a passage that is the first and the classic affirmation of the Latin American way of life:

> We do not live by bread alone. . . . Blessings may even become curses when the gigantic power that bestows them on us scares from our midst the shy spirits of Beauty and Poesy. Nor is it solely because it appeals to the poetic feelings in us that this country endears

itself to my heart. It is the perfect republic: the sense of emancipation experienced in it by the wanderer from the Old World is
indescribably sweet and novel. . . . It is something more than these
bodily sensations we experience when first mingling with our fellow-
creatures, where all men are absolutely free and equal as here. I
fancy I hear some wise person exclaiming, "No, no, no! In name only
is your Purple Land a republic; its constitution is a piece of waste
paper, its government an oligarchy tempered by assassination and
revolution." True; but the knot of ambitious rulers striving to pluck
each other down have no power to make the people miserable. The
unwritten constitution, mightier than the written one, is in the heart
of every man to make him still a republican and free with a freedom
it would be hard to match anywhere else on the globe.

Sur's editor, Ezequiel Martínez Estrada, had hailed this passage—part
of which we quote here, and more of which we will quote later—as "the
maximum philosophy and the supreme justification of America in the
face of Western civilization." Borges, even in his early salute to Hudson's
happy romanticism, had expressed grave doubts about it. But before
considering Borges' doubts, or the mixed feelings the passage aroused in
us, we wanted to see why Uruguay had moved in the opposite direction,
and why its tremendous effort to emulate Western civilization was
foundering.

. . . and as We Saw It

Hudson wasn't exaggerating when he spoke of the brick-red sea at
Montevideo. The enormous estuary of the Plata, over which we had flown
from Buenos Aires, was turgid with the jungle mud of its tributaries that
flow out of the Gran Chaco of Argentina and Paraguay. Even along the
capital's waterfront drive, the Rambla, to which we drove from the airport, the Atlantic itself is stained. And almost as far east as Punta del
Este, where Uruguay's coastline veers northward to join Brazil's southernmost province, Rio Grande do Sul, there is no clear water. The horizon
itself is flawed by the masts and stacks of a British passenger freighter
that ran aground a few years ago.

Other waterfront symbolism is provided by the two large, city-run
gambling casinos, by the old casino with its silver-capped minaret, now
converted into a zoological museum, and by grimy concrete towers protruding from the water that were intended, in emulation of Rio, to ferry
pleasure-seekers by cable car to a small island offshore. Like the ship-
wreck that never got tidied up, the cable cars never arrived. Not all
Montevideans, close to half of all Uruguayans, live in the unbroken row of
high-rise apartments that flank the beach as far as the eye can see east
and west; but few if any are not to be found one day or another between

the Rambla and the brick-red sea. For this is a beach culture. In the morning the population flocks to the beaches like lemmings; in the evening, like a spent tidal wave, it rolls back.

The population? Yes.

With the exception of those who tend the cattle, sheep, and truck farms out in the neglected *campo*, all of Uruguay's 2.7 million is middle class. Especially labor—for in a state without mines or heavy industry, the trade-union movement has been able to keep wages high and social benefits extravagant—and the civil service—for instead of being drawn from a landed aristocracy or narrowing into a self-serving elite as in other South American countries, the federal bureaucracy has so proliferated in Uruguay that its actual functions are subordinated to its privileges and its leisure. The most recent violence in this most violent year of Uruguay's modern history has attended a sit-down strike of bank clerks; it had been preceded by strikes in the post office, the port facilities, oil refineries, gas stations, and sanitation services—all designed to checkmate the government's effort to pay its bills and avoid bankruptcy.

Whether some of this may be ascribed historically to the country's top-heavy urban concentration, or whether most of it is the paradoxical legacy of a uniquely practical visionary, José Batlle y Ordóñez, (1856-1929), the fact is that Batlle (pronounced Ba'-shay) introduced most of the constitutional reforms that turned Uruguay into the Hemisphere's most advanced welfare state. Still more importantly, it was he who established the climate of consensus under which this was accepted. He had begun by legalizing divorce, abolishing the death penalty, greatly expanding education, and establishing freedoms of speech, press, and assembly that would apply just as much to the rival Blanco party as to his own urban Colorados. Then he pushed through his advanced social legislation: the eight-hour day, old-age pensions, sick benefits, job insurance. Finally, he made provision for the dangers inherent in the weakness of the opposition Blancos by replacing the presidency with a collegium representing both parties, and even providing referendums through which the whole people could vote directly on controversial laws.

This worked, or seemed to work, wonderfully well during the first half of this century. The opportunities for free association, self-expression, and graceful living which Hudson had enjoyed so much in the *campo* now appeared to be available to everyone, and without any of the arbitrary class poverty, stealing, bloodletting, and party tyranny which Richard Lamb had glossed over. But Hudson seems to have been right in implying that political anarchy was a fair price to pay for the unregimented happiness of those capable of being adventurers, bohemians, and poets of the open road. For long before Batlle's carefully legislated utopia became a bureaucracy of clerks and finally broke down, cracks had begun to appear.

Poets and novelists were the first to detect the odor of the state's decay—and to accelerate it by their exit or alienation. Lautréamont, Jules Laforgue, and Jules Supervielle went to Paris and became French luminaries in the symbolist rejection of bourgeois society. Poets like Juan Zorrilla de San Martín and Juana de Ibarbourou found their pastoral inspiration in the remote Indian or gaucho past. Horacio Quiroga, the pioneer of literary neurasthenia, horrified his contemporaries of the twenties and thirties with his *Tales of Love, Madness and Death*. Immolating himself in the Argentine jungle, he finally succumbed to the suicide that had already claimed his father, wife, son, and daughter. Juan Carlos Onetti, the novelist who became Quiroga's spiritual successor in the forties and fifties, lives a life of solitary confinement in Montevideo; his novels of drab, urban despair grew out of disillusionment with Uruguay's prewar Axis sympathies and perhaps even more out of a shared guilt for the corrupt materialism into which Batlle's democratic socialism seemed to be degenerating. In painting, an artist of such outstanding talent as Joaquin Torres-García bore witness much more obliquely to Uruguay's sickness by contenting himself in his mature work with subtle grace notes to the pictures of such European innovators as Klee and Mondrian.

The ordinary Uruguayan citizen, needless to say, expresses his country's malaise much more directly. He is contemptuous of the responsibilities that Batlle assumed would be shouldered as a small price for the state's largesse. He cheats on the taxes that pay for it. He takes advantage of the sick benefits without being sick, of the old-age pensions without being infirm, and of the retirement bonuses while still drawing a salary. If he is a trade unionist he strikes to make his wage keep pace with the inflated prices—at the expense of the country worker and the unorganized. If he is one of the two hundred fifty thousand government employees, he works half a day to spend the other half on the beach. He saturates himself with the sun, the promiscuous sex, the sweetmeats that fall in his (or her) lap, giving back nothing in return. Democratic socialism has turned him into a hedonist or a cynic—or so we concluded after talking to keen observers inside and outside the government and visiting Punta del Este, the pride of the sand sleepers.

Batlle's Utopia

I asked a foreign diplomat, himself a liberal with socialist sympathies, what had gone wrong. (Like most others I talked to, he asked not to be quoted by name.)

"Politics is the biggest business in Uruguay," he began. "Everybody recognizes it as a plague but nobody does anything about it. Everything they did was initially sound, and then carried too far, with subclauses written in to cover every conceivable constituency and voting bloc. There are three hundred forty thousand pensionnaires out of a work force of a million, and nine hundred thousand union members. Any mother with a

Palacio Salvo, Plaza Artigas
Montivideo, URUGUAY - Jan 1969

32

baby can retire on full pay for life. A child losing its parents gets a pension—fine!—but at twenty-one that same child gets a full-time job and still draws the pension."

"Can't the Blancos pressure the Colorados to stop the featherbedding?" I asked.

"Firing anyone is political dynamite in Uruguay," he replied, shaking his head. "The Blancos are not that powerful. They concentrate on pointing out that the government is too involved in things it can't run, and should turn these industries and services over to a private enterprise. But they don't explain how private companies could possibly operate the water system, for example. No doubt private concerns could do much better with alcohol, cement, and fishing than the government does, but the trouble is that capitalists are afraid of moving into such sectors lest they be regulated to death. Do you know that the government airline has a dozen planes and fifteen hundred employees?"

"Is agriculture run any more efficiently?" Bill asked.

"No. Wheat is produced at the rate of a ton per hectare, compared to six or eight tons in your country. Look at Denmark! It's smaller, the land is much poorer, and the climate is terrible, but because it's organized efficiently it's incredibly well off.

"So it comes back to politics?"

"Yes. The government has got to get the politicians off its back and stop padding the payrolls. What Uruguay needs most is a central bank, cooperatives, an agricultural extension service, and the power to shift manpower. Some of these powers exist on paper, but they don't function. The President pushes a button and nothing happens!"

"Then it's a question of education?"

"Partly. The primary school system is good. Ninety-five percent of the country is literate. But the secondary schools, instead of training pupils for life, train them for college, and the college—at least the University with its seventeen thousand students—is communist controlled and prepares for disruption only."

"The communists are that strong in Uruguay?"

"Only in the University and the unions. But if they weren't split among six different factions they'd have twenty-five percent of the vote—a lot more than they ever had in Cuba or Russia before the revolutions succeeded. But they're amazingly stupid. The University actually blacklists people who have worked for the government! Wouldn't you think they'd want their members to infiltrate the government? But no. They attack the government on the ground that it throws the full weight of economic failure on labor—which just isn't true. If anything, the unionists are the elite. Income is distributed too evenly in Uruguay. Nothing is held back for investment. So nothing new is ever built."

"And who suffers most from the inflation?"

"All classes. But the unemployed, the farm workers, and the landlords most, because they are unorganized. Just like Germany between the wars—remember what happened?"

View from the Top

One government official who had no objection to being quoted was José Maria Traiba, Secretary to the Office of the Presidency—the hopelessly permissive collegium having been scrapped a couple of years ago in favor of a single chief executive with some powers. Traiba ascribed the economic crisis of the past decade to an historical dependency on the exploitation of wool and hides which simply couldn't finance the social welfare of all the people. He was not afraid to admit, either, that the privileged public employees and trade unionists flatly refused to give up any of their gains for the common good once prices began to skyrocket and the squeeze was on. When these pressure groups balked over President Jorge Pacheco Areco's efforts to halt the galloping inflation by calling a halt to wage boosts, the government was finally forced to act.

"How?" I asked.

"By calling up strikers tor military service."

I laughed. "Our government could never get away with that. . . . It worked?"

"Magically. And now, I think, there is a growing consensus that the right to strike must be controlled. Of course," he added with a smile, "the University doesn't go along with that at all, since the communists' objective is to destroy the government at any cost."

I asked him as we were leaving whether the University trains any agronomists who might be expected to shift the emphasis from sheep and cattle to consumer products and increase the low yield of the farms.

"Four percent of the graduates are agronomists, as against thirty percent lawyers and twenty-four percent doctors," he replied, shaking his head sadly.

A Bovine Society?

One reason we decided to spend our last day in Uruguay at Punta del Este was that we were eager to swim. The waters at Bariloche (and before that, those of the Pacific in Chile) were much too cold. The red surf at Montevideo was said to be polluted with sewage, though few in the capital seemed to mind. Carrying their beach umbrellas, inflatable mattresses, fins, masks, and hot water for the *yerba maté*, the lemmings were in occupation of every square inch of sand from the Rambla to as far east and northeast as Solis, Piriápolis, and Atlántida. "There are no strikes this time of the year," explained a friend from the Peace Corps who was accompanying us, "because all the strikers are on the beach or in the water."

The Peace Corps, it had long been apparent, was no longer the band of dedicated young social revolutionaries I have traveled with over the past five years in the Dominican Republic, Guatemala, and Peru. (We took with several grains of salt the words of yesterday's Embassy spokesman: "Seventy percent of the boys are draft dodgers disseminating anti-US views on Vietnam; only good connections in Washington have prevented a full-scale probe that would disclose the smuggling, dope peddling, and homosexuality now rife in the Corps.") But it *was* true that the self-sacrificing zeal of the Kennedy era was gone; and gone too was that desire to make such traditional American virtues as optimism and industry contagious. In Uruguay, where the Corps had been reduced to a pitiful complement of six, it felt especially lost, for no program to help a literate country had ever been worked out. "They say that what we've always done is psychologically good for the countries we're assigned to," said our companion, "but isn't it actually humiliating for a proud nation to have us prying into its sore spots? Practically speaking, we accomplish nothing of lasting value. Wouldn't it be better to put all that effort and money into fertilizer, dams, irrigation works? . . . So they won't love us for that! Why should they? Maybe it would be better to have them respect us."

We were passing a development in the outskirts called Cabañas Tio Tom, and I asked our friend how this squared with Uruguay's reputed freedom from race prejudice.

"Their lily-whiteness is an unspoken obsession," he said. "Ask them why they don't import a few thousand unemployed Brazilian Negroes to help with their labor shortage in the *campo*!"

Punta del Este, a two-hour drive from Montevideo, is a fine-grain white-sand beach with moderately heavy surf and little undertow. The water is clear blue, and except for a beached freighter going to rust at

one end of the boardwalk, the view is exhilarating. It is "the place to go," not only for *Orientales* but for Argentinians as well. It has a social cachet that Mar del Plata, like Jones Beach, has lost. But it won't have it long. Towering apartment hotels along the waterfront are choking it to death, and the town behind the waterfront has something of the appearance and atmosphere of Miami Beach. While Bill was sketching the cabañas, I photographed the sunbathers and asked our disillusioned Corpsman why so many of the Uruguayan women have such enormous bottoms and calves.

"It's a bovine society," he said. "They live to eat beef, and their consumption of sweets is terrifying. Once married, they're on the payroll, so there's no limit to the amount they can consume. So they balloon. And so do the men. I know one who's five foot six inches and weighs two hundred sixty-four pounds; they say he hasn't been able to cross his legs for twenty years. But it's a male-dominated society for all that, with most men keeping a chick or two on the side at eighty dollars a month. Yet only the women, who outnumber the men, can start a divorce action. They get it on any grounds at all, and with alimony."

"Does the Church stand for that?" I asked in surprise.

"The Church has ceased to exist here, except as a social institution," he replied. "People aren't atheists because they don't think or care enough about the future to take a position of any kind. Yesterday was Epiphany: they call it Children's Day now. Christmas is Family Day. Easter is Tourist Week."

On the way back to the capital our companion unburdened himself of a final observation:

"It must be the only country in the world where the police have to protect the poor against the middle class. Last May when the students from the University were burning buses—*they* travel in *cars*—curious crowds looked on, doing nothing to help the victims. Then the well-heeled rioters began throwing rocks at the street vendors and overturning their carts. If the police hadn't stepped in there would have been a massacre."

Back to Hudson

I cannot believe that if this country had been conquered and recolonized by England, and all that is crooked in it made straight according to our notions, my intercourse with the people would have had the wild, delightful flavour I have found in it. And if that distinctive flavour cannot be had along with the material prosperity resulting from Anglo-Saxon energy, I must breathe the wish that this land may never know such prosperity. I do not wish to be murdered: no man does; yet rather than see the ostrich and deer chased beyond the horizon, the flamingo and black-necked swan slain on the blue lakes, and the herdsman sent to twang his romantic guitar in Hades as a preliminary to security of person, I would prefer to go about prepared at any moment to defend my life against the sudden assaults of the assassin.

Hudson's sweet anarchy, we had now come to realize, was about to be reincarnated in the Uruguay that had spurned his injunction. It didn't matter at all that the message was as old as Rousseau. Prosperity (affluence) is a nightmare from which the man of sensibility—in his successive incarnations as romantic, *enragé*, bohemian, symbolist, beatnik, hippie—will do anything to escape. Whether it requires merely sacrificing "security of person . . . against the sudden assaults of the assassin" (Hudson) or the forcible imposition of a dictatorship of the elite (Robespierre, Lenin, Hitler, Marcuse) to give the masses what is deemed best for their welfare, the price is right. To save "the flamingo and the black-necked swan" (even though in the bloody showdown they become victims too, along with Hudson's herdsman "twanging his romantic guitar" and his *señora* with her "innate courtesy and grace of manner,") capitalism, the organized boredom that feeds it, and the bovine leisure that seems to be its end product, must go. Burn those buses!

Arrival in Asunción

On the plane to Paraguay, a country that makes an indelible impression (good or bad) on everyone who visits it, I read an editorial acknowledging the blandness of Montevideo and Buenos Aires, those capitals that envelop their countries like manta rays. The following was in the Buenos Aires morning paper:

"One looks at the streets of Buenos Aires and the impression one gets is of the incessant erasing of "yesterday" and a constant activity which always leaves something inconclusive "today" which will be done "tomorrow." . . . And immediately "today" is here again, and other "todays" take its place, and in this way the city grows and rises and expands, and when one wants to see what happened "yesterday" one can scarcely find a trace of it, and that trace is fragmented.

Asunción couldn't be more different. Nothing is new except the Hotel Guaraní, and even that exaggerated piece of modernism is beginning to have a run-down, comfortable look as if ashamed to be caught snubbing its venerable elders. The travel brochure in our seat, though no doubt sensationalized by some Madison Avenue hand, makes the best of a good thing, Paraguay's primitive bravado:

You've never sipped caña on the rocks where two guitars and an Indian harp come up with an exciting new sound a century old?

You've never watched the rainbow-costumed Guarani women puff big black cigars as they paddle a dugout canoe up the Pilcomayo? . . . Never explored the primitive beauty of the Chaco jungles where you can chase sleek jaguars, glide a canoe past 25-foot alligators playing in the sunshine? . . . Never seen a technicolor world where a President once built a palace to look like the Louvre so his mistress wouldn't get homesick? . . .

Of course that palace doesn't look a bit like the Louvre, and alligators are a lot easier to find in Florida than in Paraguay, and the Chaco is mostly biting insects, scrubby *quebracho*, and mud, yet few can resist the charms of Paraguay's lush countryside, quirky architecture, and spirited people—once the decision is made to abide the dictatorship long enough to see for oneself.

Dictators have a way of monopolizing the foreground of a small country, particularly when they have been in power unopposed for as long (fifteen years) as Alfredo Stroessner. As in Haiti, which Paraguay resembles in many ways, the dictator's frowning visage confronts one on every wall, lamppost, and newspaper in the capital; though in the countryside it seems to have no presence and very little reality at all; and certainly abroad, where the political exiles are vociferous, the two dictators' cruelty to their enemies provides the only news ugly enough to make the headlines. Not that Stroessner, except for his iron grip on the tarnished throne, is anything like Duvalier. Papa Doc, as everyone knows, is a psychopath, a racist, and a hopelessly incompetent administrator. The Paraguayan dictator is an efficiency-minded military man whose pride in his country's martial past impels him to make it shape up. Within the limits of an unimaginative drillmaster's soul—poetry, art, and most things foreign are regarded as subversive—Stroessner is tireless in his efforts to modernize Paraguay. He has given it safe drinking water for the first time in its history. He has eliminated the chronic plagues of inflation and trade deficits. He has encouraged light industry, and to impress visitors has built a hotel as deluxe as any on the continent. There are no festering urban slums (in all South America only Montevideo can compare with Asunción in that respect), no racial discrimination, no beggars in the streets, no Indians in the backlands treated as a race apart as in Peru and Chile. But what price do Paraguayans pay for these modest achievements? And how long will they be willing to pay it?

Background to Brutalism

We had gotten off the plane at 10 P.M. in total darkness, and it was like stepping into a sauna bath. Asunción is actually higher by one hundred fifty feet than Montevideo and Buenos Aires, but one is closer

Palacio Nacional Asunción, Paraguay 1969

to the equator and there are none of the sea breezes that cool the Plata estuary. The Paraguay River, up which ocean-going freighters ply to the otherwise landlocked country, contributes to the clammy heat. The city, a half hour from the Aeropuerto General Stroessner, is low-slung, tile-roofed, and rich in well-tended tropical gardens. Some of these *quintas* are elaborately wrought of painted stucco with spindly wooden columns. Many are wreathed in yellow-bell hibiscus, and there are flaming flamboyants, lime trees and orchids, bananas, and mangoes in the yards. But the militaristic pall is immediately apparent, quite apart from the "Peace and Work with Stroessner" posters of the bemedaled dictator plastered everywhere. In a square near the Presidential Palace, a baby-blue wedding cake, soldiers were goose-stepping around an ancient tank with a flagpole sprouting out of it. The tank was one of three that the German-led Bolivian Army deployed during the Chaco War; a second was blown up, and the third captured and given to France—Paraguay's supplier of arms during that vicious struggle in the thirties. The Pantheon of Heroes on the Plaza Independencia is devoted to the generals of that war and of the even bloodier War of the Triple Alliance that preceded it.

The latter conflict was sheer madness. Paraguay was older, and at the time (1865) more densely populated than either Argentina or Brazil. It had the temerity, however, to provoke war with both of them at once, and with Uruguay for good measure—though defense of "defenseless little Uruguay" was the excuse that Paraguay's dictator, Francisco Solano López, gave for invading Argentine territory to get at Brazil. Amazingly, Paraguay came close to winning. But losing cost it almost its entire male population and a century of development. When the fighting started in 1865, there were 1,337,493 Paraguayans. When it ended five years later, there were 28,746 men left, 106,254 women—the women had been used to haul the artillery and food, and were shot by the roadside when they faltered lest they be captured and "dishonored"—and 80,079 children.

It all took place at the whim of the Irish mistress, Madame Eliza Lynch, whom López had met in Paris, and for whom he built his "Louvre" and the "Pantheon" (designed by an Italian architect to remind him of the tomb of his hero, Napoleon) which was soon to hold his remains. Before being killed by the Brazilians, as he was attempting to swim out of the country with the remnant of his army, López' last piece of paranoia had been to snuff out a conspiracy he suspected was being plotted behind his back. Leaving the field for Asunción, he had rounded up his brothers and brother-in-law, the cabinet, the chiefs of the armed forces, the judiciary, the bishops, the civil servants, and two hundred assorted diplomats and foreigners, murdering them all. One survivor, an English army doctor, was seized in the American Embassy, and remembered as he was being led away to torture in the Chaco, "the air fragrant with the perfume of orange blossoms, and the flowering orchids which hung in festoons from the wayside trees, brightened by the fireflies." Perhaps it could be said that this doctor's poetic sensibility was the only good thing that came out of the War of the Triple Alliance, for he escaped López' executioners, and his memoir became the basis for Joseph Conrad's *Nostromo*.

From the equally pointless and costly Chaco War sixty years later there were assets for the loser, Bolivia (a social revolution, the first in South America), but none for Paraguay. Marshal José Félix Estigarríbia, a military genius whose swift moves and envelopments the Nazis studied and emulated a decade later, reposes with López in the Pantheon. But Paraguay, though it retained the Chaco, lost the flower of its manhood again and any chance it might have had to escape its pride of dictators. This war of the thirties began as a dispute over the ill-defined colonial border separating Paraguay's inhospitable northwest territory from Bolivia's uninhabited lowland jungle. Chile—to deflect Bolivia's attention from regaining its outlet to the sea, seized by Chile in the War of the Pacific (1879-83)—encouraged Bolivia to believe that it could secure an outlet to the Atlantic by way of the Paraguay River, and sold it arms. Argentina, Chile's traditional foe, armed Paraguay. And the Germans and French, with big military missions in the two small countries, sharpened their weapons for the coming European conflict. Because there was presumed to be oil in the Chaco, and Standard Oil of New Jersey had been invited to Bolivia in 1922 to make explorations, it was alleged (long afterwards, by Bolivian Marxists who became the heirs of Bolivia's defeat) that "American Imperialism" had fomented the conflict.

We had these tragic holocausts in mind when we set out to see for ourselves whether Paraguay, so richly endowed with brave men and good soil, could look forward with any optimism to peace and poetry. The best informed American—for we knew our country to be unhappy with its tolerance of Stroessner—might give us some insight into the current dictatorship. The most respected Paraguayan poet should be able to provide clues to the cultural future. The hardiest critic of the regime inside Paraguay could tell us whether a transition without more debilitating violence was possible.

A Case for Stroessner

Our friend from the Embassy drove us to Lake Ypacaraí. The most attractive visual feature of Paraguay is its country architecture. Every house—even the barns, even the filling stations—is ceramic-tiled with adobe or brick walls. In the lush landscape everything except coconut palms seems to grow effortlessly. The pineapples—*ananá* is a Guarani word, they say—are the juiciest and least fibrous. Apples, pears, and peaches thrive in the cooler parts of the country. Bill bought a basket of ripe mangoes, but after several sprayings decided to eat them later in the only place adapted to eating mangoes—the shower. The single eyesore along the well-paved macadam road was the new "West Point" Stroessner is building—huge, featureless, and tin-roofed.

"You'll hear all the bad things about Stroessner," our friend remarked. "I'll be the devil's advocate and give him his due. It's obvious enough that he has no culture, no tolerance for his enemies, no respect for democratic rights as we think of them. What is not so obvious is that he walked into a state of anarchy and has given Paraguay stability and a measure of economic development. The assumption made by even so intelligent a liberal as John Gunther is that South American dictators either impose themselves on an unwilling people by force, or are imposed by us. This fantasy of the liberals presupposes that there are plenty of good democrats hiding somewhere who could govern these countries effectively if given the chance. Stroessner did not create the situation here in Paraguay; the situation in Paraguay created Stroessner."

I interrupted to ask him whether Stroessner, with his German background, had had Nazi sympathies.

"If he did, they were less conspicuous than those of Perón and the other South American leaders of his generation. Stroessner did have a German-immigrant father, but he is wholly Latin in temperament and method, from his identification with the Guaranis to his dislike of the United States." And he went on to say that there was no racial schizophrenia here, as in Peru, Bolivia, and Ecuador, "because the people are intermarried to a uniform light-tan hue. City and *campo* are undifferentiated in Paraguay."

"What made it so easy," I asked, "for an authoritarianism like Stroessner's to be accepted?"

"In Latin America," he answered, "the only real sense of responsibility is to one's family. Never to society. There is no sense of social obligation at all, and the educational set-up is designed to keep it that way. Just consider that out of seven thousand university students in Paraguay, twenty-five hundred study law—the last thing Paraguay needs. Where are the democrats going to come from? Not from the schools, where everything is taught by rote, and there is no emphasis on free inquiry, objectivity, or self-discipline. Even less are these traits acquired among the political exiles—Stroessner doesn't kill many of his enemies, he dumps them across the river into Argentina—for exile has always bred conspiracy and fanaticism. So even if the franchise here were universal, it wouldn't produce democracy or good government. After all, look at Uruguay; democracy, yes, good government, no. The basic Latin system of values still operates. Petty theft, bureaucracy, and monstrous inefficiency are the rule. Both countries have all that it takes in resources: Both are farmers' dreams; yet here only two and one half percent of the soil is cultivated, and in Uruguay not much more."

I interrupted him again to ask whether there was oil in Paraguay and whether oil had been one of the causes of the Chaco War.

"Not really," he said. "As in Plato's cave, the idea became the reality. There is no oil in Paraguay, but the Bolivians had built forts one hundred fifty kilometers inside Paraguay when hostilities started. The outnumbered Paraguayans beat the well-equipped, German-commanded Bolivian Army—after losing the equivalent for our country of ten million dead—because their leaders were not foreigners and they were proud to fight under them, even with machetes. Stroessner emerged from that war; its veterans are his pampered children. But it would be a mistake to think that he's not popular among other classes as well. He sees and talks to Paraguayans all over the country. In last year's election an opposition party of Blancos was permitted to campaign for the first time. It was a tame opposition, of course, and Stroessner took seventy-five percent of the votes. But my guess is that in a free election he'd still have taken sixty-five percent. He also allows that part of the opposition headed by the clericals to talk social revolution because it's no threat to him. If it had any program besides distributing the plums to a new set of bureaucrats, it would be a threat.

"Stroessner," he concluded, "is a very uncomplicated man. He sees everything in blacks and whites. 'The communists try to kill me, so I kill the communists.' But when the communists mounted their two-pronged, Soviet-trained guerrilla offensive in 1960, it failed not because Stroessner was ruthless, but because the *campesinos* rounded up the *guerrilleros* and turned them in—just as they did last year in Bolivia, which was Ché's undoing."

I had been surprised to see a eulogy of the martyred Cuban in one of yesterday's Asunción papers and asked him about that.

"It was in the Catholic paper where they print things like that to provoke Stroessner. But he won't be provoked by such romanticism as the cult of Ché. Of course any cult can catch on if conditions deteriorate enough, and in Latin America it's always a race against time. The billion dollars spent under the Alliance for Progress hasn't helped do away with anti-Americanism for a very simple reason: the population growth has more than wiped out the economic gains. Education is the answer, but not the kind they're getting; education to change Latin America's basic values. You've both been in Peru. When you go back there next month you'll see what I mean. Belaúnde had all the right ideas, but to put them across sacrifices had to be made. No one was ready to make them, to give anything up. He spent all the funds he had, and more, but grafting went on behind his back. He cracked down on the grafters. They retaliated by smuggling, and with lies. The Standard Oil contract was the excuse for the coup, not the reason. Have you ever heard a Peruvian ask why Peru signed a give-away contract like that in the first place? Leguía's ministers must have gotten huge bribes or kickbacks for signing such a contract. But they're never blamed. We are.

"Stroessner isn't an idealist like Belaúnde so he stays on top. He plays the Latin American game, rewarding his friends—the Army, the Chaco War veterans, the Colorado Party hacks—and developing Paraguay very, very slowly with what's left over. At least you can say that he's more of a patriot than the Trujillos and Batistas and Peróns; he doesn't put the surplus in a Swiss bank account."

A Poet in Paraguay

That evening we met Josefina Pla, Paraguay's best-known poet, quite unexpectedly. We had gone to an exhibit of contemporary artists and I had bought a tall ceramic jar covered with an intricate scratched design

of alternating birds and fish. I was told that it was the work of Josefina Pla.

"The poet? You mean she's not in exile?"

"She's right here. You'll find her at home if you want to talk with her."

She had already talked to me, out of an anthology I carried with me:

> A leaf facing the sun, falling toward the shadows
> Tired of being so distant, tired of its height, tired
> Of being the cutting edge of the wind,
> Of being a wing that cannot fly,
> Of being a song without echo, without accompaniment,
> A leaf falling wearily from its height
> And from its solitude among a thousand leaves
> All with the same song, chained when they would take flight . . .[1]

I reread the poem, and the brief biographical note: ". . . her first sensitive volume [had come] at a bad time . . . the Chaco War that brought out newspaper verse more patriotic than poetic. So her work took a long time to shock writers out of their ruts. Meanwhile she continued writing, experimenting, introducing Surrealism to the Paraguayans, and being regarded . . . as the nation's greatest poetess."

The poet was in her library when we arrived, with grandchildren racing in and out of the tiny garden on which it fronts and the kitchen on which it backs. Books, pictures, manuscripts, photographs, newspapers, and ceramics in every stage of creation, littered the dusty premises; but there was sunlight filtering through the shadows, and sunlight on the children's faces, and sunlight in the restless eyes of Josefina Pla.

Well aware that Neruda was the only poet in South America who supports himself by his poetry, I congratulated Señora Pla on her capacity to make a living in ceramics without sacrificing her creativity. She brushed a lock of gray hair off her eyes to see whether I was joking. Seeing that I wasn't, she explained that her tiny electric kiln holds three pieces, one or two of which may crack in each operation. "The cost of electricity is so high I barely break even."

"Then you make a living—?"

"By teaching." She didn't elaborate or complain, but I heard afterward from a friend that in order to support herself and her family she teaches eleven courses, and on some days as much as twelve hours a day. Those at the high school bring her seven dollars a month; those at the University, eleven dollars.

---

[1] Josefina Pla, "Forever," translated by Willis Knapp Jones in *Spanish American Literature in Translation*. Edited by Willis Knapp Jones. New York, Frederick Ungar Publishing Company, 1963.

I asked her if it was true that most of the poets and artists were in exile.

"Of course. If I didn't love being an artist, love Paraguay and its folk arts, and have a pretty good sense of humor, I'd never have survived in this country of one hundred and fifty generals."

"The generals take everything?"

"I wouldn't say that. I'm not a political person. I don't know what they take. But everyone knows what they don't like to hear. A publisher of a newspaper was given a month of hard labor in the Chaco for reprinting the well-known joke about the Chaco War, the one about the greenhorn private arriving at the front, seeing the Bolivians, asking a corporal who they were, and getting the response 'They're imbeciles, like you and me.' "

"Could one get away with a joke like that about the hundred-year-old War of the Triple Alliance?" I asked.

She laughed. "No!"

Months later, reading a poem by one of the younger Paraguayan poets entitled "Awakening," I wondered whether it could be a veiled tribute to the indomitable Josefina Pla:

> *Because someone wove the dawn*
> *With new-made dew*
> *And dazzling limes*
>
> *Because someone embroidered alternating fish*
> *On the river's back*
> *And unwound the tangle of misty leaves*
>
> *Because someone roused the fog drip's web*
> *The cycling of the zodiac*
> *And crushed the stars like lightning bugs*
>
> *Because someone stripped the tower of its soundless leaves*
> *And peopled the bell with crystal*
> *The foliage*
>
> *Because someone propped open the eyes of memory*
> *And lifted the linen sheets*
>
> *Because someone wove the dawn*
> *With wet grass threads*
>
> *Because someone sounded the horn of day.*[2]

[2] Ruben Bareiro Saguier, translated by John Upton, in *TriQuarterly*, Fall-Winter 1968-69. Evanston, Illinois, Northwestern University.

The Voice of the Opposition

Courageous as he is, the only Paraguayan sounding "the horn of day" in broad daylight gets away with it because of his protective garb. A measure of immunity is supplied to Padre Luis Ramallo in part because of his Harvard education and other North American accouterments, but in larger part because he is a Jesuit.

Paraguay's Golden Age was in the seventeenth and eighteenth centuries when the Jesuits, in successful defiance of the autocrats in Asunción, organized the Guaranis into communal agricultural-industrial *reducciónes* and protected them from the slave-hunts of the Brazilian *paulistas*. When the Jesuits were hounded out of the country in 1767, the prosperity of the back country disappeared, and the Guaranis fell prey to the Argentine absentee-landlords who exploit them to this day. But there is a difference of opinion about the Jesuit presence in Paraguay. Gilberto Freyre compares their authoritarian techniques to Nazi-Fascism and describes the fearsome images inside which the priests were wont to hide, laying down the law in cavernous tones to their superstitious charges. Freyre doesn't deny that the Indians were well treated and taught to be industrious and honest, but he argues that "it was the sort of good treatment that tends to keep a human group mere children." It stifled the Guaranis' self-reliance—which might have been a brake on the two centuries of dictatorship that lay ahead.[3]

Padre Luis Ramallo is a different kind of Jesuit. He is one of the new breed of Catholics in Paraguay—ranging all the way up to and including the bishops—who have abandoned the paternalistic approach. Many are Marxists, almost all are opposed to capitalism, and not a few charge the United States with complicity in the dictatorship for continuing to recognize Stroessner and give him loans. Their educational technique, called *conscientización*, involves teaching the illiterate through pictures, plays, and choral music, with pointed social content related to their grievances. The clergy's political tactic is to side with the students and make university reform an entering wedge in the struggle to bring down the dictatorship and achieve a social revolution. Stroessner no longer forces rebellious students to scrub slogans from walls with their fingernails, but the twenty-five-dollar draft-deferments given them if they are sons of Chaco War veterans (and who isn't?) can be canceled, and this is a real club. One of the recent demonstrations was over the seizure of a student who had tangled with the *pyragues* (Guarani for hairy feet, a synonym for the secret police) and been sent to the Chaco for a two-year enlistment.

I asked Ramallo why he thought Stroessner was permitting demonstrations, like the one last week demanding removal of the Interior Minister.

"Stroessner," he answered, "is now so dependent on international agencies for loans that he can't afford the image that violent countermeasures once gave him."

"And the eulogy of Ché Guevara in your newspaper, *Communidad?*"

"Another test case. The government doesn't want an open clash with the Church. Even the military chaplains joined the protest when an issue of that paper was seized last August."

We told him the good and bad things we had heard about Stroessner's regime since its liberalization two years ago.

"His big mistake," Ramallo mused, "may have been not to establish a military technocracy. His government is authoritarian rather than totalitarian. He balances power between the military on the one hand and his old political cronies, the Colorados, on the other. He is a consummate politician at this game, but since he can't really offend either faction he is trapped. Corruption and bureaucracy infect not only the Colorados, but the tame opposition parties—the Blancos and Febraistas whom he permits to function legally. So that leaves the students, and us. The students would hold the key to change in Paraguay if only they made contact with the people in the *campo* where the bulk of the population is. But

[3] Gilberto Freyre, *Brazil: An Interpretation.* New York, Alfred A. Knopf, 1945, 1951.

since most of the students don't know Guarani, how can they be committed to serious change? Their major complaints are (1) being had by a stupid, antiquated educational system, and (2) being integrated by this system into the larger one they despise. Our commitment to fundamental change goes deeper, but theirs must come first if we're to have the educated on our side. Without University reform, the future has no future."

Hudson Redivivus: Uruguay's Underground

In Uruguay, we discovered after returning home, youth holds the key to change too, but in a style characteristic of that parasitic society where four fifths of the people live in cities and are guaranteed full-salary retirement at fifty-five. There the Tupamaros, a band of Robin Hood *guerrilleros*, rob the rich to give to the poor—or so it is said. They take their name from Tupac Amaru II, a descendant of the Incas who led the revolt against the Spaniards in eighteenth century Peru. When the Tupamaros held up the Casino San Rafael at Punta del Este recently, the part of their 220,000-dollar haul which would have gone to the employees was returned. There is no sign that the Tupamaros, who are reputed to get their paramilitary training in Cuba, will make democracy part of their social revolution against the welfare state if they take over; but at least it is refreshing to see an organized underground that shuns gunplay, and that has what our American friend called "a sense of social obligation." The Tupamaros give as well as take; that has endeared them to the public as much as their sense of humor and swashbuckling style.

Tupac Amaru . . . how odd that these latter-day Richard Lambs should call themselves after the last of the Incas! For Hudson, in his famous celebration of adventurous anarchy, had paused to contrast it with:

> the Inca system of government, founded on that most iniquitous and disastrous doctrine that the individual bears the same relation to the state as a child to its parent, that its life from the cradle to the grave must be regulated for it by a power it is taught to regard as omniscient—a power practically omnipresent and almighty. In such a state there could be no individual will, no healthy play of passions, and consequently no crime. What wonder that a system so unspeakably repugnant to a being who feels that his will is a divinity working within him fell to pieces at the first touch of foreign invasion, or that it left no vestige of its pernicious existence on the continent it had ruled!

But it is obvious that the Tupamaros see no resemblance between the socialist empire of the Incas and the police states that profess to be replacing capitalism with socialism today. And surely Hudson, that disciple of Thoreau, would be on the side of the Tupamaros should he return to the materialistic Uruguay of today:

> I hate all dreams of perpetual peace, all wonderful cities of the sun where people consume their joyless monotonous years. . . . The state is unnatural, unspeakably repugnant: the dreamless sleep of the grave is more tolerable to the active healthy mind than such an existence. . . . May the blight of our superior civilization never fall on your wild flowers, the yoke of our progress be laid on your herdsmen.

Had he lived in warlike Paraguay, Hudson might have regarded perpetual peace with less dismay, but can anyone doubt that in the Paraguay of Stroessner he would have joined the awakened priests, poets, and students to keep the repugnant state from imposing its dreamless sleep?

3

POET AS PRESIDENT: ANATOMY OF THE COUP THAT OUSTED PERU'S BELAÚNDE

Modern Peru is overshadowed by the irrefutable superiority of the ancients in the battle to win land from the desert. . . . The [pre-Columbian] builder does not destroy or mistreat the topography, but rather seems to caress it. . . . On to Iquitos we went, impelled by the water from the melted snows of the Andes. The pilot steered his ship with gentle movements of his hands on the wheel, and he treated the water almost as a lover. His gaze penetrated the depths, while ours was lost on the surface. . . . Behind its primitive exterior, Belén is a community already incorporated into civilization, vibrant with Peruvianism, enthusiastic and determined, illuminated more by the diaphanous and everlasting light of faith than by the tropical sun.

—Fernando Belaúnde Terry

At 2:30 A.M. on the Thursday morning of October 3, 1968 the daughter of the poet who had written these words roused her father from his bed in the National Palace:

"Daddy, I think we're being surrounded by tanks!"

"Nonsense, my dear," replied the President after a look down into the darkness below, "they're garbage trucks."

Depending on one's point of view, these words expressed the faith or the naiveté of Fernando Belaúnde Terry who, a half hour later, was hustled from his bed by a squad of soldiers led by a colonel with his insignia removed.

50

President Fernando Belaúnde Terry, Peru
April 28, 1969   Harvard University

"Who sent you here?" the outraged chief executive asked.

"General Velasco, Mr. President."

"He is no longer a general. I demote him! Who are you?"

"Colonel X, Mr. President."

"I demote you, too!"

But the President who was no longer President was already on his way to the waiting car, and a few minutes later was in the plane, thoughtfully loaned to the traitorous Army Commander by the airline, one of whose biggest shareholders had heard that the nationalization of the company was imminent. On its way to Buenos Aires the plane was ordered to land by the air force control tower in Pisco, but word was radioed back that its load of armed men would surely kill the President if any attempt to force it down was made. The coup had succeeded, the Congress was dissolved; and a few days later, to forestall the possibility of a popular reaction, General Velasco expropriated Standard Oil's hated International Petroleum Company (IPC).[1]

The Coup of October 3, 1968

There are as many explanations of what brought on the *golpe* as there are interested parties—and neutral observers. Oil, though it was later made the excuse, was certainly not the cause. President Belaúnde had just extracted from the American company an agreement highly favorable to Peru under which IPC relinquished all its subsoil claims—an agreement which would have terminated with Peru in outright ownership of the pumps and refineries as well. The refinery at Talara, the only working asset that Velasco seized, was so antiquated and inefficient that Belaúnde, rather than ask for it, had extracted an agreement from IPC to replace it with a new one at the American company's expense. The agreement he had signed with the company August 12 was generally approved in Peru. Carlos Loret de Mola, director of the Empresa Petrolera Fiscal, was the government's negotiator at the meetings with IPC; and a few days later at a ceremony in Talara celebrating the recovery of the wells, he had congratulated Belaúnde in an emotional speech for "restoring the sacred soil of Peru." Then suddenly this nonpolitical conservative—because he was impressed either by the defection of the left wing of Belaúnde's party or by the virulent anti-Yanqui campaign that the Miro Quesada family had been carrying on for years in its powerful newspaper, *El*

[1] Since this chapter was written, the Velasco military dictatorship has moved appreciably to the left, nationalizing the big sugar estates and moving in on the American copper interests. So far, the Nixon administration's response to expropriations without compensation has been mild—on the theory, presumably, that when all foreign investors in Peru's industrialization are frightened away and Peru is left to its own inept and corrupt managerial bureaucracy, Velasco will have second thoughts. Meanwhile, Velasco has taken away from the communist factions their two principal issues, and the democratic center is underground or in exile.

Commercio—made a dramatic appearance on television. Charging that page eleven of the contract was missing, de Mola left millions of Peruvians with the suspicion that Belaúnde was conniving to sell Peru down the river to the United States. (Page eleven was, and still is, missing. It contained de Mola's signature and the fixed price per barrel that he insisted IPC must agree in advance to pay the government. But whether the page was slipped out of the contract by an IPC man who didn't want his company committed to a fixed price that might mean bankruptcy later, or whether it was stolen by an Army stooge to topple the teetering government, may never be known. Belaúnde accuses de Mola of bad faith.)

Disgruntlement with Belaúnde among the military is another explanation for the coup given in Lima. By seniority, General Juan Velasco Alvarado had been entitled to the post of War Minister, but when General Julio Doig, who had been caught plotting a *golpe*, resigned with the rest of the cabinet earlier in 1968, Belaúnde appointed General Roberto Diánderas to the post. Velasco, who was very close to Doig, was enfuriated even more when Diánderas was reappointed on October 2 to the cabinet of the multimillionaire gold collector, Miguel Mujica Gallo; and this second enfuriation may have triggered the coup, for Mujica Gallo's cabinet lasted just twelve hours. All the high-ranking officers of the Peruvian Army have a pathological fear of Haya de la Torre and his APRA movement, and the fear that APRA would succeed to the presidency more or less by default when Belaúnde's term ended in 1969 was given as still another motive for the military take-over. This explanation seems bizarre in view of the fact that APRA's clash with the military dated back thirty years; APRA had now become so conservative that it had allied itself with the party of the former rightist dictator, Manuel Odría, to deprive Belaúnde's radical reforms of funds.

Still another explanation of the coup was advanced by Velasco's friends on the far right. Velasco was a white knight on a charger restoring morality to a country that was being drained of its resources by the corruption of Belaúnde and those around him. Belaúnde himself was never charged with any dishonest act, but for months there had been whispered innuendos (never substantiated) that the President's sister and children were involved in smuggling. For this reason, and because his Marginal Highway and other visionary projects were "bankrupting" Peru, Belaúnde had to go.

Return to Lima

All of this, and much more, we learned from a variety of anti-militarist sources in the underground soon after landing at the capital's multi-million-dollar glass and steel airport. The airport is supposed to impress visitors with Peru's modernity, but the impression vanishes the moment

one gets into a cab and starts driving along Avenida Faucett to the City of Kings. Shantytowns flank both sides, their alleys clogged with rubble and refuse. A facade of sorts is supplied for the tourist by mile upon mile of stalls displaying typical straw hats and embroidered *bolsas* woven by the picturesque Indians whose life in the freezing Andean plateau is so miserable that they flee to these noisome slums as to a paradise. Further along, on Avenida Salaverry, there is a tricornered park planted with multicolored flowers which spell out

BIENVENIDO JESUS MARIA JANVIER 20, 1969

The date, with that startling efficiency which Latin Americans sometimes lavish on matters inconsequential, changes every day. Closer still to the center of the city are monuments to Peru's three heroes of modern times: a captain who went down with his ship in a losing naval engagement, a colonel who exhorted his troops to "fire to the last cartridge" in the decisive battle won by Chile in 1879, and a pilot who flew over the Alps only to crack up on the other side. There are no monuments in this strange country of lost causes and fierce nationalism to Peru's real heroes: Tupac Amaru I and II, who led the Indian insurrections against the Spaniards; Manuel Pardo, a wise and gentle civilian President of the late nineteenth century who tried to save Peru from its ruinous *caudillos*, anticipating Belaúnde's visions; or of course to Belaúnde himself.

Belaúnde as President

I had talked to Belaúnde three years before about this anachronistic love of the Spanish heritage. We were cruising on the Presidential yacht to Frontón Island in Callao harbor, from which as a political prisoner under Odría's dictatorship Belaúnde had once tried to escape by swimming. To my surprise he seemed to concur in the adulation of the Spanish. I had been shocked to see the equestrian bronze glorifying Pizarro, the swineherd who butchered the Indians. It dominates the Presidential palace in Lima; and I remarked that Cortés, a much more intelligent and farsighted conquistador who saved the Indians from extermination in Mexico, was regarded as a villain in that country. "There isn't a single monument glorifying him," I observed, "but there are many to Cuauthémoc, the Aztec prince who led the resistance." Belaúnde thought that was childish; and he wasn't enthusiastic about my suggestion that in the city of Cajamarca, from which I had just returned, the government could help make the neglected Indian proud of his past by staging annually as a Peruvian "passion play" Peter Shaffer's *The Royal Hunt of the Sun.* I gave Belaúnde my copy of the pageant play, and we talked about it later. As a Catholic he seemed to be offended by Shaffer's portrayal of Pizarro's chaplain as a cruel fanatic and disturbed by Pizarro's sense of

guilt for having strangled the Inca at Cajamarca after promising him his freedom. "Foreigners don't appreciate the conquistadors," said Belaúnde, his eyes flashing. "These were the bravest, most indomitable men who ever lived. Can you imagine two hundred men today doing what they did: marching without any base of supplies into an unknown land of glaciers and jungles, defeating a well-organized empire with a population of millions? Their spirit is part of Peru! We must not divide the Spanish heritage from the greatness of the Indians."

Then he had taken me back to the Presidential Palace to show me a scale replica he had set up in the courtyard: the Stone of Saihuite from the Andes behind Cuzco. The stone, as big as an Indian hut, was badly mutilated by the conquistadors' priests, but enough is left to show a sort of scale model of a socialist community with all its dams, irrigation canals, terraces, and temples. Around the edges are religious effigies, animals and serpents with their heads hacked off. The President gave orders to have an overhead spout of water turned on, but the stream missed most of the ditches and poured over the hills. "It hasn't been set up correctly," Belaúnde apologized. "The tilt is a little off. But in their time it must have worked perfectly. The Incas were not tyrants. They thought in terms of human welfare. And today their descendants believe in us because we are trying to relearn that forgotten lesson about husbanding our water resources for the common good. We are trying to make Peru work again. Not just for the Indians but for all Peruvians. I call it *mestisaje*, the fruitful mingling of the races."

Upstairs in his office, Belaúnde sat at his desk under a huge painting of Francisco Bolognesi, the colonel who had died exhorting his troops to "fire to the last cartridge" in the disastrous war with Chile. In front of the President was an electrically lighted relief map of the projected Marginal Highway by which he hoped not only to open the rich eastern slopes of the Andes to colonization but to link in fruitful comity all the neglected Indian lands from Colombia and Ecuador to Bolivia and Paraguay. I asked him about his ancestor, President Diez Canseco.

"To connect Peru by railways, the Andes with the coast," the President said, "was my great-grandfather's ambition and life work. A worthy ambition, don't you think? . . . Ah! those were the days when Americans were poets, creators, builders, pioneers, doers. They thought nothing of scaling our highest mountains, like the one we call Mt. Meiggs. Today they send out teams to make reports on feasibility, and the end is that their reports are bound and buried in a Washington office almost as big as the Pentagon."

"Who were Peru's best presidents, Mr. President?"

"We had two very good ones," he answered. "Ramón Castilla and Nicolas de Piérola. Castilla was a military man and had a strong personality. Piérola—what a life he had! It was like a novel. At one point President Pardo wanted to give in to some British man-of-war, but Piérola went out—over there to the left—in the only ship available, attacked

their squadron, and set one of their ships afire. He was that kind of man."
(He was also, according to the historian R. J. Owens, a man who "like
Castilla, saw himself as the messiah and saviour of his country, and he
was quite prepared, when revolution failed, to try assassination . . ." [2]

On another occasion in 1966 I told Belaúnde the disquieting things I
had been hearing on my trips with Peace Corps volunteers to every part
of Peru, things about the deceleration of the major components of his
program: agrarian reform; *Cooperación Popular*, a Peace Corps-like
youth enlistment designed to teach the lethargic Indian communities to
help themselves; and the Marginal Highway, with its feeder roads to the
industrialized desert coast.

I told him about the Corpsman in Huancayo who had watched the
agrarian reform break up the Fernandini and Cerro de Pasco *haciendas*
in the Andes. My companion had seen the new peasant-proprietors starving as a result of their slaughter of the cattle and their inability to farm
properly, but he had asserted that this program of land expropriations
must be accelerated if only for psychological reasons, to avert an Indian
insurrection being promoted by Cubans and Cuban-trained infiltrators.
Belaúnde seemed to agree.

I also told him of the complaints that his most promising *Cooperación
Populár* was choking to death on red tape, and in many instances doing
no more than provide jobs for his party functionaries. I described the
school I had seen under construction in Cajamarca with Indians plaster-
ing the ceiling by throwing mud at it, and the adobe one in Puno that
was washed away when the roof ordered for it in Lima never arrived.
I told him of the dairy farmer who compared the two thousand *soles* per
kilometer it cost him to build a farm-to-market road with the million
soles the government was paying. I didn't tell him of the complaint I
had from *Cooperación Populár*'s Director (Luis Vier)—that a billion
soles (rather than one tenth of that out of a total budget of 2,300,000,000)
was needed to properly finance the program—because that was something
the President must be aware of. Nor did I tell him of the Director's complaint that the biggest landowners—the Beltráns, Gildemeisters, Mujica
Gallos, and Larcos, in the coastal lowlands—were exempt from expropriation because they were politically strong. But Belaúnde could hardly be
blamed for these shortcomings in the land and self-help programs; it
was the Aprista-Odriaista majority in Congress that kept cutting the
appropriations to properly finance them.

As for the Marginal Highway, it was no news to the President that
everyone from Haya de la Torre to the Army was scornful of it. Haya
described it to me as "Belaúnde's private fantasy. . . . Everyone knows
that it makes no sense to transport Ecuador's bananas to Bolivia's banana
plantations." The Army was said to be helping only with the west-east
feeder roads because these had a military potential.

[2] R. J. Owens, *Peru*. New York, Oxford University Press, 1963.

It was when I had suggested that the redistribution of land might be speeded up by negotiating a loan from the United States to cover the payments, that the President's bitter dilemma over the oil impasse became apparent.

He had smiled grimly. "Your country is doing as little to help as possible. The State Department is blocking us at every turn."

It was true. Even then our aid to Peru was being cut to a trickle in an effort to force a settlement with IPC—not necessarily on IPC's terms, to be sure, but even so, what a piece of political insanity! For what did it profit us to save this arrogant fief of a New Jersey corporation, if in the process it cost us our friend at the helm of Peru, one of the handful of committed democrats in the hemisphere? I mumbled lamely that Peru had received two hundred million dollars in aid, and that our Congress would surely not appropriate more with the potential expropriation of IPC in the offing. "I don't have to remind you, Mr. President, that our Congress is bound by a stupid amendment to the Foreign Aid Bill to stop all assistance if that happens."

"I know," Belaúnde replied bitterly, "but we are not going to be pressured into a settlement either. Politically speaking," he added with a smile, "it would be so much easier for us to nationalize our fields, wouldn't it?"

"Much easier, and much wiser perhaps, Mr. President, because right now you're not pleasing anyone—not IPC, not the American Embassy, not your people. If you nationalized the fields, you'd be pleasing the Peruvian nationalists and undercutting the Left, wouldn't you?"

"We're bending over backward to be agreeable to the U.S.," he said.

"Don't bend too far. I'm sure most Americans would rather let IPC sink without a trace than have to deal with a Peru headed by the Miro Quesadas or the Army or the communists!"

He laughed, and I laughed, but it turned out to be no laughing matter. Neither of us really believed that the worst would happen, but I did leave Peru wondering whether Fernando Belaúnde Terry was too much of a poet for the office, or not enough of a one. Was he too much in love with the glorious Indian past to appreciate what four centuries of servitude had done to the descendants of the Incas? When I asked him once whether the constant chewing of cocaine in the highlands hadn't drugged their minds beyond a capacity to help themselves, he had answered that he chewed coca leaves too when walking in the Andes as the best specific against the thin air and freezing temperature. When I told him about the Indian I'd seen at the fountain in Huancavelica, pissing on his hands rather than bothering to wait in line to wash them with clean water, he had kidded me about the American preoccupation with sanitation. The architect in him could be so bemused by the poetry of Belén's Venetian canals that he could call that rat-eating slum of Iquitos "a community already incorporated into civilization, vibrant with Peruvianism." On the other hand, the Belaúnde who loved bullfights and had once fought a

sabre duel over a matter of pride, could be so enamored of the conquistadors and their heritage that he could tell me in all seriousness that
the social-minded Army would be on his side in any showdown.

Back to the Present

Just after the coup that ousted Belaúnde, and just before leaving for
my second trip to Peru, a friend from that country came to visit me in
New Jersey. Fernando Szyszlo is Peru's foremost modern painter. His
big, dazzling abstractions on pre-Columbian themes have won awards all
over South America and have been highly praised in the United States
and Europe as well. His wife, Blanca Varela, is a fine poet, and I had just
translated one of her poems, also on a pre-Columbian theme:

How was it here in those days?
We have barely touched their remains,
The vase revealing through distant obstinate silence
The wounded bird in the fruit tree, under the glaze.
Punctual in our indifference, we come
Sideslipping misery with the precision of athletes.
Ignorant of the stars, under borrowed light,
We have lost all sense of time.
Paracas, Chavín de Huantár, Ancón:
Words, words in a song . . .
How was it in those days?
We who have discoursed of sorrow, walking from ruin
To ruin, think not of the words: the air is compounded
Of words, a man's breath forced from him by a blow
Of a stone, his blood in the earth
The color of emptiness.
Here, among the graves without name
The scintillating rags reveal their truth.
Red stars blaze at the bottoms of jars.
Ambling about by the same changeless paths
As clouds and trees, corroded by the same
Circular timelessness of time and light—
By what forgotten seeing shall we see?

Blanca worked for President Belaúnde's housing administration, and with her husband I had visited the new homes—rising everywhere to accommodate the middle classes on the theory that the slum dweller would move up a notch into their vacated dwellings. We had also visited the *barriadas*, as well as the pre-Columbian ruins surrounding Lima; and always I had sustained my optimism about Belaúnde's capacity to rejuvenate Peru by taking deep drafts of their enthusiasm for his vision.

Greeting Szyszlo in New Jersey with the words "Isn't it terrible, the news about Belaúnde's overthrow?" I could hardly believe my ears when he replied:

"Terrible? What's terrible about it?"

"You mean you think that's the way to change the guard?"

"No, of course not. But for us, in the underdeveloped countries, perhaps the only way."

"But why Belaúnde, and just as his legal term was running out?"

"Belaúnde and those around him were becoming so corrupt after you left. You can't imagine!"

"I can't. But I'm going to see for myself in a few weeks. The new regime is popular?"

"Very. For the first three days or so it wasn't. There was some demonstrating and rioting. But as soon as the expropriation of IPC and Cerro-de Pasco was announced there was cheering and waving of flags every-where."

"Cerro de Pasco?" I said in surprise. "Velasco took over the copper mines too?"

"No, not yet; but the lands around the mines—hundreds of square miles. This land had been made totally uninhabitable a few years ago by the fumes, causing thousands of Indians to evacuate. The result was that the American company bought the lands for next to nothing; and then, finding a way of not poisoning the air with their pollutants, made a paradise of gardens for their employees, and refused to let the Indians return."

"Weren't the employees Indians?" I asked in surprise.

"Perhaps. But the high-handed way it was done made Cerro de Pasco very unpopular all over Peru—and Velasco very popular for giving the original owners back their land."

"Then Velasco is a reformer?" I asked.

"Velasco is the radical one of the generals who took over, though one of the others is quite radical too."

"How did they get that way?" I asked, having just read Mario Vargas Llosa's novel [3] of the sadistic and reactionary military school that pre-pares most of Peru's officers.

"It was an early training program, during the Second World War, I think, that gave them socialistic ideas. Your program, maybe!"

I laughed. "I suppose we won't get any more credit for that than we did for having supported Paz Estenssoro's social revolution in Bolivia," I said. "But why didn't Belaúnde do these things?"

"He was afraid. Only the military are not afraid of being called com-munists."

Szyszlo himself had taken part in the coup to some extent, he added, by being one of a score of prominent intellectuals of all parties, except APRA, who had signed a public denunciation of Belaúnde for coming to terms with IPC. "The scandal broke a week earlier," he said, "when it was discovered that page eleven of the agreement was missing—a clear indication that there were secret clauses, perhaps giving IPC preferential treatment in its purchase of the oil, or kickbacks."

My wife asked Szyszlo how Pope Paul's recent anti-birth-control pro-nouncement had been received.

"Nobody, not even the Catholics in South America, is as concerned about birth control as you are," he said. "You are concerned about it, and possibly the Soviet Union is too, because you want the status quo in the underdeveloped countries—in your case, as an outlet for your cheap

[3] *The Time of the Hero.* Translated by Lysander Kemp. New York, Grove Press, 1966.

manufactured goods. We recognize that the larger the population, the greater the pressure for revolution. When I was born, the population of South America was less than the population of the United States. Now it is greater, and by the year 2000 it may be two or three times as great. You don't fear Cuba or North Vietnam, but you do fear China, don't you? Just because China's population is so huge. If thirty, or even a hundred million, were wiped out by nuclear weapons, it wouldn't hurt China at all; she'd still keep attacking. . . . Internally it's the same: the greater the population, the more irresistible the pressure for social change."

Nothing we could say about the cost in suffering or the futility of a revolution by the crippled and uneducated could sway him. He smiled and shook his head, and we shook ours.

Poets as Revolutionaries, Revolutions Without Poets

On my way back to Peru I thought about this disillusionment of the Latin American intellectuals with democratic values. In the twenties the Peruvian poets and painters in Trujillo had grouped around the young student rebel, Haya de la Torre. Haya's APRA was essentially a demo-

l Haya de la Torre   Avril 1966   Lima

cratic movement; and the first poems of César Vallejo as well as the earthy novels of Ciro Alegría were filled with a love of Peru and a faith that its Indian majority would rise up and demand equal opportunity. Moreover it was assumed that this could happen without outside interference or alien ideologies. Haya, a constant traveler, had flirted with communism and fascism, but had finally rejected both in favor of a legal seizure of power and democratic socialism. So why had Haya's movement failed to catch on, or to spread abroad as he had hoped? Partly because the Peruvian Army repeatedly denied Haya the fruits of his electoral victories. Partly because a Marxist dictatorship has more visceral appeal to the Hispanic temperament with its tradition of *caudillos* than pragmatic nose-counting. Partly because American foreign policy made the mistake of recognizing dictators as well as democrats—as long as the dictators left such high-handed corporations as IPC, Cerro de Pasco, and United Fruit alone.[4] And partly because the poets and artists copped out.

Late in the thirties the Aprista intellectuals took divergent roads. One road led to Marxism and Moscow, the other to compromise with the oligarchic establishment. There was no middle road.

Before he left for Moscow via Paris and Madrid, Vallejo had already begun to despair of remaking Peru with the materials at hand. His poetry was becoming less topical, less particularized, more concerned with developing a new poetic language, more subjective:

> I want to write but from my mouth comes foam;
> The more I have to say the more I choke;
> No words add up to any simple sum;
> Meanings are buried under cones of talk.
> I want to sing. So, doubtless, does the frog.
> I reach for laurel—and clutch onion peel.
> My speaking voice is thinner than the fog.
> My gods and sons of gods are unborn still.
> Let's go, then, so let's go! Crop on your shins
> The grass, turn tears to flesh and groans to fruit,
> Preserve your melancholy soul in tins.
> Let's go, let's go! Be wounded and arouse
> Yourself to drink what you have drunk last night.
> Come on, old crow, inseminate your spouse.

The poem I translate, "Intensity and Altitude," was a forecast of what happened to Vallejo abroad and to most Latin American poets of his

---

[4] It was not that these corporations "ran" the countries to which they had been invited, or that they manipulated the State Department or the Pentagon in their behalf, as the Marxists claim. It was rather that their personnel were so aloof from the people of the countries in which they operated, and so indifferent to Latin American aspirations, that the fantasy of an evil conspiracy was readily accepted.

generation. The Ciro Alegrías made their peace with the status quo—and stopped writing. The Vallejos went to Spain, flared brightly for an instant with the hopes of the embattled Republic, joined the Communist Party in the aftermath of that tragic debacle, and fell silent in Paris. Only Neruda, of that generation, survived as a poet by returning to his homeland and renewing himself at its wellsprings. Vallejo's "speaking voice" became truly "thinner than the fog." In Paris he "inseminated" his "spouse" (muse) by feeding upon his despair compulsively. His poetry gained in intensity but it lost any capacity it might have had for communicating with the people of Peru. Vallejo's "gods and sons of gods are unborn still." And today, thirty years after his death, Vargas Llosa, Peru's outstanding novelist, lives in exile where he writes brilliantly but without love or hope of the scabrous urban decay in Peru. And Peru's best young poet voices the same rejection:

> My mother, myself, my two brothers
> and many little peruvians
> dig a deep hole, deep down
> where we hide,
> because up on top everything's owned
> everything's locked up,
> sealed tight,
> because up on top everything's taken:
> the shade of a tree, flowers,
> fruit, a reef, wheels,
> water, pencils,
> so we prefer to sink down
> into the bottom of the earth,
> deeper than ever,
> far, far away from the bosses,
> Today Sunday,
> far far away from the owners,
> among the feet of small creatures,
> who write, sing, dance,
> who speak beautifully,
> and red with shame
> we want only to disintegrate
> into tiny little pieces.[5]

I was not really surprised when Belaúnde, in the spring of 1969 at Harvard, confessed that he had never heard of Carlos German Belli; and that although he recognized Vallejo's eminence as a poet, he found him

[5] Carlos German Belli, "Segregation No. 1 (in the manner of a primitive cult)." Translated by Maureen Ahern Maurer, *TriQuarterly No. 15*, Spring 1969. Evanston, Illinois, Northwestern University.

unreadable. "Perhaps unenjoyable is the better word," he said to me, and added: "I must confess that I prefer to read Neruda." The fact that South America's two greatest poets were communists is reflected hardly at all in their poetry; but the fact that Vallejo is read mainly by other poets, whereas Neruda appeals to every Latin American who reads at all, is a tribute to the Chilean poet's humanity, vulnerability, normality, humor—qualities disprized in most poetry today.

The Dictators

I spent my last day in Peru trying to find out what the military men who overthrew Belaúnde stood for, and whether there were any Peruvians who felt inclined to give Belaúnde's poetic approach to the nation's problems a second chance.

Who were the men who overthrew him? General Montagne is the son of the second-in-command to Luis Sánchez Cerro, the despot who declared himself President in a rigged election over Haya in 1930, and then massacred the Apristas. General Artola is the son of Armando Artola, a minister in the cabinet of the dictator, Manuel Odría, who kept Haya imprisoned for six years in the Colombian Embassy. General Benavides is a son of Marshal Oscar Benavides who seized the presidency following Sánchez Cerro's assassination in 1933, once again destroying the ballots by which Haya had won a landslide victory. Only General Velasco, the leader of the military junta, comes from the lower middle class, having risen through the ranks in Piura as an enlisted man.

Just before we arrived in Lima, Velasco had made his first public speech. He chose to make it in the *barriada* called "28 de Octubre" in honor of General Odría's *golpe*—Odría having been the first to concede squatters' rights to the Indians pouring in from the Andes. The *patrón* of this particular *barriada* is Enrique León Velarde, a millionaire aristocrat who is its Mayor. But Velasco, though he chose his ground, and brought a regiment of enlisted men in trucks to cheer him, was not well received. To defy the Yanquis, Valasco had growled, rivers of blood would flow if necessary, and the Marines would have to climb over mountains of corpses. The press was told not to print these remarks but to content itself with the histrionic conclusion: "A soldier knows how to die." It was also told to make no allusion to a series of demands for radical reforms presented to the General by a representative of the slum dwellers.

I talked with Andrés Townsend Escurra, Deputy from Lambayeque and leader of the Apristas in the dissolved Congress. I asked him why Belaúnde's staunchest backers in 1964, the Army and the Miro Quesadas, had turned against him.

"Both for the same reason," he said. "The elder Miro Quesada has always believed that the assassin who killed his brother and his brother's wife during the Sánchez Cerro confrontation was an Aprista. He and the

Army, with its pathological fear of Haya, backed Belaúnde in 1964 to prevent Haya's election, just as they joined to overthrow him last fall when it looked as though APRA would inherit Belaúnde's tarnished mantle."

"Is there any truth," I asked Townsend "in the rumors going around Lima that Velasco is getting advice from the Moscow-oriented communists?"

"Velasco's closest advisor at the moment," Townsend replied, "is the dean of our bar association, Alberto Ruiz Eldridge, a Marxist who is notoriously anti-Yanqui." He thought that Artola might go along with that kind of advice, but not the more conservative Benavides or Montagne. "Velasco reaches retirement age at the end of this month."

"I've heard that his consuming ambition is to be a marshal. Couldn't they make him one?"

"They'd have to bring back the Congress they dissolved to do that!" he laughed. "Maybe the proximity of Velasco's retirement date hastened the coup."

"But what really brought it on?" I said. "They must have been plotting a long time."

"The Peruvian Army has always had a vocation for power," he replied. "they have a sort of university they call CAEM (*Centro de Altas Estudios Militares*), the excuse for which is national defense. It appeared with the change from the old order to the new messianic complex. It prepared the ground for the *golpe*. This is only one of the many "institutional" military coups taking place all over Latin America. To forestall popular revolts and necessary changes they pose as anti-Yanquis preserving the national patrimony. What they are actually defending is the status quo— for the old oligarchy."

"And your party?" I asked.

"It is the Army's tactic to hold on while Haya gets older and older. He'll be seventy-four on February 22. But the National Executive of APRA is only forty to fifty years old. Our paper, *Tribuna*, has been against the *golpe* consistently. But we're losing ground to the Peking-communist students and they may soon have strength enough to force the Aprista Rector out at the University of San Marcos. These perpetual coups are destroying confidence in moderation. Peru is becoming polarized between extremes."

Townsend is a dapper, ingratiating man who could have been a Papal secretary in another incarnation. The only possible incarnation-occupation that would fit J. Wesley Jones, the American Ambassador, would be village grocer. This shrewd, quizzical roly-poly knows his customers and his stock, but has he ever been out from behind the counter? When I talked to him in 1965, he was reluctant to admit that we were shamelessly backing up IPC's claims or putting the squeeze on Belaúnde. "It's not so much a question of this company," he had said, "but the avalanche of expropriations that would follow from here to Arabia, and the provisions of the Hickenlooper Amendment which would force us to crack down—not merely withdrawing aid, but military missions, health programs, sugar quotas, finally, perhaps, even diplomatic personnel." He rolled his eyes and threw up his hands. "God knows we don't want to, but now you can see why I'm so busy, why this nightmare takes precedence over everything!" If ever a man of good will was the prisoner of his country's self-defeating policy, it was J. Wesley Jones. Four years later, after we'd compounded the error of undercutting Belaúnde over IPC by penalizing him again—to the tune of eighty million dollars because he wouldn't take our fatherly advice about arming Peru with jet interceptors,[6] Ambassador Jones was still defending the policy which had not only left Belaúnde defenseless, but cost IPC (the object of our solicitude) its very existence.

"Why didn't Belaúnde take over IPC himself?" I asked Jones in 1968.

"Why? Because he didn't believe that the state should get mixed up in the expensive business of refining and exploration, and because he didn't want to lose our aid. Belaúnde should have settled the IPC issue long ago."

So why didn't we make it easy for him? By withdrawing our support for IPC, for instance?

But our shortsightedness doesn't absolve Belaúnde either. The Ambassador had a point. Not to have settled the oil issue for fear of losing American aid was more than enough of a pretext to make Velasco's bulldog face shine like a benign patriot's!

My last interview was with Enrique Zileri Gibson, editor of the influential picture magazine, *Caretas*, which had defied Velasco's censorship the week before. Velasco had closed it down briefly for printing a cover picture of Artola looking like Himmler under the caption "Artola? Mamacita!" But the magazine reappeared the following week with a cover photograph depicting the secret police rifling *Caretas'* files. I asked the young editor how they got away with defiance of the dictatorship.

"There was such an uproar over the crackdown," Zileri said, "not only here but all over the continent, that they decided it wasn't worth the bad publicity they were getting."

Zileri was another one who thought that the seizure of IPC was a grandstand play to immobilize the Left while ruling in behalf of the Right. A law protecting the bankers had been passed the same day the Talara refinery was occupied. "But Velasco's mistake may be in believing that Peru can survive in isolation, without aid, without loans, without markets abroad. He's gotten himself into a position where he can't afford to make even a token concession to the American position."

"I think we've gotten ourselves into a worse position," I said. "So you think Belaúnde has a future?"

---

[6] The classic, perhaps apocryphal explanation for this second slap in the face was given by the American official who is supposed to have said haughtily, "The Latins aren't ready for supersonics yet."

"Definitely! Even now he has twenty-five percent of the people with him, though his party is underground. When Velasco's popularity reaches a low point, Belaúnde will be regarded as the only clean political figure left—even a hero. Like Prado, Pardo, and others, he will then return from abroad in triumph—probably backed by APRA!"

Belaúnde in Exile

Belaúnde himself, when I visited him at Harvard shortly after returning to the United States, is just as confident that he will return to power in Peru.

I asked him whether it was true that some of Velasco's advisors are Marxists.

"Yes. But not enough to worry his principal backers—who backed him to avoid my taxes. Fear of APRA was only the excuse for the *golpe*. Ambition, greed for power, and the desire to keep things as they were, without taxes or other sacrifices, were the real motivations." As for devaluation of the *sol*, it had been forced upon Peru by the rich who took their money out of the country to avoid taxes, and then brought it back to make fortunes out of the devaluation itself. They could shout their heads off about corruption in the government, but they knew it wasn't true, and so did Peru. "How many other deposed presidents have been so penniless that they have had to teach to make a living?"

Sitting behind his desk in the Department of Urban Affairs, where he teaches a course in city planning, Belaúnde had lost none of the witty self-assurance and youthful handsomeness that charmed visitors to Lima. I asked him whether the current occupation of Harvard's administration center by rebellious students made him feel at home.

"Of course," he said with a laugh. "But compared with what goes on in our bullrings, this is a *novillada!*"

"In retrospect," I asked him, "does your Marginal Highway seem wasteful?"

"No. It was a ten-times cheaper way of providing new land and jobs than the big irrigation dams on the western slopes of the Andes—which, by the way, I built more of than any previous president. It was beginning to provide land without men for men without land, as they say. And the proof is that the road continues, as do the branches in Colombia-Venezuela and Paraguay-Argentina. Moreover, the oil discovered in the course of building the road has a potential far exceeding the exhausted Talara fields. In the virgin jungle north of Cajamarca, near the airport I named after Ciro Alegría, there is a deposit they're now calling 'a second Maracaibo.'"

"Then you think the Marginal was your greatest achievement?"

"I think the climate of openness was my greatest achievement," he replied. "The press was completely free. I had no spy apparatus. I was much too busy for such nonsense. Perhaps, you might say, that is why I am here! But I wouldn't have it any other way. There were nine hundred Indian communities when I took office. When I left there were two thousand—with communal and individual land provided for each of them. I'm proud of that. I'm proud of having restored municipal elections; and I'm proud of having constructed more housing than in all the previous years of Peru's history."

"And Peruvian culture today?" I asked. "What is most valuable in it?"

"Our folklore, and our craftsmen in the folk arts," he answered without hesitation. "Nothing else approaches them in importance. They are the only poets in touch with reality. They are the real Peru."

Is it in the nature of the poet to see too many possibilities, to know too much history, to fear so much betraying the individual human being, that he lacks the ruthlessness to act decisively for the common good? I remembered Belaúnde's moving description of the man picked up on one of his campaign trips over the Andes who had lost his hands building a

government road, and of the government's glacial and diabolical indifference to this individual who had been given no pension. "This suffering man loved his children tenderly," Belaúnde had said. "He did not have hands to care for them, but his sensitivity and kindness proved that they were not necessary to cherish his children. Perhaps he, like Christ, atoned for the faults of others." Belaúnde's first act as President—when he might have been building that spy apparatus—was to see that that forgotten man got his pension.

In the Dominican Republic, I had seen the poet-novelist Juan Bosch, starting out with a nation behind him, overthrown by the military without a hand being lifted in his defense. Had Belaúnde, the poet-architect, been as vulnerable for the same reasons? There had been a day early in his term when enthusiastic laborers had contributed one hundred thousand shovels to the program to rebuild Peru and it had been suggested that they be permitted to parade through Lima. Belaúnde had turned down the suggestion as demagogic; expectations might be raised too high, the promise might not be kept. I felt after leaving Belaúnde at Harvard, that he wouldn't make that mistake again. That had been "the real Peru," the Peru that needed not only poets in touch with people, but people in touch with poets.

4

THE ANTI-POET AS REVOLUTIONIST: THE BOLIVIA CHÉ GUEVARA MISSED

Bolivia, a country of legendary riches with the poorest, most primitive people in South America, attracted the world's attention when Ché Guevara attempted to make it the springboard for his "continental revolution." To understand why the Argentine revolutionary tried and failed, something of this country's tripartite geography and history must be appreciated.

Landlocked, and as large as California and Texas combined, Bolivia lies between Chile, Argentina, and Paraguay on the south, Peru and Brazil on the north. Its eastern half, consisting of the huge provinces of Beni and Santa Cruz, is a jungle wilderness, mostly roadless, sparsely populated, but rich in oil, lumber, and tropical foods. The narrow northwestern section, known as the altiplano, is high, dry, treeless, cold, and densely populated; it shares Lake Titicaca with Peru and contains the twelve-thousand-foot-high capital, La Paz. The southwestern corner of Bolivia with its towering mountains has the fabulous silver and tin deposits that have brought only grief to Bolivia, and the beautiful colonial cities, Sucre, Potosí, and Cochabamba.

In the days when Bolivia's silver enriched Spain, and on into the nineteenth century, when tin began to supplant silver, the Quechua-speaking Indians of western Bolivia whose great pre-Columbian empires had been destroyed, lived in serfdom. But although they worked the mines and fields for the rich (and often absent) *patróns*, these squat, barrel-lunged,

stony-faced descendants of the Incas retained a rich folk culture and a relatively high productivity.

In 1952 Bolivia was convulsed by a fundamental social revolution, the first in South America's history. Ever since Bolívar liberated the colony from Spain and gave it his name, Bolivia had been ruled by a succession of military despots, one giving way to another by *golpe*—sometimes as many as five in a single year—but all enriching themselves at the expense of the land and its people. Then in 1933 the disastrous Chaco War with Paraguay unhinged both the oligarchy and the military establishment through which the oligarchs had maintained control. In 1937, declaring himself "Totalitarian Dictator," Major Germán Busch took over the decimated, bankrupt country. Before he shot himself in August of 1939, Busch prepared the way for the social revolution that was to follow by giving the tin miners representation in the government, declaring war against the millionaire monopolists, Patiño and Hochschild, and campaigning against foreign industrial enterprises, "Yanqui Imperialism" especially. In the period of anarchy that ensued, the Marxist-oriented Movimiento Nacionál Revolucionario (MNR) came to power, and under its socialist leaders, Víctor Paz Estenssoro and Hernán Siles Zuazo, the mines were nationalized and the big landholdings broken up and sub-divided among the Indians who tilled them. As in Mexico, where the Revolution of 1910-14 made economic conditions a great deal worse for the peasants and workers before they began to get better, Bolivia's mines and fields virtually stopped producing. Inefficient management, feather-bedding, and constant wage boosts priced tin out of competition in the international market. The peasants, lacking cooperatives, fertilizers, or credit, now produced only enough to feed themselves. And the govern-ment, deprived of revenues from both traditional sources, became so demoralized and corrupt that it was finally overthrown by a *golpe* in its own army. The air force general who succeeded Paz as President, René Barrientos Ortuño, had been a partisan of the socialist revolution from its inception, but he was anti-communist and pro-American. The United States had supported Paz Estenssoro with loans, but Barrientos carried this friendly liaison further by giving an American oil company a contract to explore and develop the oil in the eastern wilderness. He also sent his Ranger commanders to Panama for counterinsurgency training to fight the Castro-trained *guerrilleros* he expected momentarily.

First Visit

Bill Negron and I flew to Bolivia for the first time in 1966, just before the arrival of Ché Guevara and his Cuban comrades. We were on our way back to Peru after a brief visit with Pablo Neruda in Chile. "Open your eyes, offended peoples!" ended a poem about Puerto Rico the Chilean poet had given us as we boarded the plane for La Paz, "there is a Sierra Maestra all around you!" A year later, when Ché was winning his first skirmishes with the Bolivian Army, those lines would have seemed prophetic; but two years later—when Neruda's party, the Moscow-line communists, had refused to support Ché and abandoned him to his fate, they seemed ironical. In 1966 Bolivia seemed very remote from subversion or counterinsurgency. An ambitious road-building program was under way—Lake Titicaca to La Paz, La Paz to Cochabamba, Cochabamba to Santa Cruz—and Ambassador Douglas Henderson, a Kennedy appointee who had served in Lima, was telling us that Bolivia's future, like Peru's, lay in industrialization—giving jobs to the millions flocking into the cities from the Andes, and rehousing these slum dwellers. When Hender-son said scornfully that Belaúnde's plan to move the city folk back up and over the mountains to colonize the jungle was "sheer mysticism," we half believed him, for we had heard of the superstitious terror of the jungle, its diseases, its insects, its savages, which has been in every highland Indian's heart since pre-Inca times.

But emerging from the efficient, antiseptic embassy into the streets of La Paz, we were less sure. What rational American solution, spurning "mysticism," could possibly take care of Bolivia's hang-ups? It was

"General Abaroa Day," [1] and down the crooked mountain streets poured men in uniform and civilians in their Sunday best, government workers, student lawyers, veterans of the Chaco War, carrying banners and sandwich-boards with the slogans "For the Reconquest of Our Sea," "Antofagasta Is and Always Will Be Bolivian," "Bolivian Naval Might," etc.— till they converged in the Avenida 16 de Julio parade. There, the center of every admiring gaze was a float with a dreamboat ocean-going passenger liner, *La Boliviana*.

"When the hell are you hicks going to catch up with the rest of the world?" we heard one of these young patriots taunt a group of gaping Indians near the corner of San Francisco Church. In their homespun shorts, white boaters, and thonged sandals, the *campesinos* stared sullenly back. Obviously they didn't understand a word of Spanish, and if they could have read, the sign "For the Reconquest of Our Sea" would have meant nothing to them. The Cholo women in their derbies, sitting on the curb, understood vaguely what was being said, but surely knew nothing of Antofagasta, that thriving port that had been Chilean now for almost a century.

"Will they ever get it back?" I asked Henderson later.

"Of course not," he said. "This is their folklore. We have ours. What do they need a seaport for, with all those rail lines to the Pacific, and soon an Atlantic outlet by river through Paraguay? They'll have this inferiority complex—and hate gringos and breed communists in their universities—just as long as they are weak. It's our job to help them help themselves to be strong. And to ignore the brickbats."

The Ambassador, in addition to pushing for bigger loans and teams of engineers to get those roads built to the oil-rich lowlands, had done his bit by contributing ten thousand dollars' worth of paints and brushes to the capital's school children. Blocks and blocks of fences in the center of the city were covered with murals of dolls and demons in brilliant colors. They were the only fences in La Paz that didn't flaunt the airbrushed slogan of the student communists: "Yanquis Go Home!"

We learned a lot of other things about Bolivia, trivial things perhaps but illuminating, during that brief first visit—things which might or might not have helped the single-minded Ché the following year when he failed so signally to make contact with the people. ITEM: The biggest turnover in the Indian market is in llama fetuses. One of these must be buried at each corner of a new house to insure fertility. ITEM: The equestrian statue of General Sucre, the national hero, has been stripped of all its brass lettering. Windshield wipers disappear instantly if left on parked

---

[1] Eduardo Abaroa, we discovered later, was the Bolivian equivalent of Peru's Francisco Bolognesi, a young hero from San Pedro de Atacama who had fought to his last cartridge in that hopeless war against Chile when Bolivia had lost not only her nitrate deposits, like Peru, but her seaports as well. The young martyr was made a general posthumously.

cars. We watched a gang of six-to-eight-year-old boys stealing the tiles and plastic seat covers from a vestibule in the Cathedral where some repair work was being done. ITEM: Until our American hosts imported a lawnmower last month, their lawn was cut with the lid of a tin can; the same instrument was used to cut the wool from alpacas and llamas until our AID program provided shears. ITEM: The brown derbies worn by the Cholos date from 1900 when an English merchant had to unload a stock of these hats shipped him by mistake; he saw to it that word got around that the derbies increased fertility. ITEM: A Swiss trader, whose route includes Andean Peru, noted that both Bolivia and Peru are richer in natural resources per capita than the United States, but that their people don't have a tenth of the income of the Swiss, who have no natural resources at all: "When you don't have anything, you have to be more industrious than anybody!" The Swiss trader disagreed with Henderson about Belaúnde's colonization scheme. "Modern industry means machines, not millions of jobs. But land grants and credits could mean that cash crops like tea, which is in short supply all over the world, might serve to lure some of these parasitic hordes out of the city *barriadas*. The biggest drawback is the pollution of the rivers down in the *junglas*. There's no healthy drinking water in that whole vast area. The legend of the *sierra*, that those who go over the top never return, is true!" ITEM: We'd been drinking coca tea to counteract our *soroche* (altitude sickness). The Indians, in addition to chewing this narcotic constantly to anaesthetize themselves against cold and hunger, clamp a leaf to both temples to keep the evil spirits out. What evil spirits, we asked a Quechua-speaking friend. The answer was predictable: "The spirits that prevent fertility." ITEM: The tin miners in the socialized mines are now getting their "featherbedded" wages paid again—out of an American loan.

From our bedroom window one morning we watched the sunrise gild

La Paz, Bolivia - 1969
W. Nagron

the beautiful, ramshackle city in its cup of steep hills, mist hanging over
the clumps of dusty eucalyptus, with snowcapped Illimani in the distance.
White roses gripped the red brick walls descending in three leisurely
stages to a picket fence. Over the rose-draped walls is a scraggly corn
patch. Over the picket fence, Rebecca, the Aymará maid, tosses the garbage into an open sewer which finally reaches a tunnel under the center
of the city. Before the Americans built the tunnel, typhus epidemics were
frequent. It embarrasses us that Rebecca answers our questions by lower-
ing her eyes and addressing us "Caballeros. . . . " The stucco walls of the
house are pitted with bullet scars from last year's coup; and in the dining
room there is a neat hole in the window where a stray shot recently just
missed a guest. Yet nowhere in Bolivia, and least of all from the Indians,
were we to encounter the slightest gesture of hostility; and our host, who
crisscrosses every part of the country on his monthly rounds, confirmed
our impression.

We returned to Peru in 1966 on the bus that circles Lake Titicaca, accepting an invitation from a fellow passenger, a Maryknoll priest, to stop
off overnight at his parish house in Juli. The road over the capital's valley
rim first passes tiny settlements of Indians tilling their patches of wheat
or potatoes, or tending sheep. As the road descends into the lake basin,
the isolated adobe cottages coalesce into villages, and the low rolling hills
of the altiplano are covered with the yellow of wild mustard, the blue of
lima beans, the patato's purple, and the variety of reds of the tasseled
quinoa. As we reached the vast lake itself, *totora* skiffs could be seen
sailing between the islands; and cattle, up to their bellies in the reeds
from which the boats are woven, slurped the green algae.

For all this apparent agricultural bounty, these are the worst nourished
people in the world, Father Macri told us. Their diet is all starch: eighty-
five percent dehydrated potatoes (out of which they have stamped the
water, to subsist through the harvestless months), *quinoa* soup, cereal,
and bread; no meat at all. A few scrawny chickens are kept only for their
eggs. The cows give at most a quart of milk a day (compared to sixty in
the U.S.), which is used entirely for cheese; and the sheep are herded for
their wool alone. "Land is the Indians' biggest asset," said the padre
from Rutherford, New Jersey, "but the tiny individual plots, once the
father dies, can't be divided among his five sons, so the other four drift
to the *barriadas*."

"What's their recreation?" Bill asked.

"Drinking—" the Father replied, "pure alcohol, made from sugar.
Twenty cents' worth is enough to get drunk on."

"How do they treat their animals?" I asked.

"Lovingly," the padre answered. "They wouldn't sell one to save a sick
child—and I mean that literally. An aspirin or two is as far as an Indian
will go in that department. Though, of course, he wants our prayers, and

a mass for the little dead one. One of our aims is to discourage the idea that religion is something you seize and pay for when in desperation—like sickness, or forestalling a hailstorm that might level the potato patch. There weren't more than twenty-five churchgoers in this village when we came here a decade ago. Now there are close to a thousand."

Second Visit

Father Macri had exaggerated when he said that drinking was the Indians' only diversion. The Peruvian city of Puno, a few miles west of Juli, is the focus of festivals with costumes, masks, music, and dance rivaling anything described in the *Thousand and One Nights*. And to the east, depending on the day of the year, highland Bolivia's church fiestas can be as gaudy as anything depicted in the paintings of Quattrocento Siena. The black goatskin men's helmet of Tarabuco, with red and yellow lines intersecting on top, and the matching dish-shaped rhomboid worn by the women of that town, heavy with spangles and tufted with old coins, are positively medieval. A coca bag from Cochabamba is worthy of holding a queen's jewels: the shoulder strap intricately stitched in red and purple; the sack an abstract pattern of ancient symbols in green and gold; the lime pouchlet black and green; and the sixteen hanging pompoms multicolored to complete the dazzling harmony. In the church of Jesus de Machaca in the *yungas* north of La Paz, Indians in full dress costume with headdresses and parasols of feathers dance the *cueca* to keep on the good side of the gods of the sun and rain, just as they have for a thousand years.

The Bolivian Government, naturally enough, is less concerned about preserving the country's matchless folk arts than are the wives of American missions with plenty of time on their hands to develop aesthetic sensibilities. Yet oddly enough—a switch on the American imperialism war cry—U.S.A.I.D. was being criticized by Bolivians in January of 1969 for turning over its pilot save-the-folk-arts project to the Bolivian Government! "*Artesinas Bolivianas* was your only program," its former Bolivian director, Daisy de Wende, told me reproachfully, "that put you in touch with the people, the only one for which Bolivians were grateful. For who's grateful for a road? or a piece of machinery? Who even knows where they came from? But these *campesino* craftsmen were aware of your help. For the first time in their lives they got a fair price for their textiles. And for the first time in history they were invited to come in and sit down with the gentlemen and ladies—a revolution in Bolivia! They were treated like human beings!"

"And now—?" I asked.

"And now our politicians have moved in. Already they've used AID's twenty-seven-thousand-dollar terminal fund to buy themselves cars! The new director cares nothing for peasants, or people of any kind. The Minister of Culture was smart enough to see Bolivia's loss and asked me to stay on, but I refused. I prefer to start all over again from scratch, on my own, even without capital. Why, oh why did AID do this to us?"

But this was only the most peripheral part of the tension hovering over Bolivia as we arrived for our second visit, though AID seemed to be involved in all of it. The night before, the residence of our new Ambassador, Raul Castro, had been bombed; and the day before that a similar device exploded in front of our consulate in Cochabamba. Alleged motivation? The government had fallen behind on paying its agreed share (ten to fifteen percent) of the various projects; AID (lest the U.S. Congress strip it of its appropriations) was insisting; ergo, the various communist groups, to score such an "imperialistic" insistence on payments, had tossed a bomb or two.

Since our host, as before, was quite close to all this, we asked him what it signified.

"The difficulty," he said, "springs from the fact that all these under-developed countries accept loans of no matter what magnitude, figuring that over the generous forty-year period of interest payments, the money will be found—or they'll be long since gone. We're following the contract to the letter, but if the Bolivians go on refusing to pay their minimal share and we cut back on the key road projects, it could cause a revolution and the overthrow of Barrientos—which of course is the last thing AID or the State Department wants. It's partly our fault. We're so enthusiastic about what we're helping them accomplish, we may have caused them to overextend themselves. But we have to find out whether they really can't pay, or are dragging their feet and pocketing the money."

"How can they pay their share," I asked, "revenues from tin having dried up?"

"By cutting salaries, by firing those employees who do nothing, and by taxing the *campesinos*—all unpopular measures.

"Another problem," he went on, "is that the roads they're building have to be maintained. We insist on a maintenance budget; they resent that. The Santa Cruz-Cochabamba road we built for them in 1948-54 is a shambles—no maintenance. And this is economically Bolivia's most important road. We've loaned them money to repair it and it's still unrepaired. Until U.S.A.I.D. came along, the only Bolivian roads were those built by Paraguayan prisoners during the Chaco War—just as the only Paraguayan roads were those built by Bolivian prisoners."

While Bill was arranging our trip to the colonial cities, I went to see Ambassador Castro whom we'd met in El Salvador two years before. We had already heard how well he was getting along with Barrientos, the swashbuckling, wenching, Quechua-speaking President who had been trained as a fighter pilot in the United States.[2] They had gone to Santa Cruz together a couple of weeks ago, and in the evening Barrientos had disappeared with some local girl leaving Castro waiting. Finally Castro announced he was going to bed. "You can't!" the shocked staff told him, "You've got to stay up with him." "I'll stay with him," the American Ambassador said, "as long as I'm doing what he's doing." Barrientos, hearing this later, had been delighted.

Born near the Mexican border, Castro is probably our only Ambassador who speaks English with a slight foreign accent, and looks like a Latin. He is a jovial, no-nonsense type. He thinks the Bolivian government's biggest problem is collecting taxes—even token taxes—from the *campesinos* who have never paid any. A bill to collect from them is now before the Congress: it is called "The One Farm Tax." Out of four million Bolivians only twenty-six thousand are on the tax rolls, not nearly enough to pay the government's bills, for there are very few wealthy people in Bolivia since the Paz Estenssoro Revolution, and no millionaires. The Ambassador wasn't at all disturbed by the weekend's violence, which he called marginal, and which didn't spring, he told me, from the eighty percent of the people who are for Barrientos and share his pro-Americanism. "It's much safer here than in Guatemala, that other direct-action country," he said, "where they use machine guns and kidnap you. In this mining country they use dynamite sticks. Barrientos is very popular everywhere except in the mines, which his army now controls, and among the students. There are no moderate democrats among miners or students."

Castro was very high on Bolivia's potential, which he considered greater than that of any South American country of its size. "The mestizo population of the lowlands, Argentine-influenced, is very enterprising. The one hundred thousand people in bustling Santa Cruz are hard workers. The land is very rich, and of course there is the oil, exceeded in South America only by Venezuela and possibly Peru and Ecuador. But this area and the unexplored jungles of the northeast, bordering Peru and Brazil, are underpopulated, and it's hard to get highlanders down there. They blow up with reverse *soroche*. United States Air Force regulations, re-

---

[2] On April 27, 1969, three months after our second visit to Bolivia, President Barrientos was killed in the crash of a helicopter which he was piloting. His legal successor, Vice President Luis Adolfo Siles Salines, was overthrown in September, eleven months short of the expiration of Barrientos' term of office, by General Alfredo Ovando Candia, the Army Chief of Staff who had been Barrientos' comrade in the coup against Paz Estenssoro. Taking a page from the successful script of the Peruvian military, the right-wing Ovando was quick to gain favor with the radical student left by seizing and nationalizing Gulf Oil's Bolivian subsidiary, operating in the Santa Cruz fields under agreements signed with Barrientos. In charge of this operation was Ovando's Mines and Petroleum Minister, Marcello Quiroga—interviewed in this chapter.

member, insist that you inhale oxygen at ten thousand feet, and we're two thousand feet higher than that right now. Mining, lumbering, farming, furs, are all big comers, but at the moment it's oil, and the problem is how to get it out of this landlocked country. Thirty-five thousand barrels a day go out over the railroad to Arica, but there are no storage facilities there for any more—unless Chile provides them. The same railroad takes out the tin and some lumber. There's an even costlier haul from Santa Cruz to Puerto Suarez and then down the Paraguay River to Buenos Aires—but that is over fifteen hundred miles! A pipeline to northern Argentina is under construction; and Argentina has generously given Bolivia a free port at Rosario on the Parana River, but that, too, is a fifteen-hundred-mile haul."

"I wonder if Ché would have been so optimistic about settling the future with guns if he'd known about these problems," I said.

"Ché," he replied with a laugh, "knew only that Gulf Oil was here."

Journey to the Silver Cities

If Ché had taken time out to visit the three provincial capitals that are the pride of Bolivia—they can be visited in three days, we discovered; and in his disguise as a balding, bespectacled salesman, Ché would have passed as unnoticed as he had in La Paz—what would he have seen? Would their glorious configurations and noble architecture have humbled him? Would it have profited him to blame the monkish orders for over-populating Sucre with churches? or to condemn the Spain of the avaricious Philips for establishing their mint in Potosí? Simón Patiño, who built his tin Tuilleries in Cochabamba out of the blood and sweat of an army of Indians, was, unfortunately, a poor Bolivian who struck it rich. No. It was better for Ché not to see these celestial cities. In the hellish ravines of Nancahuazú and Quebrada del Yuro, where not even a human foot had left its mark, he could go on blaming the Americans for all the continent's afflictions. And South America's intellectuals, from Santiago de Chile to Caracas, who have been hanging scapegoats in effigy ever since the liberators abdicated and pronounced the continent ungovernable, could be counted upon to applaud his martyrdom.

"Patiño was generally regarded as a stupid Cholo," remarked a Bolivian engineer who took us to see the tin king's Portales Palace in Cochabamba. "We wished we had been so stupid. At the time they built this for him he was living in Paris as Ambassador. No doubt he owned the Bolivian Government as well as the Embassy. . . . One day he had been minding a company store in Oruro for a *patrón* who warned him not to give credit to some prospectors who had just arrived in town since their claim to a certain hill was known to be worthless. The prospectors arrived and talked Patiño into accepting half the claim for an armful of groceries. When the *patrón* returned, Patiño dutifully handed him the claim, but the furious *patrón* threw it in his face. 'The mortgage is yours, you stupid Cholo! You pay it off!' Patiño did, and the half-hill, which turned out to be all tin, became his. Years later, in 1925, he became the dominant figure in the Chilean combine that had acquired the other half."

The baroque palace was built for Patiño in the eary twenties out of Italian marble by French architects. Its cornices are embellished with appliquéd gesso, white on gold. Thirty-seven interior decorators from France were employed on the interior fittings. The grand ballroom, forty feet high, is graced with golden cupids bearing the "S.I.P." emblem. The adjoining billiard room is a miniature multicolored Alhambra, and still standing in the racks are the dozen gold-leafed cues. Was the palace ever occupied? Perhaps for a week, perhaps only for a single christening party, as in the case of Rafael Leonidas Trujillo's "El Cerro" outside the Dominican capital, which it approaches in opulence and bad taste. "Portales" was seized by the Bolivian government after the 1952 Revolution, along with the many other Patiño mansions, and of course the mines. To cast doubt on the legality of this move, the Patiño family quickly presented it to the University of Bolivia, and it was perhaps at that moment of touching generosity that the two white marble mastiffs guarding a modest pile of books were added to the entrance gate as a symbol of the "learning" the family had hastily decided to patronize.

Eight months before our visit, Antenór Patiño, the tin king's son, returned to Bolivia with the body of his mother to inter beside Simón's remains at Pairumani, their *estancia* outside of Cochabamba. Christian Democratic students greeted him at the airport, slinging pails of pigs' blood. He then held a press conference at which he announced that he had come back to spend some of the family's five-hundred-million-dollar fortune on benefits for Bolivia, but that he was now returning to France. The students' answer was that they would rather starve than accept his blood money.

This commendable pride, and a somewhat disparaging attitude toward the less gently favored cities of Bolivia, came out in every Cochabambino we talked to. The bleak chill of La Paz, Oruro, and Potosí, is not here; nor does Cochabamba sweat with Santa Cruz' steamy *calor*. The soil is rich. The landscape undulates. And there is a busy social life for those who can afford it at the Club Cortijo and the Cochabamba Hotel. Monday nights the streets are deserted for there are double features at no extra price in all the movie theaters. President Belaúnde had prepared me for the Cochabambinos' toploftiness when he told me of the greeting Barrientos and his staff had received when they came here to open the federal highway: "Gentlemen, we have been waiting for you three hundred years!" The Revolution, a local businessman assured us, had been necessary, but it had left the liberated Indians more animal and individualistic than ever. Barrientos was still the *campesinos'* hero, but he had done little to give them the producers' cooperatives they needed.

"His biggest failure has been his inability to set an example. He is building big homes for himself all over the country, enriching his family, and permitting outright theft among his friends."

A young English businessman staying at our hotel was more optimistic about Bolivia's future. He had spent a year traveling all over the country and he thought the Indians, especially those in the altiplano, would oppose any revolutionary movement. "They are relatively well fed, with a traditionally balanced diet, and they are disciplined because of their centuries-old system of having a village dictator whose term expires forever after one year. He has to be honest, and as a result they're honest; and one may travel anywhere in this country in perfect safety. The communists get nowhere with the Indians. But I'd go further and say that Marxism doesn't go down with the *macho* complex of Latin Americans. Nobody wants to be collectivized. Everybody wants to be at least a little *caudillo*. No, Marxism appeals only to the intellectuals—and they don't really believe in it either!"

Sucre, the ancient capital which has never relinquished its claim, is the most unspoiled colonial city in South America. Even from a distance, rolling with the folds of its valleys, it has an enchanted look. It was a perfect day when we arrived, the sky a C-major blue with cadenzas of billowing cumulus, and far away dark chords of rain hanging from thunderheads on the jagged horizon. Every roof is of terra-cotta tiles, and this low-lying plain song is counterpointed by the bell towers of the thirty churches and monasteries, dazzling white. Parks, here and there, of emerald *piño*, complete the symphonic poem.

Dropping our bags at the keyless Gran Hotel, where you get in and out of your room by putting your hand through a hole in the glass door and lifting the latch, we climbed the Cathedral's square tower accompanied by six beautiful Indian children who asked for nothing but copies of the photographs we were taking. Then, in the bucking Toyota of Gladys de Costa whose architectural knowledge was formidable, we visited San Lazaro, the oldest church with its colonnades dating from 1534; La Merced (1540-80) with a great gold retablo behind its altar and a golden pulpit intricately carved; the Monastery of San Felipe (1694) with splendid cloisters and notable woodcarvings of its own; La Recoleta, a Franciscan church with carved choir stalls as fine as any in Peru, dating from 1602-07; and San Francisco (1564-70) with its ornate multicolored and spiked ceiling in the Mudejar style the Moors brought to Spain. On top of one church we saw blocks of stone held together with silver clamps.

The *Chuquisaqueños* (so-called from the province) are proud of their city, as well they might be; but their pride goes more to announcing its "capital" status hourly on the radio, than to preserving its visual beauty. In fact a hideous dormitory of cinder blocks had just been built next to one of the churches, completely destroying the inviolability of its cloister.

I asked an American resident whether the Church has any real hold over the *campesinos* and he answered obliquely by telling me this story of his maid. Finding her drinking garlic tea last week, he asked her why. It seems she'd seen a dragonfly the week before, and dragonflies, "it's well known," steal a single hair from one's head to give to a witch in the pay of one's enemies. Sure enough, two days later her sister was stabbed in a brawl. The *ajo* infusion would set matters straight.

But the Church, as everywhere in South America, is on the move to replace superstition with education for self-improvement. And especially in such areas of widespread unemployment and near-starvation as south-west Bolivia and northwest Brazil, it is anxious to identify at long last with the underdog. It was significant that when Barrientos' soldiers smashed the communist labor union in the state-owned tin mine at Catavi, alleging that an insurrection was being organized to mesh with the Cuban *guerrilleros'* offensive, the priests in that area waited until Ché had been killed, and then denounced the suppression of the union. It was significant, too, that in doing so they invoked this reputed declaration by Recife's "Red" Archbishop, Helder Cámara: "Those who categorize as communist any courageous, intelligent, daring action in defense of truth and justice are simply serving as propagandists for communism." The point the Bolivian miners' padres seemed to be making was that if Barrientos was turning the Bolivian Revolution into a military dictatorship that excluded the hungriest people in Bolivia—the unemployed tin miners—it would be no better than the Rightist military clique that had stifled all protest in Brazil.

There were communists, too, in Potosí—the ancient mile-and-a-half-high silver city—plenty of them. Especially the grade school teachers

San Bernardo, Potosí, Bolivia. January 1967

with a receptive clientele of hungry children. And understandably, because all the money that wasn't going into those roads west was relieving the pressure on La Paz, ringed like every Andean capital by hordes of mountain migrants. Potosí, like Cochabamba and Sucre, was getting almost no relief, yet the province of Potosí contained (contained very poorly, one should say) seven hundred thousand people: seven hundred thousand people who felt they were being unfairly discriminated against. No doubt only a handful of them blamed Barrientos for this, but that handful had airgunned its slogan in purple or red on every peasant hovel along the twisting upland tracks from Sucre: *Gloria a Ché*!

It had been a wearisome, depressing, and yet exalting ride in the iron cab of the *ferrobus*, a clanking diesel-powered contraption on narrow-gauge tracks that we boarded in Sucre before dawn. An hour's wait in the overcrowded darkness, the aisle jammed with stinking peasants and their animals, promised hell on wheels—especially since our seat was over the wheels. Yet five hours later in sight of Potosí we were singing with the rest of them. The red river valleys and striped cliffs were majestic, and the Indians in their brilliant ponchos and Victorian top hats, crowding in on us at every whistle stop with buckets of chicken and rice and onions and unidentifiable stews were not to be denied. We stopped once for *saltañas* (meat-filled buns), and at Betanzas for beer; and when we finally arrived, there was Juan Aitken, who asked us to call him "Jack," and who made the most amazing statement we'd heard in South America ("Our problem is underpopulation"), a statement only exceeded by his response when Bill remarked that his own father in Puerto Rico was a Lion too: "He must be a good fellow."

Jack was the local representative of Turismo who had heard that we were coming, and a companion more knowledgeable (about Potosí) and *simpático* would be hard to imagine. First he talked the *ferrobus* company into squeezing us aboard the next day's eight-hour haul to La Paz, booked solid for six weeks ahead. Then he took us at my request to see the cut-stone facade of San Lorenzo (1728-44), swarming with Indian-faced cherubim, which is even richer than its celebrated twin in Arequipa (Peru) though not as well placed, being cramped inside a projecting arc of the nave's barrel-vault, facing the marketplace. And then we visited *La Moneda*, the enormous sprawling palace that turned out those millions of pieces-of-eight for Spain from the sixteenth to the nineteenth centuries. Its colossal wooden wheels and wood-geared presses, once driven by teams of mules on the floor below, are still intact. Here the silver was pressed into bars, sheets, and wafers for stamping. The dies still exist, but there are very few coins. The Museum (Jack's brainchild) is too broke to afford them, or even to illuminate its gloomy picture gallery, although it has assembled as fine a collection of colonial arts and crafts as any in Bolivia. We were especially fascinated by the ancient miners' lamps with crucifixes, the crude spikes with which the chunks

of ore were dislodged, and a bellows-shaped device called a *culero* (ass-seat) on which the Indians slid down the muddy tunnels. We were also intrigued by Jack's explanation of why one high-vaulted chamber was blackened. "This was always a favorite meeting place for our revolutionaries," he explained. "We've had 1.5 revolutions per annum since Independence, you know. And to keep themselves warm they made bonfires of the archives."

Silver and tin are still smelted at Potosí, and the sinister conical mountain of precious metal makes a perfect tourist photograph through the city's arched gateway; but mining no longer pays. The government took over that half of the industry controlled by Patiño, Hochschild, and Aramayo, leaving the smaller producers unmolested but too thoroughly unionized to modernize or expand. "The private sector," Aitken said, "operates far more efficiently than the government's. Do you want to see the symbolism, and the only work of art—if you can call it that—produced in Bolivia in our time?"

Out in the dazzling sunlight of the main street we contemplated the bronze pyramid of miners, its topmost figure brandishing a gun. "When they put it up in the forties," Aitken explained, "he was brandishing a shovel. When the more militant MNR took over in the fifties they substituted the gun. What next?"

Politicians and Poets

Back in La Paz, I asked one of our top officials in AID why the mining country was getting so little help. He put it this way. "We—that's to say the Bolivian Government and AID—are putting the money where the future lies, in the oil and agricultural lowlands. The Revolution expected the nationalized tin mines to support all its reforms. Instead, the mines have run at a loss ever since, and at the expense of the rest of the economy. Bolivia is fourth in the world in tin production, but the cost of production, where miners still pick the tin out of the hills with their bare hands and get higher and higher wages for doing it, is $1.48 a pound compared with $.85 in the three big producers, Malaysia, Indonesia, and Thailand, where the deposits are alluvial and are taken out with dredges. Understandably, since he's cutting back on the featherbedding, Barrientos is not popular in the tin country, and by the same token that is the only sector of Bolivia where Ché is something of a hero."

"Is Barrientos popular enough with the peasants to get away with taxing them?" I asked.

"Nobody knows. But no other Bolivian politician could even try. Remember, the tax will affect only those forty percent who have land titles—the four hundred thousand out of nine hundred thousand who've received titles since 1953."

"Are the others getting them?"

"Constantly. Last month Barrientos signed fifteen hundred new titles at a single sitting."

"You mean he has to sign each title personally?"

"If he didn't they wouldn't believe what they were getting was for real!"

"How do you account for their trust in him?"

"Because he's *muy macho*. He pilots his own plane. He flies all over the country, landing in places where you drop into the fog and count ten. He never fears to face his enemies. He directed the action against Ché in person—they were yards apart in one skirmish near the end. I saw a Chola at an airport once come up to him holding a kid, claiming it was his. He was wearing his stocking cap and talking Quechua a mile a minute. He acknowledged paternity, gave the girl some money and hugged them both. It may be corny, but they love him for that sort of thing. It was one of Ché's many drawbacks that he and his intruders couldn't speak a word of Quechua—much less Guarani, the dialect of the sector they were operating in."

We went to see Fernando Díez de Medina, Barrientos' idea man and speech writer when he isn't in the *campo*. A poet and novelist, Díez de Medina was Minister of Education under Paz and Siles Zuazo. He had no official position in the government at the moment, but proudly displayed in his office a photograph showing him standing between Barrientos and Ovando, the Army chief who was expected to succeed Barrientos in 1970. I told him about the communist slogans we'd seen all over the southwest, and the report in Potosí that communists dominated the school system there. He thought the percentage was greatly exaggerated. "As for the slogans, the trouble is that the democracies don't spend money on propaganda. The Moscow, Peking, and Havana people get their simple-minded message to the masses at any cost, and if it's the only message the masses see—well, a lot of people are taken in. Why don't you try the same thing?"

I said I'd been arguing the point at our embassies, and in Washington, for years but always got the impression that it was considered somehow indecent or un-American to label our constructions, claim credit for our assets, or advertise our heroes.

He laughed. "If you don't, they will. In fact they do, as you've seen for yourself. The signs ought to read *Gloria a los Kennedys*, no?"

"And *Gloria a Martin Luther King*," I added.

"Precisely."

We went next to talk with Marcello Quiroga, a revolutionary nationalist *Diputado* who wants to set up a *frente civica* of all leftist groups. He was jailed a month ago for being the only speaker at a students' mock-trial of Barrientos and Ovando, making the usual leftist charges of repression and a sellout to Gulf Oil. Though he is not permitted to occupy his seat in the Congress pending his trial on unspecified charges, he is quite free to write for *El Sol*, an opposition newsletter, and to broadcast on Radio Altiplano. I asked him if he considered himself a Marxist.

"I am a Marxist only as Marx interprets reality," said the young novelist who won the Faulkner Prize some years ago, "not a party man. I represent the Nationalist Left in Latin America."

I laughed. "Is there a Latin American who is *not* a nationalist? Or who will admit to being a conservative? Borges perhaps. Certainly not Barrientos! Aren't you in favor of Barrientos' continuation of the Revolution's land program?"

"It's true," he said, "that our peasants have the land or are getting it, but most don't have clear title. Barrientos wants to distribute titles only so he can tax, and at the rate he's going it'll be a century before all the titles are signed. But the point is that distributing the land isn't enough. They must produce, and without producers' cooperatives they can't."

"I agree. . . . And Barrientos' bet on the hot lowlands?"

"The lowlands can only be colonized via industrialization. Cochabambinos go voluntarily to Santa Cruz for the cotton harvest because the wages are good. But that isn't solving the problem where the people are. Under Barrientos, the whole tendency is toward uneconomic individual plots, *minifundia*. A tractor can only be bought by many *campesino* families working together. And without tractors. . . ."

"Would you favor expropriating Gulf Oil?" I asked.

"No. But I'd insist on a better contract. Under the present one, Gulf gets an excessive share of the profits. The Petroleum Code of 1956 was forced on Bolivia by the United States. It gave twenty-five percent to the oil companies in depreciation allowances. Paz took over Standard Oil, but

Siles gave it back—to Gulf. I say: Better no contract at all than a contract prejudicial to Bolivia! . . . When you return, come and see me. If you don't find me in Congress, you'll find me in jail!"

Quiroga has a more winning personality than Díez de Medina, doesn't hand out mimeographed biographies and inscribed copies of his books, and expresses himself much more frankly. But like most of the leftists he tends to talk in clichés and disdains practical solutions to specific problems. "Many think Bolivia is two camps," Díez de Medina had said to us, "those for the Government and those against it. I don't agree. I see grays. And I prefer our way, and Chile's, to the mailed fists of Argentina and Brazil and Peru. We have complete freedom of the press. We've saved the mines. We're building roads and pipelines, with your help."

We showed Díez de Medina's books to Eduardo MacLean, a literary critic from Cochabamba with whom we had drinks later that afternoon. He had nothing but disdain for the wily politician as a literary critic, but conceded that Franz Tamayo, subject of one of the books, was Bolivia's best poet. "But for God's sake!" exclaimed MacLean, "he wrote poems out of Greek mythology! None of our poets or novelists write about Bolivia. The new ones write about political ideas." And as if to prove his point, a young poet named Pedro Shimose came up to our table, introduced himself, and presented us with a copy of his *Poemas para un Puebla*, the opening lines of which were as follows:

> *In order to speak about my country, one must name you.*
> *One must say: Camillo Torres, Ché Guevara, Josue de Castro*
> *as one says Yucatan, Machu Picchu, the Amazon.*
> *In order to understand my country, to love it, to know what it is*
> *one need not attend social receptions, read papers or visit libraries.*
> *It is enough to say: slums of Rio, farms of Caracas*
> *(while the generals plan their headquarters),*
> *slums of Santiago de Chile, Mexico, Buenos Aires, Lima*
> *(while the Papal Nuncios take their siestas)*
> *mining camps of the Bolivian highlands*
> *(while the ministers make big deals).*
> *And when a Brazilian Archbishop protests injustice*
> *the marshals tremble with fear and call the CIA . . .*

Ché

He was a brave man, unsullied by the materialism that flaws our civilization, dedicated to delivering the oppressed from bondage even at the cost of his life. He was pure and selfless in the context of his calling. And he was the anti-poet though none of the poets, or priests, who envied him for his capacity to substitute action for doubt, were aware of it.

Cuba's Guillén recited an ode followed by a twenty-one-gun salute. The

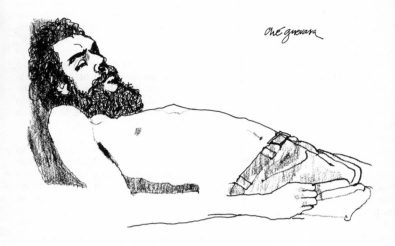

Brazilian Archbishop expressed his "great respect," and Evita Perón's confessor in Buenos Aires compared him to El Cid. Julio Cortázar promised that his pen would be guided by Ché though they "have cut off his fingers." The Ecuadorean poet, Adoum, proclaimed that Latin America had been ennobled, and Jean-Paul Sartre announced that Ché had been "the most complete man of his time." Robert Lowell, seeming to recognize the ambiguous truth that he had been slain "for truth, for justice," nevertheless called him "the last armed prophet."

The painters fell in love with his death image, strapped naked to the laundry tub at Vallegrande so reporters could inspect the wounds. They painted him with the traditional full beard, the lustrous brown eyes rolled inadvertently heavenward (Christ entombed), or lashed to the helicopter's skis, an airborne redeemer in the clutches of Hell's Angels. They painted him realistically, with the stigmata; or abstractly, in a sunburst of red.

He came to Bolivia armed with cash, automatic weapons, and statistics. These should suffice, for wasn't it enough that this strategically placed little country was poverty-stricken and receiving help from the archenemy? In all Ché's voluminous diaries there is no mention of anything in Bolivia's history, past or present, that could have provided a clue to what the people really wanted. If he caught even a sidewise glimpse of the landscape's awesome majesty, the ancient monuments or living folk arts, or the beauty of common faces or figures of speech, he maintained a silence that was absolute. The mission, as he saw it, could be accomplished with rifles, grenades, bazookas, rocket-launchers, walkie-talkies, and the syllogisms of the prophets, Marx and Lenin, "correctly" interpreted—by him.

Vanity, arrogance, and lack of the poet's eye were his undoing.

His vanity betrayed him into abandoning the disguise of a paunchy, close-shaven Uruguayan salesman that had permitted him to wander the streets of La Paz undetected. It also insured the disastrous indiscretion of all those photographs later captured in a cave: posing with weapon at the ready, chatting with comrades whose identities would thus be revealed.

His arrogance developed out of the stunning Cuban triumph; if he had it in Argentina, in Guatemala, in Mexico, in the Sierra Maestra, it was well concealed. It led him not only to misinterpret the quick collapse of Batista's forces—he credited a peasant uprising, when in reality it had been the total defection of the Cuban middle class with its resources in money, technology, and arms that had unhorsed the corrupt dictator—but into compounding the error by ignoring the fact that Bolivia's peasants had already won their revolution against the landlords and were prepared to defend it against him. (He gained not one single *campesino* recruit.)

Even so, with a poet's eye and ear, Ché might have survived—at least escaped—to fight another day. But the little band of Cuban revolutionaries who hadn't bothered to learn the local languages was as isolated in its armor of abstract dogma as if it had been on the moon. The diaries reveal a lack of empathy for anything Bolivian, any reference that might have provided a bond with a native man or woman, any suspicion that individual human beings might retain a "retarded" love for their country or its traditions. Even Bolivia's communists were spurned as too backward or nationalistic; they were told to participate under Cuban leadership or withdraw, and when they withdrew the last possible link to the real world, the last hope of survival, was gone.

It may be argued that all true apostles of violent revolution are antipoets. Lenin's remark to Gorki after listening to Beethoven—about rejecting the music because it made him want to stroke heads rather than break them—is well known. "We are good revolutionaries," said Lenin on another occasion, "but I don't know why we also feel obligated to prove that we stand on the heights of foreign culture. As for myself, I don't hesitate to declare myself a barbarian." Mao wrote poetry once, and perhaps still does, but the surviving verses are hermetic in the neoclassical tradition. Szyszlo, when he came to see me, told me that he had just visited Fidel Castro with Cortázar, and that when the Argentine novelist asked the Cuban what he thought of Mao's xenophobic "Cultural

Revolution," the *lider maximo* had answered surprisingly: "What is the point of a cultural revolution if the students aren't taught to read Shakespeare?" But there is considerable evidence that in the executions-without-trial that set the tone of the Cuban Revolution after the entry into Havana, Castro's romanticism and human warmth yielded to Guevara's single-minded ruthlessness. "Hatred as a weapon," he wrote just before leaving for Bolivia, was the best means of turning a human being into a "selective and cold killing-machine."

Which is not to say that Ché enjoyed killing his enemies, as Hitler and Stalin did—he released his Bolivian prisoners, without exception, unharmed—but only that in contrast to the poet, preoccupied with seeing life as he finds it, celebrating it, creating it, the anti-poet, concerned with proving himself right and forcing all men into the image of that rightness, accepts death without compunction as the price of victory.

5

BRAZIL IN FIVE CANTOS

Introduction

Everything bespoke the fact that Miguel had been born for greatness. His carriage was virile, his face radiant, and his whole person distilled an air of self-confidence and tranquil identification with the world.

The greatest of Miguel's capacities was his ability to avoid developing any of them, and one day his family realized that he had neither learned a trade, nor acquired a profession, nor discovered any of the modern techniques for procuring sustenance. . . .

—CARLOS DRUMMOND DE ANDRADE, "Miguel and His Theft"
translated by William L. Grossman

The most unpopular classic in Brazil is Vianna Moog's *Bandeirantes and Pioneers* (1943), a book that explains the vast, richly-endowed nation's retarded economic development and failure to develop democratic institutions by comparing its stagnation with the unprecedented progress achieved by the United States in both directions in the last two centuries.

The fact that the Brazilian sociologist told the unpleasant truth about both countries, foreseeing the neuroses that plague the affluent, guilt-ridden North American society today, and even tipped the balance of the future in Brazil's favor, was beside the point. Moog had not only exposed the sickness of Brazilian society and the veil of sham that covered much of its vaunted culture, he had proclaimed flatly that culture in the United States (culture, mind you!) was so incomparably rich compared with any

92

to be found south of the Rio Grande that it was absurd to claim that citizens of the United States did not have the right to call themselves "Americans."

Such a devastating self-appraisal could not possibly have been published, or probably even conceived, in any other Latin American country. Yet in tolerant Brazil it was immediately hailed as a classic, went through many editions, was used in the schools; and within two years its author had been elevated to a seat in the august Brazilian Academy of Letters. If *Bandeirantes and Pioneers* is unpopular today, it is because tolerance itself has been proscribed by Brazil's military rulers, polarizing society to fanatical extremes and exposing the intellectuals in their ivory towers or underground bunkers to the same perverse cliché that dominates the rest of Latin America—helplessness vis à vis the United States, a world power "without culture or ideals" devoted to extracting the last ounce of material profit out of its weak neighbors.

Moog's thesis, briefly, was that the usual explanations for the two countries' unequal rates of development—climatic, geologic, racial, geographic—did not hold water. The difference must be traced back to the early settlers. The *bandeirantes* (flag-bearers), who explored the Brazilian heartland, were the last wave of the colonial *conquistadores*. They came for gold, cattle, and Indian women. They introduced epidemics of disease. They depopulated every part of Brazil except the narrow strip between the coastal range and the Atlantic. They had no public spirit or will for political self-determination. And their "intermezzo of adventure" left behind a land fit only for exploitation, a world where the only principle was the principle of authority. "The strongest man was not the man who mastered himself but the one who dominated others, and had the capacity to possess the greatest number of women."

The North American pioneer, in contrast, was a reformation settler. In the beginning he was a Calvinist whose God told him that only labor makes the body strong and cures the sicknesses induced by idleness. The Lutherans, Wesleyans, Quakers, and Unitarians who followed were as devoted to the virtues of frugality and punctuality, and they had the capacity to organize for communal benefit. Unlike the Catholics, they believed in the perfectibility of man here and now. They had no use for pessimism or tragedy. Accomplishment—a word significantly untranslatable into the Brazilian tongue—was the focus of the pioneer's dynamic culture. He resented being called an intellectual, that summum bonum of all Latin societies. His eyes were not on Europe. He was preoccupied with making new institutions, inventing things with his hands, holding conventions. Although he glorified business and equated even beauty with it ("she looks like a million dollars"), his ultimate goal was altruistic—a society free of classes and race domination, with plenty for all—and not one of his presidents was a banker or industrialist.

That Spanish and Portuguese "incapacity for economic matters which seemed almost inspired," as Tawney put it, was compounded by the expulsion from the Iberian peninsula of the Jews, "the only people in both empires trained in the handling of wealth." The Portuguese emperors followed the Spanish monarchs in helping the Church combat usury, thus bypassing the industrial revolution originally (and ironically!) founded on those very fortunes in gold and silver extracted in the Western colonies. Brazil, and the rest of the Latin countries, fell back into feudalism. According to Moog, there followed, from the lack of belief in the perfectibility of man, "a lack of any collective ideal, the nearly total absence of the individual's belonging to the place and community in which he lives . . . *the blame always attached to others.*"

In the society of the sugar estates, and on into the Empire of the nineteenth century—and the independence that was independent of these authoritarianisms in name only—nothing fundamentally changed. Science was suspect. Art (with one major exception) was imported. Erudition, humanism, universalism, were concerned with forms only. "Applause and approbation, the satisfactions of vanity and self-conceit," said Alberto Torres as late as 1920, "compose the whole ambition of men's minds. To attain to the truth, to be capable of a solution, to train the mind or character to resolve and to act, are things alien to us." So far had Brazil's dislike of useful work, invention, and cooperation gone, Moog observed, that the Catholic Church itself had to import its priests from abroad—even from the United States, of all places!

Yet while Vianna Moog was coming of age and preparing to write his book, the Brazil he describes was changing. The novels of Machado de Assis, revealing the old order so perfectly in their disenchanted irony and profoundly European pessimism, were yielding to the lusty extraversion of such masters of social fiction as Jorge Amado. The Vargas dictatorship was giving the middle class and organized labor a share of the oligarchs' pie, just as the Alessandri regime was doing in Chile and the Perón dictatorship was about to do in Argentina. German and Italian immigrants, especially in the southernmost Brazilian state of Rio Grande do Sul and in the mushrooming industrial metropolis of São Paulo, were giving Brazil a new breed—go-getters untainted by those social graces through which the landed had justified their culture, immune to that cosmic terror in which the Catholic *mozombo* had cowered.

In the quarter-century that has elapsed since Moog's book appeared, Brazil has experienced a degree of parliamentary democracy, Brasilia has been built, Rio and Recife have become ringed with *favelas*, and Marxism has gained a foothold not only among the students and intellectuals but even in the Catholic hierarchy. And in the arts—the poetry of Carlos Drummond de Andrade, Jaõa Cabral de Melo Neto, Vinícius de Morais; the prose of Graciliano Ramos and Guimaraës Rosa; the architecture of Oscar Niemeyer; the painting of Portinari; music from Villa Lobos to the bossa nova; the cinema of Vinícius and Dos Santos—provincial conservatism and French-oriented *modernismo* have yielded to a sophisticated self-assurance which, if not yet influencing the rest of the world, seems entirely at home there.

The question, as we arrived in Brazil, was: How to equate this coming-of-age with the dictatorship of a small military clique which, with hardly a ripple of protest, had just swept aside the parliamentary system and every outlet for dissent and experiment?

What would the poets and novelists have to say?

Would the seeds of the future be found on the beaches of Rio or in the *favelas* above them? Or in Brasilia? Or in the colonial splendors of Minas Gerais? Or in the exuberant Africanism of Bahia, the Black Rome? Or in the radical pronouncements of Dom Helder Camara, Archbishop of the impoverished Northeast, who alone the dictatorship feared to muzzle?

What would Vianna Moog himself have to say?

Canto I: Rio de Janeiro

The Poetry of Pleasure

> *That girl who flings herself so cold*
> *And wanton to my arms, who aims*
> *Her breasts and kisses at me, stammering bold*
> *Verses, and vows of love, and ugly names;*
>
> *That girl, that flower of melancholy, who*
> *Laughs at my colorless suspicions (two),*
> *She, only, who would never have to shun*
> *Caresses lavished on another one;*
>
> *That woman who to every love proclaims*
> *The misery and greatness of her aims,*
> *Proud of the signature my teeth inbled,*
>
> *That woman is a world!—a bitch, a trull*
> *Perhaps . . . but for the impression in a bed*
> *Never was any quite so beautiful!*
> —VINÍCIUS DE MORAIS[1]

"They were on the beach," the Englishman from São Paulo explained as we touched down at that city on our way to Rio. "They're a fun-loving people, and when they're not whooping it up in Carnival, they're out there soaking up the sun, not grubbing about in politics or planning for

[1] "Soneto de Devoção" from *Novos Poemas* in *Antologia da Moderna Poesia Brasileira.* Edited by Fernando Ferreira de Loanda. Rio de Janeiro, Orfeu, 1967.

some problematical future. Does that answer your question about how they reacted to last month's military crackdown? Some call it apathy, but it's more a devil-may-care indifference, as though this was something that had been done to them before and couldn't be avoided. Brazilians don't look for scapegoats, the way they do in the other South American countries. I've never heard you blamed for supporting Castelo Branco, and now this chap who's succeeded him. The way they explain it is that it's a Brazilian eccentricity, deplorable but inevitable, to yield to the generals in a time of crisis. No excuses. Like the man who never showed up to dinner: 'I'm weak, that's why I didn't show up!' And like Brazilians generally, he was so loaded with charm his hosts couldn't find it in their hearts to blame him.''

Vinícius de Morais, the Brazilian troubadour to whom I carried letters from Neruda and Elizabeth Bishop, was nowhere to be found. Characteristically, the ageless romantic poet had just left troubled Rio in the company of a young girl who wanted to see Italy. The boîte at Copacabana where he was usually to be found with his guitar, singing such of his famous songs as "The Girl from Ipanema," was closed. A revival of the celebrated Carnival film, *Black Orpheus*, for which Vinícius wrote the scenario, had been postponed—by order of the puritanical military government, rumor had it. But we were lucky enough to meet on the beach that afternoon a young bossa nova composer who knew Vinícius well and promised to guide us through one of the labyrinthine *favelas* tomorrow. Virgílio Nova, as we shall call our friend, lest his frankness get him in trouble, began our instruction in the pleasures and pains of his city by assuring us that we could indeed afford to miss Carnival next month.

"Transvestite dances have been forbidden for the first time, and there's a regulation not to remove any part of your clothing—even, presumably, your necktie."

"How did it all start?" Bill asked.

"Carnival?" he said. "Way back. The Portuguese thought it would be a good idea to make every slave king for a day. It's still a good idea from the ruling class point of view, even though the slaves are nominally free now. An unemployed black from the *favelas* who spends the whole year putting together a costume of satin, furs, and semi-precious stones weighing forty-five pounds and calls himself "Czar of all the Russias" hasn't much time for revolution, has he?"

"Then why are they cracking down on it?" I asked.

"The military have always had this moralistic streak," Virgílio said, "ever since General Dutra succeeded Getulio[2] after World War II and made gambling illegal. That particular puritanism cost them millions in revenue—and of course it didn't stop gambling, our national pastime. Now they express their prissiness in many ways—all petty. Here, on this beach, paddle-tennis players were arrested last week for molesting the bathers. Almost all the leaders of the pop music craze have been jailed for a day at least.[3] Carlos Imperial got it for imitating John Lennon's record-album nudes on a Christmas card with the caption 'Hope YOU are better off New Year.' "

Virgílio's attitude toward politics reminds me a little of intellectuals during our Jazz Age of the twenties; like Scott Fitzgerald and Mencken, he regards politics with sardonic amusement. The best of his stories about the President, Marshal Arturo da Costa e Silva,[4] has him visiting Salazar, his (then) opposite number in Portugal. Doctor Salazar impresses his guest: 'You want to see how stupid the Portuguese are? Come here, boy,' he says to an attendant, 'go up to the fifth floor and see

---

[2] Getulio Vargas—political leaders are often referred to thus familiarly in Brazil. Vargas was the most progressive dictator of this century, and the most ruthless.

[3] Six months later *bossa nova* was virtually banned, and the two most important innovators in Brazilian popular music, Gilberto Gil and Caetano Velloso, who had fused the hard beat of rock music with Brazilian rhythms in their songs, went into enforced exile because of police orders forbidding them to work in the principal cities. Both had begun fifty-seven-day jail sentences in Rio during our visit.

[4] Marshal Costa e Silva suffered a stroke shortly after our visit to Brazil and was replaced by another general chosen by the Army's executive committee. At least well into 1970 there has been no relaxation of the Army's authoritarian dictatorship.

if I'm there,' and the boy returns to report in the negative. 'You see how stupid the Portuguese are?' says the laughing Brazilian dictator to his fellow-generals when he returns to Rio, 'All Salazar had to do was *phone* the fifth floor!' And Virgilio goes on to tell the story of Costa e Silva's suppression of constitutional government last month in terms of the futility of efforts to stop it. "Senhora Bittencourt's paper was the chief voice of the opposition until then, but the Senhora had lists of people she didn't like whose names were never to be printed. One was her own chief editorial writer! Another, unfortunately for her, was the Foreign Minister. She survived the Institutional Act[5] for a few days by expressing her opposition through the weather reports,[6] but one day the police called and asked her to interpret these and she asked saucily why they didn't arrest her. They did, and she's been in jail ever since, refusing to undress, going on hunger strikes and sit-downs, her spirit unbroken. Or take the governor of this province, Carlos Lacerda. He took sleeping pills and had himself removed to a hospital, but they woke him up and carted him off anyway. The big pitch of this regime is that it is saving democracy—and it really believes it!"

"Didn't Costa e Silva's predecessor, General Castelo Branco, try to establish an opposition party?" I asked.

"They called it the 'Yes Party' and the 'Yes, Sir! Party,' " said Virgilio with a laugh. "But you're right. He did try. And he was generally respected, and as popular as any head of government in our country can ever be. He was honest—something unprecedented in Brazil—and he did stop the inflation that Goulart had been encouraging to let the communists in by the back door. But Costa e Silva is unpopular with everybody—even with the military. Even its own paper had an editorial last month, 'The Nation Yawns.' "

"Then there'll be a revolution?" Bill Negron asked.

"The liberal wing of the Army might take over in ten years or so. Then there could be free play between the only two real alternatives we have, another liberal regime headed by Kubitschek—"

"You mean Kubitschek is popular still, after all the millions he's supposed to have made out of Brasilia?" I asked.

"At a reception for Castelo Branco several years ago," Virgilio replied, "Kubitschek was cheered so wildly he had a heart attack and had to be carried out! Of course he's under house arrest now."

"—and the second alternative?"

---

[5] The decree under which the President in December, 1968, closed Congress, canceled all individual political rights under a state of siege, waived writs of habeas corpus, and received the right to seize assets of those who "illegally enrich themselves."

[6] "Weather black . . . temperature suffocating. The air is unbreathable. The country is being swept by a strong wind, . . ."—*Jornal do Brasil.*

"A left but not Marxist regime supported by the Church. Meaning Dom Helder Camara, the Archbishop of Recife—another reason you must pass up Carnival and visit the Northeast. Dom Helder is the only outspoken critic of the regime they haven't dared gag. At least he hasn't been arrested, so far. And he'll talk to you frankly, even though he's a bit anti-American."

One trouble is that opposition politics in Brazil has always been a luxury of the well-to-do. The *Esquerda Festiva* (Festive Left), to which Virgilio and Vinícius belong, spends half its time inventing protest songs for fashionable singers, driving to nightclubs in sports cars to applaud them, and the other half sitting on beaches discussing, as Virgilio put it, "books by Marcuse, Sartre, and Régis Debray which nobody reads anyway." All about us as we talked, the superbly limbed coffee-colored girls in their bikinis were discussing the latest fashions, the newest discotheques, and the problem of paying live-in maids an exorbitant fifteen dollars a month. It is estimated that a member of the Festive Left spends more money drinking beer on the beach on a Sunday afternoon while discussing the plight of the poor than the man from a *favela* makes in three working days. The will to change is there, but how do you establish communication between the fifth of Rio's population that is regularly employed and the four fifths of those four million who scrounge for a few *cruzeiros* in or near the *favelas*?

"Are the poets reaching them?" I asked Virgilio.

"They were when bossa nova was going strong and the radio was open to protest songs. Vinícius deserves a great deal of credit for that shift, which cost him his diplomatic career. Before that, in his 'Girl from Ipanema' period, the boîtes were full of bolero-type despair over love, though one song in Kubitschek's time earned its author a one-way ticket to Italy—'To be President you just have to keep smiling while flying your relatives to big blasts in Brasilia.' But then came the Beatle craze—that made Roberto Carlos our first rock-and-roll millionaire—and the great folk singers like Jair—who got jailed for their protest songs. But our best non-popular poets, like Carlos Drummond de Andrade and Jaôa Cabral de Melo Neto, have always sided with the opposed—obliquely."

I remembered that Moog had cited Drummond de Andrade among others for introducing humor into Brazilian poetry for the first time— "perhaps the great dividing line in the definitive emancipation of Brazilian from Portuguese and European poetry"—and that Gilberto Freyre had praised this poet and Vinícius as well for a daring "association of social problems with poetical art" begun a generation ago, comparing them with the composer Heitor Villa-Lobos and the painter Candido Portinari for emancipating Brazilian art from "the colonial echo of a purely European philosophy of life."

I especially love this prologue of Drummond to an early declaration of independence, which I translate as freely as Vinícius' sonnet:

Never to rhyme the word 'sleep'
with the uncorresponding 'deep';
I shall rhyme 'flesh' and 'beautiful'
with anything that's suitable.
So much for rhyme. Words were not made to be
tied together; They jump, they kiss each other,
dissolve, not always in a clear sky but
a clean one, authentic, and unfathomable . . .

So these are my poets, united in the pride
of their precision; I incorporate
them to my fatal left side. From Vinícius
I steal his clarity. I drink Murillo.
Toss me your flaming necktie, Comrade Pablo.
Let me drown in you, Apollinaire. Goodbye
Vladimir Mayakovsky: Brothers all,
and not for a free ride, gliding among the camellias.
This is the landscape where I stake my life.[7]

We made the round of beaches from Copacabana to Ipanema and Leblon and back. It was like Montevideo, but more relaxed, more opulent. Some were surfboarding, others were fishing. At least ten games of soccer were going on, end to end—blacks, browns, and whites like brothers, kicking the sand in golden bursts, or sipping cokes through straws on the crumbling mosaic "waves" that separate Copacabana from Atlantic Avenue. Round and round the arcs of blue the highrise apartments go, with here and there a little humpbacked chalet or drawbridged castelet to mark some typcoon's power to resist the taxes. Even the *favelas*, running up the steep balding buttes behind the beaches into jungle, lack the depressing squalor of San Juan's "Fanguito" or Lima's inhabited garbage dumps—or seem to. The smell of the city is a rich compound of beer, sweat, perfume, mangos, and salt spray. And always the crowds of pleasure-seekers in their lemming-assault on the rollers. . .

Our car broke down. We piled into a taxi. We relaxed no more:

They call it the Battle of Rio, and though I'd had basic training with the sideswiping *machos* circling Mexico City's *glorietas* and leapfrogged the traffic islands on Lima's Avenida Arequipa, I had never known fear like this. Drivers pass on the left or right, considering it chicken to tip their hand or slow down. Volkswagens, like swarms of angry ants, cut through the tunnels carved by overloaded buses and teetering lorries, barreling along at a speed of fifty or more. Bus drivers are paid by the

[7] These are the first two stanzas of "Consideração do Prema" in *Antologia da Moderna Poesia Brasileira, op. cit.*

number of fares they pick up and so race three abreast for the stops. Pedestrians are considered fair game, and it's always open season. Drivers who cut you off are admiringly called *fechadas*, and those who cut off the cut-offs (without shearing more than a fender or wheel) are the *quebras de asa*, or terranauts. Stop signs had been changed to read STOP OR DIE! by Rio's traffic chief who concedes that his city's drivers are the world's worst. If he released the death toll it would stop tourist traffic cold and discourage the insurance companies from ever writing another policy.

The Arts of Immunity

In view of this apparent propensity for lawlessness, excess and death-defying recklessness, it's amazing that Brazil's contemporary artists are as tame as pussycats. Either they work within the Renoir-Cézanne-Matisse orbit that circumscribes that least adventurous of "modern" collections, the multimillion-dollar Assis Chateaubriand museum at São Paulo; or they ape the latest New York chic—op, pop, kinetic, minimal, pornographic—a year or five years too late. So, at any rate, we were forced to conclude after visiting Senhora Bittencourt's Museum of Modern Art.

"It's the sad state of criticism in Brazil," Virgilio remarked apologetically, as we headed for the apartment of the one critic reputed to be both sophisticated and impervious to politics. "Standards of honesty and objectivity simply don't exist here," he added. "I was beaten up by a composer's friends last year for suggesting in print that his latest composition was less than original."

"You couldn't prosecute him?" Bill asked in astonishment.

"It would have been in the courts for years," he replied, "and in the meantime they'd have done much worse to me than break my glasses."

Mark Berkowitz was on the phone when we arrived at his apartment. "Yes, of course," he was saying as we entered, "if somebody here in Rio were to buy a stone Picasso it would be much easier to display than in London. Why? Less boringly familiar. Anyone in Brazil with a million dollars to spend spends it in Paris or New York where the action is. . . ." The art critic, whose own pictures are chosen with rare discrimination, told us that the Second National Bienal that opened in Bahia last month was closed after two days by the police. "The nudes were regarded as immoral and the paintings of Ché Guevara as subversive."

We set out for Rocinha with Virgilio the next day at ten. This particular *favela* (a small yellow flower, Brazil's euphemism for the squatters' shantytowns) lies in a steep valley opening out to the sea and sheltered from the rest of Rio by a cliff. Climbing to the top, we found ourselves looking down into a millionaire's swimming pool, and across the bay at

Favela in
Rio de Janeiro
1·69

fashionable Ipanema Beach. Rocinha has a good beach of its own, but it was deserted. "They're too busy scrounging a living to swim," Virgilio explained, "and besides, they don't know how." They may learn, he added, by watching the affluent when a traffic tunnel through the cliff is completed—"that is, if the whole *favela* isn't bulldozed to keep its beach from being polluted."

For now, the slum dwellers live in a world of their own. They come from the arid Northeast, packed into closed vans for the two-week ride. The Ya-yas from Bahia bring their African cults and magic potions. We saw a table in the market selling specifics against the Evil Eye—carved hands with the thumb protruding between the second and third finger, tiny dolls, dried herbs, ordinary mothballs.

There are a few concrete steps and sidewalks in the steeply pitched alleys filled with red mud and trickles of sewage; these walks, Virgilio explained, were built by teams of university students who also initiated classes for instruction in reading and writing. "It was all stopped as subversive as soon as the military took over. Now no one pays any atten-

Boys in The
Favella in
Rio de Janeiro
Berger 1/69

tion to what goes on in these vast communities except your Peace Corps-men who are regarded as heroes. The *favelas* are full of thieves, of course, but they never steal from each other. If the police shoot a thief, the next day a policeman is shot. That discourages policing!"

At one lookout point where we stopped to take pictures there was a pile of refuse with fine wire stretched across it like gut leader.

"To keep people out of the garbage?" I asked one of a dozen beautiful children who had attached themselves to our party.

"No," Virgilio interpreted the answer, "to be waxed for kiteflying."

We were constantly impressed by the capacities of these simple people to amuse themselves, and even to beautify their environment. All the shanties had tile roofs, many had neat patios and jigsaw-decorated wooden porches, and all were surrounded by bits of jungle—trees with prickly but edible fruit, flaming gladioli, purple flag, lilies, banked bougainvillea. On the roofs, bristling with radio aerials and not a few TV antennae, dogs sprawled in the sun and children flew their kites. The houses are painted in very sophisticated pastel shades. One immaculately painted little white one had birds in cages all over its facade, and a glass cabinet filled with china birds inside.

But we were impressed even more by the human qualities of these people: by their joie de vivre, their humor, their unfailing friendliness.

Virgilio took us back to his apartment for dinner. His ambition is to write an erotic opera, and he showed us proudly his library of Sade, Masoch, D. H. Lawrence, Henry Miller, and their latter-day disciples. I told him that I was steeping myself in the novels of Machado de Assis and João Guimaraës Rosa, Brazil's great novelists of yesterday and today. Machado, who was a nearsighted and epileptic mulatto, and a Jamesian dissector of middle-class pretensions, reminded me of Borges. In his disenchantment with all the rewards of this world, he had even anticipated the "aleph," Borges' symbol of circular time:

Just imagine, reader, a procession of all the ages, with all the human races, all the passions, the tumult of empire, the war of appetite against appetite, and hate against hate, the reciprocal destruction of human beings and their surroundings. This was the monstrous spectacle I saw [in my nightmare]. The history of man and of the earth had thus an intensity that neither science nor the imagination could give it, for science is too slow and imagination too vague, whereas what I saw was the living condensation of history. To describe it one would have to make the lightning stand still. The ages moved along in a whirlwind, but nevertheless, because the eyes of delirium have a virtue of their own, I was able to distinguish everything that passed before me, afflictions and joys, glory and misery, and I saw love augmenting misery, and misery aggravating human debility. Along came voracious greed, fiery anger, drooling envy, and the hoe and the pen, both wet with sweat and ambition, hunger, vanity, melancholy, affluence, love, and all of them shaking man like a baby's rattle until they transformed him into something not unlike an old rag. . . . My tired eyes finally saw the present age go by and, after it, future ages . . . a ball of paper.[8]

With his casual, chatty, but always precise talking to the reader, so much in the vein of Sterne but with overtones of Flaubert, Machado presents bourgeois life in nineteenth century Brazil in all its emptiness, but he accepts it as the only life worth worrying about. How different is Guimaraës Rosa's vision! He too rejects the establishment, but by going to the backlands and creating out of that raw frontier a mythic kingdom with its own laws and language. In real life Guimaraës remained a diplomat, restrained, punctilious, a member of the Academy, dying characteristically at his desk surrounded by his files and dispatches; but the world he created is as self-reliantly individualistic as Emerson's, as yea-saying to everything in the universe as Whitman's, as full of ribald humor (and tortuous verbiage) as Faulkner's. The protagonist of his major novel who talks for all 492 pages without a chapter break expresses the philosophy of the *sertão* "where the strong and the shrewd call the tune" and "God himself when he comes here had better come armed":

Everything in the world is there because it deserves to be and needs to be . . . I keep thinking about all this. I enjoy it . . .

The most important and nicest thing in the world is this: that people aren't always the same, they are not all of a piece and finished but changing.

I share my land, what's mine is theirs, we are close as brothers . . . What we want is to work, to live in peace. Me, I live for my wife —who deserves nothing but the best—and for religion . . . Love inspires love. I tell you it's so . . .

When you dream, sir, dream on these things. The smell of flowered fields, strong in April: the purple little gypsy, and the yellow nhiíca and the broom. This, in the Saririnhém . . . The cicadas shrill their music. Ho, and the cold! The hoarfrost collects even on the backs of the cattle, and on the housetops. Or on the Meaomeão—beyond there the earth is almost blue, not like the sky, but a vivid blue like that of a partridge egg. Winds that don't let the dew settle. A gust of hot wind passing between the fronds of palm trees. I remember, I disremember . . .

Do you think that I sold my soul, that I made a pact? . . . Don't

[8] Machado de Assis, *Epitaph for a Small Winner*. Translated from the Portuguese by William L. Grossman. New York, Noonday Press, 1952. Cf. the quotation from Borges' "El Aleph," p. 14.

worry about that. It is the future that matters. To buy or to sell, sometimes, is almost the same thing . . . There is no devil . . . It is man who exists.[9]

Virgilio thinks that Graciliano Ramos, who lived in Alagoas near Recife, was as good a novelist. "If Jorge Amado in Bahia is our Steinbeck, Ramos is our Faulkner. His best book is *Vidas Secas* (Dry Lives), about the poor in the Northeast who are driven to eat the dogs and parrots they love. Ramos died as a result of years spent in one of Getulio's prisons and his *Memorias de Carcere* is an account of that terrible experience."

I told him I'd been stirred by Nelson Pereira Dos Santos' movie based on *Vidas Secas*, and stunned by the restraint of the peasant protagonist who, when he has the government bully who has ruined him in his power, lets him go. "But I suppose that's true to the Brazilian reality like the rest of the picture," I said. "There were no signs of revolt in the *favela* yesterday either, were there? And your popular social philosophers like Gilberto Freyre and Vianna Moog only explain the gentleness of the people and the lack of crusading idealism in the rulers."

"Freyre has become an ultrareactionary," said Virgilio bitterly. "When a photographer took a press photo of him he didn't like recently, Freyre denounced him to the police as a subversive and he's still in jail. We regard Moog as very old hat, too. Much of what he says is true, but he's too journalistic and low-brow to attract the youth. But he is here in Rio, and you can visit him and see for yourself where he stands. For an antidote, talk to Dom Helder in Recife!"

The Politics of Pain

Vianna Moog is a handsome, solidly built, graying man of partly Swiss extraction. His mother, a friend told me, is still living in Novo Hamburgo and after more than half a century in Brazil, doesn't speak a word of Portuguese. Moog himself still has a post in the Education Ministry. He sees the nineteenth century ending in Brazil only with the Vargas dictatorship. And he sees the military, faute de mieux, "the only class that cares about the unity of Brazil."

"They have no vocation to be dictators," the sociologist told me, "any more than you Americans have a vocation to police the free world. You accept the responsibility reluctantly, just as they do. Before last month's crackdown by Costa e Silva, they always preserved the civil, constitu-

---

[9] João Guimaraës Rosa, *The Devil to Pay in the Backlands*. Translated by James L. Taylor and Harriet de Onis. New York, Alfred A. Knopf, 1963. This is the major novel; but the subdued and mystical stories, collected in *The Third Bank of the River* (Knopf, 1968) are an easier introduction to this Joycean creator whose punnings, alliterations, and ambiguities are evidently untranslatable.

tional forms. Now for the first time they're trying to do the job without intermediaries."

"What class do the generals come from?" I asked.

"Most of them, including Castelo Branco and Costa e Silva, come from the lower middle class that Vargas created. None of them are millionaires, or even rich men. They have the morality of bourgeois Christians and more national conscience than the civilian leaders who always thought of their city or state first. I mean: a *paulista* thinks first of São Paulo; a *carioca* of Rio; a *mineiro* of Belo Horizonte; and so on. Originally most of the military were from Rio Grande do Sul since that was where the Triple Alliance War against Paraguay was focused.

"Without national parties there will be no democracy in Brazil," Moog continued. "Castelo Branco made the last of many attempts to create an opposition party, but he couldn't even get the approval of his own party to make national reforms."

"And the unions—?"

"The unions have no independence here. They have always been creations of the government. When President Goulart gave their leftist leaders a free hand, the government was forced to intervene lest their wage demands bankrupt Brazil—which almost happened, as you know."

"Will the military turn right or left?" I asked.

"They're bound to turn left, with land reforms and more education, to satisfy the masses." [10]

I asked him why the intellectuals scorn his *Bandeirantes and Pioneers*.

"That's a complicated question," he said with a smile. "It's still getting around, in its ninth edition now, and is used in the schools. But you have to know, for instance, that our newspapers, though owned by capitalists, employ leftists to write their columns and book reviews."

"Because they write better?" I suggested.

"Unfortunately, yes, they often do."

"What triggered Costa e Silva's Institutional Act?" I asked.

"Deputy Mario Moreira Alves' charge that Castelo Branco's prisoners had been tortured."

"Was it true?"

"No. But no one in Congress had the guts to disprove it. It was easier to keep plaguing the President by claiming immunity for the Deputy; and perhaps I too would have voted for congressional immunity on principle had I been a congressman. The military asked only for permission to sue him, to force his charges to the test. So when permission was refused the question was posed: does this forum give one total

---

[10] I learned later that education's share of the national budget had dropped from 11 percent to 7.7 percent, and that the number of illiterates, already half the total population, is increasing.

immunity? total license to make irresponsible charges? Congress voted yes, and then celebrated the victory with cheers and champagne. That did it!"

At the American Embassy, where I spent the following morning talking to our two top officials, there hung a mobile with ten hands pointing in ten different directions. "It's the perfect symbol of our foreign policy," said one of the officials, "but don't quote me!" (I mention this for the benefit of those who think our policy is malevolently monolithic and that our officials pursue it uncritically.)

"The Institutional Act was not necessary," one official said. "There has been terrorism by the extreme left ever since the 1964 revolution of Castelo Branco, but it wasn't that which caused Costa e Silva to outlaw the remaining freedoms; it was the strikes and peaceful demonstrations by left-of-center liberals—strikes and demonstrations that we would consider perfectly normal. The feeling that the leader of the liberals, the tarnished but still popular Kubitschek, could have won any election hands down, may have triggered the coup—if it had a trigger other than the wounded pride of the military. The resulting suppression of the law-abiding opposition has been followed by no diminution of the far left's terrorism. Therefore, the only gainers have been the Peking and Havana factions, and on the extreme right such fascist organizations as the *Compañía de Caçar Communistas* (Society to Hunt Communists).

"Basically," he continued, "it boils down to this. There is absolutely no faith in democratic processes, no feeling that there must be an opposition to insure health. The Army feels that any opposition means subversion and must be stamped out ruthlessly. The concentration of leftist sentiment almost exclusively in the universities, where the leadership is pro-Mao or pro-Castro, assures a temper just as unyielding as the Army's."

I asked a Brazilian educator later in the day what alternatives he saw to the Institutional Act. "None," replied Guilherme Figueiredo, the Executive Secretary of the Fulbright Commission. "Before, they always made the mistake of turning over the government they had seized to civilians. With the result that we floundered from the morass made by one group of corruptionists to the next one. Brazil needs basic reforms—agrarian ones especially. The military may fail to make them, but they are the only group disinterested enough to try. Why, then, you will ask, are they concentrating on stabilizing the currency? Because that has to come first. Without that, it's ridiculous to divide up the land because there wouldn't be any credit or tractors or fertilizer with which to make the land produce. In place of malnutrition, we'd have starvation."

One of Brazil's foremost businessmen, with whom I talked the following day, agreed that there was no alternative to the military regime in the foreseeable future, but he thought a great mistake had been made by the Costa e Silva group. "They've thrown out the baby—how do you say?—with the dirty water? I mean their too severe denial of civil rights. They can enter my home, take it away, put me in jail for life, even kill me with no protest on anyone's part. To be sure, they haven't done any of these things, but the fact that they have such total power tends to freeze our economy. No one dares invest any more. The risks are too great. I don't even dare buy a new car, lest it seem that I'm part of the new crowd profiting from it all. The money in Brazil is fleeing the country as never before. Even if they give assurances, it may be too late to restore confidence."

But it was an American, a *Time* editor assigned to Brazil, who had least to say in justification of the military. "How can they be sure," he said to me, "that Goulart's inflation hurt the little guy? After all, everything in 1964 was going up, from the worker's wages to the shoeshine boy's fee, along with the prices. Look at the inflation *we're* having, and everyone admits that we're more prosperous than we ever were. Maybe this deflation is hurting Brazil more. Anyway, it's ripe for revolution—if there were anyone capable of leading it. Discontent is universal. Ask anyone from a beggar to a millionaire. Or get the record of Geraldo Vandri's song and listen to the words that it's a criminal offense to listen to now."

I'd already heard the words of "Caminhando" ("Walking"):

> *Here we have soldiers*
> *All under arms,*
> *Some of them lovers,*
> *Some of them not;*
> *Almost all lost,*
> *Their guns in their hands,*
> *Who learned in the barracks*
> *An old, old lesson—*
> *To die for the fatherland*
> *And to live without reason.*

Canto II: Minas Gerais—Imported Grandeur, Native Commitment

We began our journey into colonial Minas Gerais with a stop at Petró-polis, where borrowed grandeur came to a tawdry end. Petrópolis is a tidy mountain resort in the coastal massif, now not much more than an hour's drive from Rio thanks to rock tunnels that carry the highway to the summer palace of the emperors. The village itself contains the present Summer White House, heavily guarded; a cluster of elegant jigsaw cha-teaux; and the enormous Swiss chalet, Quintandinha, one of those Latin American phenomena like Lima's Country Club and Mexico's San José de Purua that can't quite decide whether they are private clubs or public resorts and so fall into genteel decay surrounded by their duck ponds.

We had a note of introduction to the Director of the Imperial Museum, Lourenço Luis Lacombe—fortunately, because the museum is so understaffed that only one wing a day is open to the public. Donning the outsize felt slippers that are obligatory for all Brazilian museums, we glided over the glassy parquet floors of brazilwood and jacaranda, inspecting this repository of Victorian taste that can only be compared with the Emperor Maximilian's Chapultepec Palace in Mexico or those hallowed halls near London where Prince Albert consorted with his demure queen.

The prime exhibit is the emperor's crown, weighing 1720 grams net with its 639 diamonds and 77 pearls in an ugly setting designed in Rio (1841) by Carlos Marín. Set beside it is the blue, silver-threaded royal mantle collared with toucan feathers. The two most suggestive relics of the imperial fantasy, however, are the table at which the last emperor wrote his abdication—the circular marble top with a painting of Achilles dragging Hector's body behind his chariot—and a cradle for the imperial infant in the form of a golden shell supported by golden harpies, and covered with a mosquito net suspended from a golden fishing rod. In the infanta's bedroom there is a painting of a white baby (the infanta) being dandled by a black mammy. Like Cousin Max in Mexico, Dom Pedro II, with his identical fuzzy sideburns and soft eyes, was an amateur astronomer (or voyeur) and his telescope on a tripod still stands beside the royal bed.

Freyre calls the rich, deeply cultured province of Minas Gerais Brazil's Castile, with Ouro Preto its Toledo. From the provincial capital, Belo Horizonte, clogged like every Brazilian metropolis with traffic and halfempty skyscrapers, three sites of great interest are within easy driving range.

Nearest and least visited is Sabará, where a tiny chapel honoring Nuestra Senhora do O is filled with some of the finest Renaissance painting outside of Italy. No one knows who painted these dozens of wood panels covered with religious allegories in a rosy golden tonality—some Portuguese journeyman, presumably, who, if he had not seen the graces in billowing gowns of Sandro Botticelli, had eyes as glazed from dreaming a neoclassical paradise. Nothing that survives of the celebrated colonial schools of Cuzco or Mexico compares with this—and nothing is being done to preserve it for posterity. Grimed with the smoke and grease of centuries, cracked, ripped, poked with holes, and peeling, these paintings are a glory never to be forgotten by the few who have seen them.[11]

Ouro Preto, second of the triad of colonial jewels, and most visited, is

---

[11] And not even all of those—for Hanson's otherwise exhaustive guide to Brazil (New World Guides to the Latin American Republics, New York, Duell, Sloan & Pearce, 1943) joins every other that I know in mentioning the chapel and ignoring its contents.

one of those complete hill towns, common enough in the Appennines and perhaps in Spain, but in this hemisphere to be seen only at Huarás in Peru and at Guanajuato and Taxco in Mexico. It is brimming with handsome churches and quaint tile-roofed houses inhabited by artists and little old ladies. There are breathtaking views of the purplish-red earth and viridian groves of Minas Gerais. But in the gift shops crowding the lordly plaza there are folk crafts that look as though they were turned out on assembly lines.

Third of the triad is sui generis not only for Brazil, but for Latin America: a sculptural masterpiece as impressive as anything conceived by the pre-Columbians, a treasury of religious art as moving as the Gothic. There are baroque churches in Ouro Preto, Bahia, and Rio as fine as the Sanctuary of Senhor Bom Jesús de Matosinhos in Congonhas do Campo that boasts Aleijadinho's sculptures—but no finer. So the setting —those immaculate white plaster walls and blue doors enclosed in coiling stonework, the noble towers and descending platforms connected with flights of steps, the clouds billowing over the undulating hills—is part of the drama, but only part. Everything made by nature or man must yield here to the lifesize figures of the "Twelve Prophets." Turning this way and that on the double staircase in their richly carved robes, holding their scrolls with one hand as they gesture imperiously with the other, these

godlike figures in green soapstone with their curiously Oriental features seem to be waiting . . . but for what? As always in the greatest art, there are no answers, but many interpretations.

Freyre was the first to sense a "socially significant message." According to him, this crippled son of a Portuguese artisan and a Negro woman used the available religious paraphernalia to express revolt against the European exploiters of slave labor. On the one hand Aleijadinho was identifying himself as a revolutionary "with Christ and the primitive Christian martyrs (masochism), and on the other with the terrific Old Testament prophets who preached against social sins and made personal sinners suffer mentally, if not physically (sadism)." Freyre saw this "mulatto El Greco" with his daring distortions and social conscience anticipating painters like Orozco and Portinari, writers like Jorge Amado, Carlos Drummond de Andrade and Vinícius de Morais.[12]

Moog, on the other hand, in the most moving part of his book [13] compares Aleijadinho with Lincoln. Both iconoclasts, in his opinion, seem to have caught the secret of everything lacking in their respective cultures. The United States, if it is to escape the fate of its preoccupation with material things, must heed the voice and example of Lincoln, who disregarded his political career to vote against the Mexican War, Lincoln the mystic who communed with Shakespeare and the Bible, Lincoln the endless talker in a country too busy for conversation, Lincoln who told a land bemused by gadgets that a lightning rod would never protect a rich man against the bolts of his conscience. And Brazilian civilization?

It has Aleijadinho. Do Brazilians lack sufficient love of work? He has it and to spare; he spends his life working from sun to sun, to the extreme limits of his powers. Do Brazilians lack the associative spirit and the capacity for teamwork? Aleijadinho has both in generous plenty, to the point of making collaborators of his slaves and pupils. Do Brazilians lack belief in funds earned by useful work and in a sense of the social function of money? He has it by the handful. Never was money more usefully and painfully earned than Aleijadinho's; and the money he earns he distributes among the poor in the churchyards of the temples in which he works. Do Brazilians lack the spirit of "Brazilianity" and of initiative? He has it beyond all others; he is the first to make use of Brazilian materials in his sculptures. Do Brazilians lack the faith that moves mountains and builds empires? He has it, profound, unshakable. Is the Brazilian's idealized image the *bandeirante*, the lucky object of fortune's sudden

---

[12] Gilberto Freyre, *Brazil: An Interpretation*. New York, Alfred A. Knopf, 1951. (Lectures delivered in 1944-5.)

[13] *Bandeirantes and Pioneers, op. cit.*

smiles? Aleijadinho's image is Saint Francis of Assisi. Do Brazilians not work on account of the climate or their liver? Aleijadinho achieved his work while losing pieces of himself, moaning with pain . . .[14]

Aleijadinho (Little Cripple) was born Antonio Francisco Lisboa in 1730. He was illegitimate and his mother was a slave, but his father declared him free the day of his baptism. Until the age of forty-five he led the life of a typical prosperous mulatto of the time: pleasure-loving, dissolute, a dilettante of the arts. Suddenly one day his fingers and toes began to swell, his body arched, his face became leonine, the horrible pains that were never to leave him began: he was a leper. But he refused to die. And as his body deteriorated, to the extent that he had to be wheeled about with the tools strapped to his fingerless hands, his spirit grew stronger. His early figurines, understandably, express rage and despair. There is one on the altar at Congonhas, legless and handless with a reliquary window in its stomach, the cheekbones so exaggerated they seem ready to pierce the skin. The larger groups of polychromed wood in the six little detached chapels below the church are still grotesques, but less so; the dwarf reaches out to Christ in real anguish, and the pain on Christ's face as he bears the cross is softened by compassion. But it is in his last works, the "Twelve Prophets," when he is suffering most excruciatingly, that Aleijadinho rises above his fate, no longer reacting to it, but fusing its meaning, as Beethoven did in the last quartets, into a catharsis that comes close to expressing joy. The "Twelve Prophets" have been called classical in their serenity, but there is nothing Greek about them unless it is the spirit of health they breathe.

Canto III: Brasilia

Juscelino Kubitschek was a *mineiro* too, and before yielding at Brasilia to that megalomania that was to cause Brazil's ruin and his own, he caused a modest chapel to be erected in Belo Horizonte. It is on the shore of an artificial lake of shallow brown water, called Pampulha. It was designed by Oscar Niemeyer (before he yielded to megalomania in Brasilia) as a series of mosaiced loops, with a detached bell tower. Portinari designed the exterior mosaics of blue and white tile, and painted the mural of "Christ on Judgment Day," perhaps his finest work; and João Ceschiatti outdid himself in a remarkable bronze relief covering the confessional, the "Expulsion from Eden." For years the Catholic Church made itself look foolish by refusing to consecrate this little chapel on the grounds that Niemeyer and Portinari were avowed communists. But

[14] *Ibid.*

Kubitschek, born in Diamantina, the City of Diamonds, was not satisfied with this small hedge against mortality. He had made his fortune manipulating real estate in Belo Horizonte, and Belo Horizonte was already built.

Like everyone, Brazilian and non-Brazilian, who has thought about Brasilia and written about it, I had been impressed with two arguments in its favor. I was intrigued with the idea of building a great city from scratch, with modern architects and city planners given control down to the last aesthetic detail. And the theory of placing it far out in the central backlands seemed sensible, as a means of bringing undeveloped Brazil into the industrial age. "Surely it's a useful symbol?" I had said to Guilherme Figueiredo.

"Useful!" he snorted. "Can Brazil afford symbols at that cost? We'll be paying for that piece of symbolism a century from now. The military dictatorship is the smallest part of the price. With half those billions every *favela* in Brazil could have been razed, and the slum dwellers rehoused—and educated!" But though I felt the same way about the billions we were currently spending to send three men to the moon, I was still not entirely convinced. I wanted to go to Brasilia and see for myself. My judgment as to whether the new capital provided a useful symbol could have little value, but I'd be as good a judge as any of whether the city was beautiful and livable.

Livable? No! Beautiful—perhaps.

But can the two be separated in architecture? If we have learned anything from the styles of this century, it is that form must follow function, expressing not only a building's use and the well-being of those who inhabit it, but relating to the harmony and scale of the landscape and the other structures with which it is surrounded.

The best that can be said (or the best I could say, after walking all over Brasilia and photographing it from land, lake, and air) is that it has a clean, Euclidean elegance. This is especially true of the twin skyscraper shafts that house the senators' and deputies' offices flanked by the shallow dome and inverted cup in which they were supposed to debate. This area, with its flat palaces and reflecting pools, its fountains and dovecotes and decorative sculpture is a cut better than World's Fair styles—but only a cut. The unfinished cathedral in the shape of a crown of thorns is ingenious, but as impersonal as the public buildings: an intellectual construct that exorcises the sacrifice involved by turning the instrument of pain into geometry. From the air, by night, when some fabulously expensive artificial lighting detaches the buildings from each other and makes them glow like extensions of the stars, the overall effect of Brasilia is dazzling. But why weren't the buildings built around the artificial lake created to save the site from its aridity? From the water the profiles of the higher buildings are truncated and the lower ones cannot be seen at all.

But the greatest weakness of Niemeyer's style is its repetitious blandness. The dozens of lesser buildings are almost without exception boxes: cubes, rectangles on stilts, with minimal variations in the fenestration, placed end to end or at right angles, generally of identical height. "Machines for living," as the French father of this inhuman style put it— but who wants to live in a machine? How much less sterile is a random organism like Ouro Preto that just grew, acquiring personality in the process. Or even Rio, sprawling aimlessly about those magnificent beaches and boulders, with now and then a bizarre chateau, or a Muslim mosque, or a *favela*, to take the curse off uniformity.

In one of his stories, Guimaraës Rosa describes the emotions of a little boy "taken to spend a few days in the place where the great city was being built . . . and the lake." Instead of being delighted, as his aunt and uncle had hoped, by the excitement of bulldozers leveling the landscape, his eyes focused on a wild turkey that snaps open its tail like a fan— "its thick-buttoned armor plate of ruby-red wattles, and its head glinted with flecks of rare blue, the blue of the sky." But in a flash the bird is gone, killed for tomorrow's birthday party, and "in the infinitesimal null speck of a minute's time, a feather's weight of death entered the child's soul . . . he was discovering the possibility that there might be other misfortunes lurking in the mechanical world, in hostile space, and beginning to see that only a hair's breadth lies between contentment and disenchantment." And as he sees the great trees fall, the boy feels sick: "The tree had died with such finality." At length he sees the turkey return —or thinks he does—but smaller, and full of hatred, pecking the severed head of the original bird, and in the descending night the fireflies glimmer and disappear, and with them "happiness." [15]

The poets understand well this dislocation of man from nature, but the lawmakers who shunned Brasilia like a plague (before the reason for their settling here was canceled with a flick of a general's pen) are reputed to have resisted only leaving the fleshpots of Rio. Whether this is true or not, it is a fact that the Brazilian middle class, like middle classes everywhere, has been brainwashed to equate quality with quantity, beauty with money, progress with pollution, mobility with traffic, and architecture with cold steel and hot glass. When we were having tea the week before in Ouro Preto with Dona Lilli Correia de Araujo at her delightful Chico Rey pension, she had pointed sadly at the hideous new university creeping (illegally) over the skyline across from Elizabeth Bishop's

[15] João Guimaraës Rosa, "The Thin Edge of Happiness" in *The Third Bank of the River*. New York, Alfred A. Knopf, 1968.

house. "The people of this town," she said, "hate and despise the law making Ouro Preto a national monument. The thing they'd rather do than anything is tear down every last one of these old buildings and put in their places—skyscrapers!"

We flew back to Rio's Santos-Dumont Airport to be ready for tomorrow's departure for Bahia.

Santos-Dumont! . . . Could the tragicomic career of this little aeronaut who is regarded in Brazil as the father of flight symbolize the ambiguous ideals that mushroomed in Brasilia?

With as much inventive perspicacity as the Wrights, Santos-Dumont went to Paris and became diverted from the logical pursuit of an internal combustion engine capable of powering a heavier-than-air machine. All the Brazilian hang-ups diverted him. Underestimated at first, his fierce national pride fed upon the exaggerated reports of his prowess relayed to him from Rio. While the Wrights were shunning publicity as the devil's design on serious work, Santos-Dumont became the darling of frivolous society. No one had flown a powered dirigible before him—and he knew well enough that that was not the object. He sensed that he must get out of Paris and stop this *bandeirante* prize-hunting. He did love Brazil, this little dandy whose father was Brazil's coffee king, but abstractly, from a distance. He had a joy in flying in the early days that was irresistible; but his vanity prevented him from sharing it with any man, and the advances of women he repulsed.

The old weakness for blaming others caught up with him on the Riviera when the vehicle that was to take him to Corsica never got off the ground. Earlier in 1906, when he had flown two hundred feet at an altitude of seven feet, he had brushed aside reports that the Wrights had flown further in 1903 and were now making regular daily ascents in Dayton. Flattered to give the French War Ministry the right to use his dirigible as a weapon, Santos was soon charging that it had been snatched from his peaceful hands by "warmongers." In 1910 he had a nervous breakdown and never flew again. By 1928 he was shouldering the whole burden of guilt for World War I, suffering paroxysms of remorse every time a plane crash made the news. Returning to Brazil to celebrate his election to the Academy that year, he stood on the deck of the *Cap Arcona* in Rio harbor only to see a planeload of welcoming professors explode in the air before his eyes. In 1932, seeing his countrymen killing themselves with "his" invention in the Vargas revolution, he went into the bathroom and hung himself with his necktie.

Alberto Santos-Dumont, not Aleijadinho, is Brazil's recognized hero.

Canto IV: Bahia—Black Rome of the Artists

We could not have arrived in Bahia on a more propitious day. The Fiesta of Yemanja was being celebrated in the great arc of beach called Praia de Santa Anna (Rio Vermelho). At one corner of the arc is a flight

of steps leading to a statue of the African sea goddess—a white mermaid. Tens of thousands of blacks jammed the beach, loading their armfuls of flowers onto barges, wading into the surf to get the barges afloat so they could be poled and then sailed far enough out to be dropped where the divinity would have elbowroom to receive them. Half of the huge crowd was in bathing suits, thrashing about in the water, while the other half danced and sang encouragement. Old women in spotless white ankle-length dresses carried dollhouses covered with white spangles on their turbaned heads. Young athletes in trunks, after depositing their precious offerings, splashed the water on everyone within range while clapping children screamed with delight, falling over each other into the waves to avoid the few drops flying through the air.

Only in Haiti had we seen so many giving such pleasure with so little. And only in Haiti had we witnessed such total unself-consciousness of being black—and conversely in ourselves such a release from guilt at being white. The bathing beauties who offered themselves to us with their eyes could have been on any beach, and of any color. But the camaraderie of the men at the "restaurants" of packing crates fringing the sea wall—how to account for it? Not only were we the only whites among them, but we were obviously foreigners, and judging by our cameras and clothes, affluent. So here they were pulling up rickety chairs, offering us roast crabs and beer, and refusing to let us pay for anything. We were their guests and Brazil's, they explained, and they would be insulted if we took out so much as a *cruzeiro*. All of the linguistic resources within a hundred feet of our table were pooled to make this plain to us (for thus far, *obrigado*—thanks—was about the extent of our Portuguese), and instead of increasing our embarrassment by offering us elementary lessons in their language, they begged us for the latest American expressions—"to impress our friends," they explained, "and to make them think we've been in your great country." We laughed and they laughed, but in the presence of a people to whom laughter is a congenital trait or a centuries-old response to oppression, who has not heard his own laughter ring hollow?

"The Latins have developed the ethnic aspect of democracy more than the political," Freyre observes, "and the Anglo-Saxons, the political aspect more than the ethnic." But this does not begin to explain why African slavery, abolished later in Brazil than in the United States, left none of the deep wounds of prejudice that still scar us. The Portuguese colonizer was a compromiser type, with no absolute ideals or unyielding prejudices, and "least cruel in his relation with slaves," whom he treated in the aristocratic tradition with a "clinging tradition of ineptitude, stupidity, and salaciousness." [16]

Moog makes much of the fact that Portuguese civilization matured "not in the presumption of the superiority of the white over other races, but in the actual, present knowledge of a superior civilization created by a race of darker pigmentation." The cult of Moorish beauty was surely some psychological preparation; and so was the polygamous ideal and reality—"so common in patriarchal Brazil and so in conflict with the Christian concept of monogamy." From the beginning, Puritan and Lusitanian attitudes toward people of color seem to have been in sharp contrast. Whereas Captain John Smith in 1607 left behind him the Princess Pocahontas, who had saved his life, Diego Alvares, shipwrecked off Bahia a century earlier, carried *his* princess Paraguassú proudly home with him to Europe and then returned with her to Brazil to found a notable family. Which is not to say that the early idealization of the Indian, and later of the mulatto woman, resulted in complete equality for either of these races in Brazil—on the contrary both were enslaved, and are cruelly exploited economically to this day [17]—but only that the sexual taboo has not been operative here, and the social one only in the mildest of forms.

[16] Gilberto Freyre, *The Masters and the Slaves*. Translated by Samuel Putnam. New York, Alfred A. Knopf, 1946.
[17] According to the Brazilians themselves a policy of virtual genocide has been practiced against the Indians (75,000 survivors out of a population of millions) and still goes on. A twenty-volume report has been issued by the Indian Protection Service. The Director of the Service for 1964-66 was charged with 42 separate crimes including murder, torture, illegal sale of land, and embezzlement of more than $300,000. In Bahia state, two tribes were wiped out with smallpox injections; and in Mato Grosso, arsenic and dynamite, dropped from planes, were used to eliminate the Indians from desirable farmland.

Yemanja is a Nigerian deity from the ancient kingdom of the Yorubas whence came most of the slaves to Bahia. Dahomey tribesmen in 1866 destroyed the Yorubas' capital city of Ketu, so today the Yoruba gods survive in Bahia only. Other slaves were brought from Angola, Nago, and elsewhere in West Africa, and their gods enriched the transplanted cult. The Bahia *capoeira*, with its gestures of personal defense, is supposed to have originated as a means of subverting the ordinance forbidding slaves to carry weapons: the masters were tricked into believing that their slaves were only dancing (their arms and legs being their only weapons). But today, in a singular reversal of proveniences, the *capoeira* dancers travel to Dakar to show the Africans black choreography at its purest. It is the same with Haiti, where voodoo (the transplanted and very slightly Catholicized religion of the Dahomey and Arada tribes) flourishes, with its attendant dance lore and drumming, as nowhere in the motherland.

Through a misunderstanding over the telephone of his Spanish (which quickly trails off into Portuguese), we visited Jorge Amado after the Yemanja ceremony rather than accompanying him to it as he had proposed. Actually the house of the famous novelist is in Vermelho directly above the festival beach, and the author's collection of Afro-Brazilian folk objects attests to his interest in the cults of *candomble*. Like his friend Pablo Neruda at Isla Negra in Chile,[18] the Brazilian social realist is a compulsive collector. No other homes that we were to visit in South America compared with these two—in taste, in originality, in livability. There are points of cross-influence, such as the giant mermaid of painted wood that hangs in the stairwell of the Amado home, rivaling many such at Isla Negra; but the points of difference are as marked. Neruda's home reflects his lifelong preoccupation with surrealism. Amado's house, surrounded by a well-tended "jungle" of Brazilian flora, is most notable for its primitivistic paintings—perhaps the finest such collection in Brazil. Both are "happy" houses, reflecting happy marriages, but Amado's seems less a museum, enlivened as it is by children who are encouraged to display the rebellious symbols of a younger generation. Teen-aged João, bearded and long-haired, arrived by sports car during our first visit. Later he received us in his "pad" off the spacious, tiled veranda that surrounds the house, wearing a sort of toga striped like a prisoner's uniform. Proudly he showed us his latest posters: the martyred Ché Guevara, and "Lyndon Johnson" riding one of the motorbikes of "Hell's Angels."

Jorge (pronounced George in Brazil) was barefooted and wearing white shorts and a red homespun shirt as he graciously received us. On the sun-drenched porch, his brother James, married to Graciliano Ramos' sister, served as interpreter when necessary. While we were talking, maids, houseboys, and gardeners passed in and out in a steady procession.

[18] See Chapter 10.

Jorge Amado — 1969
BAHIA

The stocky novelist with his shock of curly, crewcut white hair, asked what we had already seen of Brazil, and mention of Brasilia started a friendly argument. Niemeyer was a genius, Jorge said, and the city had already justified itself as a crossroads to open up Brazil's heartland. When I asked him whether those billions couldn't have been better spent on the *favelas*, he frowned.

"The point is that the money would never have been spent on the *favelas*. It would have been spent on automobiles and whiskey, or banked abroad. So we must be grateful that it was spent as it was."

I had to admit that we were spending our billions on ventures still more remote from the people's needs. "Do you think, then, that Kubitschek was Brazil's best president?" I asked.

"No. Maybe Jânio Quadros could have been. He had the ideas, but he was forced out by reactionary and foreign interests who feared agrarian and structural reforms."

James Amado didn't agree. "I think Quadros was an unstable demagogue with intellectual pretensions, and as responsible as anyone for our present plight under the military."

I asked them if they saw any way out of this impasse.

"Only by a union of all democratic forces," Jorge said, "including the communists, whom I don't support, as Pablo does," he added. "Only such a union could offer free elections and the calling of a constituent assembly."

"Is anyone calling for such an assembly?" I asked.

"Only I am in favor of it," he said with a laugh.

"Are you writing a manifesto?" Bill asked.

"If I did, it wouldn't be published."

"The communists are strong?" I asked.

"Very weak. They are split into six factions. They resemble the military regime in one respect: their one idea is to survive!"

"So Brazil's problem . . ."

". . . is that it has no political leaders."

I had been reading Jorge Amado's vivid novel of frontier life in this region during the cacao boom half a century ago.[19] The key sentence in the chronicle of family feuds for the virgin forests comes at the close when the city lawyer says to one of the embattled contestants regarding the killings: "The curious thing is how you people can do such things and still be so good." It indicates the same generous optimism about human nature that Guimaraës Rosa expresses more intellectually. In fact, in his introduction to the English translation of Guimaraës Rosa's epic novel, Amado had cautioned critics not to be misled by the formal aspects of the younger novelist's obsession with language: "The outward cloak of

[19] Jorge Amado, *The Virgin Land*. Translated by Samuel Putnam. New York, Alfred A. Knopf, 1945.

this formal aspect seems to conceal and hide from certain critics that heaving universe, brutal and tender, violent and gentle . . . Brazilian and universal at one and the same time." I asked Jorge, who calls his fellow-novelist with perhaps exaggerated local pride "a novelist of Bahia rather than Minas Gerais," why their styles differ so markedly.

"I'm part of the 1930 generation," he said. "We regionalists revolted against Portuguese romanticism. The generation of the 1940s revolted against our reportorial style."

"Then you wouldn't be an admirer of Faulkner, I suppose, or of García Márquez or Cortázar among contemporary South Americans," I said.

"I have García Márquez' novels but I haven't read them yet. Cortázar, yes; but it's a characteristic of Argentine writers that they are very detached from life and preoccupied with language. They are Europe-oriented, and write with an eye to being translated, perhaps. Among your novelists my favorite is Mark Twain—as great as Dickens or Tolstoi—and among moderns, Hemingway, Sinclair Lewis, Upton Sinclair, Richard Wright, the young Steinbeck, and especially Erskine Caldwell."

"Your mention of Wright," I said, "makes me want to ask you about the sentence in *The Violent Land*—'A black man who has a daughter is only bringing her up for a white man's bed.' Is that still true?"

"No. That was more than half a century ago when some of the traits left over from slavery still persisted. Nowadays as the Negro mounts the economic ladder he is absorbed, totally, because he is accepted racially. And that is very disturbing, that fusion, to many blacks from your country who visit us, like the editor of *Ebony* who said to me 'It's terrible! Our race is disappearing in Brazil!' And it's true."

After we'd had *mangaba* under one of his mango trees, I asked Amado about the artists in his collection whose work impressed me most. Djanira, who paints black ritualists of the *macumba*[20] in white costumes against dazzling baroque buildings and landscapes, is a neoprimitive from Rio; her paintings have become fashionable and expensive. A superb watercolor of four *bandeirantes* was by the Argentinian-born painter and sculptor, Carybé, who lives in Bahia with his American wife, Nancy. A pre-Columbian put-on by Mario Cravo of Bahia, skillful enough to fool a Tamayo, was not characteristic of this artist's serious work, Jorge said.

The time we now spent in the company of these last two artists, so vastly different yet so Brazilian in respecting each other, was pure joy. And in their company we came to love more than the African side of Bahia—from the four-breasted nymphs tempting the monks in the blue-tiled cloister of San Francisco de Assis, to the *moqueca* stews of a dozen unidentifiable crustaceans cooked in *dende* palm oil.

---

[20] African rites, as practiced in Rio, with aboriginal (Indian) additives.

Carybé showed us the quick Bushman-like studies of gauchos that come out of his nostalgia for the pampas of his childhood, and all over Bahia the sculptural reliefs in a dozen media that pour out of his uninhibited creativity. I say uninhibited because this artist is as happy to borrow from Picasso, Marisol, Stankiewicz, as he is to have others borrow from him; and at his best—as in the nineteen wood reliefs he had just completed for a bank—his imitations are inimitable. In one of these ten-by-four-foot panels the life-size figure will be draped with necklaces and bracelets of real wari-shells. In another, copper plaques and mirrors are inserted. In a third, the guts of a slave will be filled with rusting chains and manacles. But the finest is the simplest: a swirl of feathers this way and that across a priestess' body, combed out of the yellow wood with *brio*.

Mario Cravo, as man and artist, is at the opposite pole from the gentle Carybé. With deep sideburns joining a pendulous moustache under gimlet eyes behind thick, half-shell granny-glasses, he is almost a caricature of an intellectual. It was not surprising at all, after listening to his rapid-fire pronouncements a few minutes, to hear that he had lived in Greenwich Village and taken a degree in fine arts at Syracuse. "I love machines," he growled as he accelerated his Porsche past six speeding buses on a hairpin turn, "but you must never let machines control you; you must control the machine!" BOOM!—we had hit a hole in the pavement and our heads smacked into the (fortunately) canvas top. Mario's entrance yard is a maze of derricks, water tanks, and steel drums that he is about to convert into sculpture; and his studio, the size of a Braniff hangar, is lined with books, folk sculpture, baroque saints, welding equipment, gas bottles, and mock-ups for such gigantic totems as his "Yemanja and Her Son-Lover" in the garden of the University's Anthropology Museum.

He had some interesting things to say about Brasilia. "You have to understand the insanity of our politics to know why a president with an ambition to make himself a monument couldn't risk not completing it in his term of office. His successor would either stop the work out of envy or destroy it. Kubitschek had to make it so fast it could neither be stopped nor destroyed!

"The builders of Washington," he went on, "made some of the same mistakes when they imported a style and fastened it on your capital. Imagine how utterly absurd it must have looked in the beginning, all those Roman orders sprouting out of that swamp! It doesn't look so bad after a hundred years, so perhaps there's hope for Brasilia . . . but our whole concept of art changes. They took two hundred years to build San Francisco which you saw this afternoon, letting it grow naturally. Carybé and I are given a few months to complete our masterpieces and get the hell out."

Mario's masterpiece, like Carybé's, is his simplest, least frenetically

MARIO CRAVO
Bahia

modish work; and it is already being shoved aside by an environment hostile to simple masterpieces. Hacked, as though with a machete, arms upraised, the man's face reduced by injustice and malnutrition to a hunted weasel's, this "Christ" worthy of Gruenewald has been placed by the Museum of Folklore (which presumably commissioned it) off to one side of its parking lot where it is rapidly being enveloped by a mango tree and rotted by the tropical deluges. Perhaps its fate is symbolic. For who in Brazil cares about its subject, Antonio Conselheiro, the backlands religious fanatic who held out with his followers for the whole year of 1897 against the Brazilian Army until not one rebel remained alive?

Canto V: Recife—Background to Rebellion

What did it matter that they had six thousand rifles and six thousand sabres; of what avail were the blows from twelve thousand arms, the tread of twelve thousand military boots, their six thousand revolvers and twenty cannon, their thousands upon thousands of grenades and shrapnel shells; of what avail were the executions and the conflagrations, the hunger and the thirst which they had inflicted upon the enemy; what had they achieved by ten months of fighting and one hundred days of incessant cannonading; of what profit to them those heaps of ruins, that picture no pen could portray of the demolished churches, or, finally, that clutter of broken images, fallen altars, shattered saints—and all this beneath a bright and tranquil sky which seemingly was quite unconcerned with it all, as they pursued their flaming ideal of absolutely extinguishing a form of religious belief that was deeply rooted and which brought consolation to their fellow-beings?

. . . It was the very core of our nationality, the bedrock of our race, which our troops were attacking here, and dynamite was the means precisely suited. It was at once a recognition and a consecration.[21]

One man did care about the bestiality of this response to Brazil's underdogs: Euclides da Cunha; and Cravo's tree-sculpture could as well be his portrait as Antonio Conselheiro's, for the author of Brazil's great epic was himself maned like a lion, uncouthly clothed, and he fell under an assassin's bullet when the Army feared new revelations from his merciless pen.

Os Sertões is quite without prototype in Brazilian literature—or in any literature for that matter, though it bears a rough-hewn resemblance to James Agee's more lyrical and personal description of North America's victims, *Let Us Now Praise Famous Men*. Like Agee, who begins by expiating his guilt with a description of every nail and knothole in the Alabama shanty on which he is spying, Cunha starts off by detailing the geology of the backlands with exhaustive objectivity. In the second chapter, "Man," he presents his protagonist emerging out of the unresolved turmoil of Brazil's predatory and hunted races—"our shamefaced feudalism" that produced the *vaqueiro* "growing to manhood without ever having been a child" and "damned to life." Then, arising out of "the insurrection of the earth against man," comes his latter-day embodiment, armed only with superstition, and finally "hallucinated, depressed, and perverted" by the missionaries into an "atavistic" bandit. Conselheiro's

---

[21] Euclides da Cunha, *Rebellion in the Backlands*. Translated by Samuel Putnam. Chicago, Illinois, University of Chicago, 1944.

career is seen as a "condensed summary of a very grave social malady"—
a paranoiac individual from Bahia who was "asked to go down in history
when he should have gone to a hospital." The mad old man appears in
the backlands and becomes the embodiment of all the frustrations,
hungers, rebellions, and suicidal impulses of the disinherited. Running
afoul of the Archbishop of Bahia (for interpreting Christianity literally
and predicting Judgment Day) and of the Army (for preferring the decent
Empire to the corrupt Republic), he prepares his followers for guerrilla
warfare, agrarian communism, free love, and the ultimate siege of
Canudos.

The story of the siege that follows is the story of all mankind's insane
holocausts. "Concerned with the fearful physiognomy of peoples amid
the majestic ruins of vast cities, against the supremely imposing background of cyclopic coliseums, with the glorious butchery of classic battles
and the epic savagery of great invasions, History would have no time for
this crude slaughter pen." But history, with two World Wars and the
death camps of Central Germany and Siberia still ahead of it, would get
the message soon enough. Ringed by fifty-two hundred soldiers, the army
of beggars at Canudos didn't surrender. "The only case of its kind in
history, it held out to the last man." Conselheiro's decomposed body—
"precious relic that it was, the sole prize, the only spoils of war this conflict had to offer!"—was dug up, and the severed head "sticky with scars
and pus" was carried around the streets of Bahia "by delirious multitudes" in "carnival joy."

No wonder that this Brazilian nonconformist who had forged a new
style to convey his unique jeremiad should be the inspirer of Guimaraës
Rosa; and no wonder the militarists of that day struck him down when
it was noised about that he was writing a further revelation of their
crimes in the *sertão*. Its title was to have been "Paradise Lost."

I saw this veritable paradise, thousands of square miles of it, green,
well-watered, uninhabited, the morning we flew to Recife, girdled by its
swarming slums. How long would today's militarists, we wondered, tol-
erate Dom Helder Camara, the only man in Brazil proclaiming that this
starvation amid plenty was intolerable? We had come to Recife to talk
to the "red" Archbishop, but long before our appointment we were hearing about him.

Checking in at the Hotel Boa Viagem, we asked the desk man to confirm
our reservations to Belém and Paramaribo. The official at the Cruz do Sul
informed him that our names were not on the list and that the plane was
full, an old story. "Is it worth twenty thousand *cruzeiros* to you?" the
desk man asked us. I handed him the four dollars. "That will be ample,"
he said. "With enough money you can buy anything in Brazil."

"Except Dom Helder?" I suggested.

"Dom Helder is a communist," he said. "Don't let them tell you anything else. The present government is exactly what Brazil needs. We're a lazy people, and every civilian government has taken advantage of it. We need agrarian reform, the kind we're getting now, with industrialization; not Dom Helder's kind, dividing up the big estates into small parcels. Taxation of unproductive land is the answer: taxation and collection."

The taxi driver who took us to the Archbishop's palace was more sympathetic. They'd forced Dom Helder out of Rio, he said, because he had worked tirelessly for the *favela*-dwellers, rehousing thousands of them and encouraging thousands more to demand services and jobs—and to fight for them if necessary. "The situation is more desperate here," he said. "When the peasants in the far west of the province of Pernambuco moved into the sugar plantations of the central part, they always ended up by owing the sugar bosses and their company stores money. So hearing on the radio about buying cars and TVs here without any down payments, they moved in on us and built these huts on stilts on the tidal flat. When the tide comes in, they're isolated half the day. When it moves out, the crabs in the black mud eat their shit, and they eat the crabs. They came for jobs, and there are no jobs."

Dom Helder confirmed the cycle. "But they're fatalistic about it," he said, "and that's our fault."

The Archbishop faced us across a long mahogany table in a sun-parlor without decoration. His iron-gray hair is thinning and his face is deeply lined. His eyes have an expression at once sly and benevolent. When impassioned, he talks with his hands. I asked him how many other churchmen in Brazil take his revolutionary position.

"About fifteen percent," he said, "another fifteen percent are reactionaries. The rest of the bishops take no position. But I am concerned about the revolution needed in the whole underdeveloped world, not just in Brazil. Understanding is more important than dollars. Last week at the CICOP meeting in New York I presented three propositions: 1) Reintegrate Cuba in the Latin-American system; 2) Admit Red China to the UN —they call me a Fidelista and a Maoist, but neither of these two propositions has anything to do with friendship for those leaders or their philosophies; 3) Have five North American universities join with five Latin American ones to make recommendations to the UN on underdevelopment. The key to the relation between developed and underdeveloped countries is justice. The underdeveloped countries need trade, not aid. Without this there can be no peace, or, as Pope Paul VI put it, the new name for peace is development. Conversely, underdevelopment means war.

"Capitalist versus socialist imperialisms," he continued, "equal Vietnam. I oppose both imperialisms. Capitalist imperialism accepts the Church, yes, but only so long as the Church follows the old charity course. I want Brazil to be a friend of the United States, not a slave. I oppose

Dom Helder

129

the foreign policy of the United States, not its people. The Pentagon exercises vast influence over government and business, even over your universities it now appears, via research. Have you read *Seven Days in May*? Yes, I fear very much that the Pentagon will one day swallow the White House—which will affect us, because all these Latin American armies that run our countries are absolutely dependent on good relations with the Pentagon, where the lie is believed that what is good for the United States is good for Latin America."

I asked the Archbishop of Recife and Olinda whether he'd been gagged by either the Castelo Branco or Costa e Silva regimes.

"I had a dialogue with Castelo Branco," he said, "but many members of his government thought it subversive to demand that the two thirds of Brazil lacking almost everything be raised to the level of the one third that has enough or more than enough." He stood up. "Do you know that one third of Brazil's 87,000,000 people are in this drought-stricken northeast hump? Am I expected to ignore that fact?"

He walked to the window, clenching his hands, and then turned to us again. "I am not better, or more human, than my predecessors in the Church who accepted African slavery for four hundred years, but I have a responsibility to Pope John XXIII and his age. *The Army's major vision is to save the social order. Mine is to change it!*"

He sat down, and continued more calmly: "Now, with this Institutional Act of Costa e Silva, things have changed. There is no freedom of the press. I don't receive any orders prohibiting me from saying this or that, but a stifling blanket of silence covers me. My personal movements are not interfered with, but the radio and TV no longer invite me to speak— or report what I say."

I asked him if he thought the military were less corrupt or corruptible than the civilian rulers who preceded them. He smiled wryly. "When civilians come back to power again," he said, "it will be to expose the very same corruptions in the military that the military are supposed to be eliminating by getting rid of the civilians! Already the military regime has been obliged to expose corruption in the Caixa Economica—which is headed by one of their thirty marshals. . . . So you see why it doesn't really make any difference whether the military or the civilian capitalists rule this country, and why I am obliged to take a revolutionary position."

At the door I came back and asked him whether he thought discrimination against the Negro had been abolished in Brazil. He told me about the conference in Rio he had attended with the late Robert Kennedy, and how the Senator had accepted regretfully the students' charge that in the United States discrimination was still practiced. " 'Many of us are trying to change that,' Kennedy said, and then looking around him at the three hundred students and educators, he added: 'I must say I'm a little surprised not to see a single Negro face at this conference.' "

We waited for the Belém plane with a beautiful Brazilian girl who had been our hostess in Olinda. She didn't mention Dom Helder, but it was clear that her point of view had changed greatly in the year since she'd left her native São Paulo. I asked her why the vast paradise we had passed over flying from Bahia couldn't be colonized by Recife's poor. "Because," she answered, "every bit of that land is owned by somebody, somewhere. A man I know in São Paulo just bought himself a farm in Matto Grosso—not to farm it, but as a hedge against inflation; he admitted it was slightly larger than Switzerland . . . and speaking of Switzerland, how terrible it is that even the modestly well off in this country send their money there for safekeeping, thus increasing Brazil's impoverishment! I didn't used to think of such things when I lived in São Paulo. I had two fine dogs that ate a pound of raw meat a day. Now I won't let my children have even a poodle. How could I feed it when every day beggars come to my back door for the scraps of bread? Yet the only man in Olinda who was teaching these people to read and write, so that they might question their status as animals, was denounced as a communist and sent into exile! If this is the only response the military can make, don't be surprised when you come back to Brazil if we've all turned revolutionaries!"

6

GUYANESE INTERLUDE

Demerara is the Elysium of the tropics—the West Indian Happy Valley of Rasselas—the one true and actual Utopia of the Caribbean Seas—the Transatlantic Eden.

—ANTHONY TROLLOPE, 1860

In Georgetown I longed for the liveliness of Port of Spain. Now I longed for Georgetown, and the people of Paramaribo told me I didn't know what dullness was: I should go across the border to French Guiana.

—V. S. NAIPAUL, 1960

Demerara? Georgetown? Paramaribo? French Guiana? Are we still in South America? Yes; but the reader who knows his way around this strange, unsung part of the continent will forgive us for providing others with the barest essential bearings. The jungle enclave in which Raleigh sought El Dorado lies between Brazil and Venezuela with its northern face the Caribbean Atlantic, and was once the property of three colonial powers, France, the Netherlands, and Great Britain.

Poorest in everything, least populous, and smallest is the eastern sector, French Guiana. A penal colony until 1946, and still a neglected dependency of France, it has no culture of its own and need not concern us.

Surinam, the central sector, is that part of the region which the Dutch of 1667 accepted in trade with the English for Nieuw Amsterdam (New York), the English remaining in what is now Guyana, with its capital Georgetown. Surinam today voluntarily retains its ties to the Dutch motherland. Its population of Negroes, descended from slaves imported by the Dutch, and other races imported later as indentured labor, has

132

begun to work out an accommodation of ethnic traditions—especially around the thriving capital, Paramaribo. This Dutch-speaking coastal culture, however, exercises a very tenuous influence over the jungle hinterland with its pockets of aboriginals (Amerindians) and descendants of escaped slaves (Bush Negroes).

Independent Guyana—once Spanish, then Dutch, and finally British—is the largest and westernmost of the three sectors. Bounded on the north by the Atlantic, on the east by Surinam, on the south by Brazil, and òn the west by Venezuela, it is watered by four tremendous rivers: the Berbice, the Demerara (hence Trollope's name for the whole then-British colony), the Essequibo, and the Mazaruni. Here, too, a polyglot coastal culture dominates a jungle hinterland with the same scattering of Amerindian and Bush Negro villages. But this English-speaking culture feels itself closely tied to the Caribbean islands, especially to Trinidad. As in that exuberant melting-pot of races, and as in Surinam, Guyana is divided almost equally between Negroes and East Indians. And the confrontation of these two races, as in Trinidad, is so increasingly hateful and explosive that perhaps the only thing that might bring them together would be Venezuela's decision to seize by force that greater part of Guyana which it now claims Britain separated illegally from Spain.

Trollope, the English novelist, and Naipaul, the Trinidadian novelist of East Indian extraction, are probably the most acute minds ever to have commented on this area in print. Yet each of them reveals a basic untrustworthiness in the quotations at the head of this chapter. Trollope was an English romantic and saw a utopia where there was none—except perhaps for the British planters. Naipaul was a disenchanted islander who experienced agonies of dullness as a reflection of his uprooted yearning for older civilizations. The region is neither paradisiac nor dull. In the post-World War II period, Surinam made a remarkable adjustment to independence within the Dutch cultural orbit. Guyana made the more adventurous decision to opt for a native culture, at least "native" within the context of all the once-British slavocracies of the Caribbean; but this decision entailed the consequence of cutting loose politically. There followed a desperate skirmish for power in Guyana between the descendants of the African slaves and the descendants of the indentured East Indians, who were in a slight majority. The latter—hard-working, frugal, cohesive—won the first round. Their leader, Cheddi Jagan, an undeviating Moscow-communist and a man of great personal magnetism, became Prime Minister. Strongly opposed by the British—for the strikes he encouraged against the sugar companies and for the threat his crusading Marxism posed in their other overseas possessions—Jagan hung on until 1964 when the British landed troops to stop the racial strife. His successor, the Negro leader Forbes Burnham—financed by the United States with British connivance, Jagan maintains—was a great orator and also a man of winning charm. He has been Prime Minister ever since, with independence achieved (1966) but the racial division confirmed.

Waterfront Street Surinam 1969

Arrival in Paramaribo

Surinam is another of those places, like Bahia, Barbados, and most parts of Haiti and Jamaica, where the Negro is unself-conscious of color. It's his country, and he's obviously delighted to have foreigners enjoy it. He even seems happy to serve them. At the Tororica Hotel, where Bill's wife and mine had come to spend a week with us before we continued on into Guyana and Venezuela, the waiters laugh uninhibitedly with the guests, and a black worker high on a scaffolding over the swimming pool smiled and waved back when I waved to him from a deck chair.

Which is not to say that there is no racial problem in Surinam. Some time ago Carnival was tried without success. Not only was it against the Calvinist-Lutheran grain, but a Dutch businessman chosen king refused to dance with the black queen—on the flimsy pretext that only kings were recognized "in the old days." This evoked outrage in the press for a few days, and then was forgotten. The prejudiced Dutchman (happily for all) returned to Holland. There are no counter-prejudices against the Dutch, we were told, though the Dutch were notoriously cruel as slave masters, and inflexible as colonial overlords. The Royal Family is adored here—as it isn't in Holland—and though the local dialect (a pidgin-English called

Talkie-talkie) is the common tongue of Surinam, there is little agitation to substitute it for Dutch in the schools. "Dutch, because of its difficulty or improbability," Naipaul says, "breeds new and separate languages which very soon destroy Dutch. There is the kitchen Dutch of South Africa, the Papiamento of the Netherlands Antilles, the *negerengels* of Surinam. A passion for bad grammar is one of the singular features of regional pride in Dutch territories." [1]

Naipaul thinks that the assimilation, offered but not made obligatory by the Dutch, tends to make the Negro bewildered and irritable—"Racial equality and assimilation are attractive but only underline the loss, since to accept assimilation is in a way to accept a permanent inferiority"— but this is a subtle point and hard to prove. Naipaul does admit, however, that Surinam has emerged from the centuries of slavery under the Dutch as the only truly cosmopolitan area in the West Indian region, and that if there is a cultural problem it is mainly a problem for the Negro who has rejected his past and all that attaches him to Africa. In the Caribbean islands where Africa (except in Haiti) is no more than a word, the search for a usable past is difficult indeed; but here in Surinam, as we shall soon to discover, the Bush Negro has preserved his African arts; the Amerindian, his gaudy dress and his cooking; the Javanese, his exotic dance. And along with these, all of them have preserved their pride.

For all the assimilation, though, there is widespread dissatisfaction with the paternalistic administration of Prime Minister John Adolf Pengel, and to understand why, it may help to break down the racial composition of Surinam's 324,000 people:

      115,000 Creoles (blacks and mulattoes of the coastal strip)
      113,000 Hindustanis (East Indians)
       48,000 Javanese
       28,000 Bush Negroes (descendants of escaped slaves)
        5,500 Chinese
        5,200 Europeans
        4,200 Amerindians (aboriginals)
        5,200 Others (Jews, Lebanese, Syrians, Americans, etc.)

Creoles were the overwhelming majority of those who voted Pengel in, and Creoles got most of the political plums. Where does that leave the Hindustanis? In limbo, so far. A small minority of the Creoles support independence, as does a small minority of the Hindustanis—but the latter are said to favor it if (or rather when) they become the majority. When Prime Minister Pengel visited Holland recently and made guarded mention of independence (for home consumption) the canny Dutch agreed with alacrity—causing Pengel to beat a hasty retreat. Only the young intellectuals who have studied in Holland favor independence vocally.

[1] V. S. Naipaul, *The Middle Passage*. London, André Deutsch, 1962.

But most of those with the means to travel to Holland stay there, with the result that Surinam loses its brightest young men.

The Chinese always support the regime in power. The Javanese have their own parties, but none of the parties have ideologies. All their programs are oriented to local problems and all make the same demands: higher wages, more schools, better roads, etc. None of them oppose the bauxite concessions, the largest of which is a joint Surinam Government-ALCOA venture, with sometimes an American as director and sometimes a Creole. And none of them cry Yankee imperialism. How unlike South America!—and indeed South America scarcely recognizes this region's existence.

Paramaribo, which contains 175,000 out of Surinam's 324,000 people, is an attractive city. The government buildings are solid examples of the Dutch architectural style, and the Catholic Cathedral, across the street from the octagonal Lutheran (Dutch Reform) Church, is unique. Inside, it is faced with a variety of polished hardwoods: even the Gothic vaulting is of wood, and the columns are Moorish! And surprisingly this eclecticism works very well. It is pointed out with relish that the Lutheran Church is built over a graveyard containing the remains of Mme. Aura van der Lith, the notorious wife of three colonial governors she was suspected of having poisoned, and another eighteenth century grand dame, Mme. du Plessis, whose gravestone was split by lightning, they say, because once on her barge on the Surinam River, she drowned a Negro baby whose crying disturbed her.

The local museum is of great interest, and as efficiently organized as the Tororica Hotel—very likely the best hotel (in décor, cuisine, and service) in South America. There are examples of Bush Negro carvings in the museum as fine as the pilaster panels in the Tororica's lobby, and a variety of Amerindian paddles with designs said to symbolize the love life and family expectations of these people. Javanese *tampans*—bells in a cage like a small bed—dolls of the various ethnic groups, bottles of surprising variety and beauty, and birchbark canoes complete the collection.

Bush Negroes and Amerindians

Ferdinand and Tony, Surinamese friends who offered to drive us up-river and as far as the French border in search of primitive artifacts, waited in the car while we confirmed our flight to Georgetown at the KLM office. The clerk gave us a preview of the threat that currently hangs over the Guyanese. "The Venezuelans," she said, "are treating Surinam very well these days. They're all smiles! . . . Why? Because they want to neutralize us if they meet with resistance when they move their army into Guyana's backlands!"

"Will the Surinamese play dead?" Bill asked.

"Maybe not. Our turn to be carved up might come next. The Brazilians are already alarmed. So much so that their Chief of Staff visited an Amerindian village in Guyana last week. He surely wasn't looking for bead necklaces. He wanted the Venezuelans to know Brazil frowns on meddling with the frontiers."

But Tony, on the drive out of town, thought that the Surinamese might be too plagued with problems of their own to help Guyana. "The Hindustanis here are out for power—their power—and when they outnumber us, we Creoles are going to be in trouble."

"What about the Javanese?" I asked.

"They're the sweetest people," he said. "No crime, no trouble, no laziness."

"Who are the lazy ones?"

"We are," he replied with a laugh. "The memory of slavery is what keeps the Creoles from farming. There's a terrible shortage of labor in Surinam, especially on the land. Everybody wants a job in industry, or in the city at the very least."

"I've read that there's a huge reservoir of unemployed farm labor over in Guyana," I said. "Why don't you invite them over here?"

"The Dutch would never permit it," he said.

"But you're independent—or aren't you?"

"Yes . . . but we Creoles wouldn't like it either. There are so many communists among their Hindustanis, so much thieving and violence in Georgetown's streets."

We had now reached the Marowijne River at Albina and could see the village of St. Laurent on the French side. "Population there is five thousand and twenty-five thousand in Cayenne, their capital, both penal settlements until a few years ago," Tony said. "Thirty-five thousand, and nothing but De Gaulle's silly missile pad to keep them alive."

I asked him what Holland's stake in Surinam really was.

"Moral," he replied. "They're expiating their guilt for the whole colonial empire they exploited and lost. And it's costing them a hell of a lot of money."

The two primitive settlements we visited couldn't have been more different. Neger Kreek, just past Moengo, is Bush Negro. Here, and in other such settlements, the tribal life of Africa was miraculously reconstituted. Even a written script (Djuka) was invented. The houses are on stilts with brilliantly painted exterior murals, abstract, geometric. The women are nude from the waist up and very comely. They seemed cheerful, easygoing, and glad to see us. The men—some say they are the most skillful riverboatmen in the world—were carving a dugout canoe. The only "cash crop," Tony told us, is fire dancing—a by-product of the African spirit worship similar to Haitian voodoo which is still practiced here. The local fire dancers had left for a nightclub in Paramaribo just before we drove in. These people are also great woodcarvers, who must

Surinam
—Negritos

have adapted this skill from their African memory, so there is a second "cash crop"—but we missed out on that one as well, for all the finished pieces had gone in the same truck with the fire dancers . . . to the Tororica gift shop.

We rented a dugout canoe to reach the Amerindian settlement an hour

michel   Joseph

Albina
Surinam

upriver from Albina. The only similarity is that the women here are also bare breasted; but neither the breasts nor the women are attractive. Both sexes are taciturn, and are said to be heavy drinkers. The only response we got to a cash offer for photography was to have our guilders snatched from us and stuffed in the thatch. The shelters are handsome and well made. The "walls" of palm-frond don't reach to the floor, with the result that there is plenty of ventilation and light inside. The several families sharing the largest structure were busy depoisoning their cassava roots and making pancakes of them on iron discs. This operation is conducted with great finesse. The pancakes are "printed" with a design of concentric circles. The women and their children wear beautiful grass skirts of many colors and bead necklaces.

"It is us they resent," Tony said, "not you." He could be right if suppressed guilt lies behind that taciturnity; for it was these Amerindians the Dutch hired out to hunt down the escaped Negro slaves.

Poets of Racial Fury

If poets and novelists are as rare in Surinam as revolutionaries that is because, as already noted, apprentices in all three of these nonconformist trades go abroad and stay there. We had already met René de Rooy, Ferdinand's brother, in Curaçao, where he shares the literary scene with such formidable Caribbean-Dutch luminaries as Boeli van Leeuwen and Governor Cola Debrot.[2] Another talented Surinamese writer of short stories is L. A. M. Lichtveld, Minister Plenipotentiary at the Royal Netherlands Embassy in Washington. Naipaul describes meeting a poet who felt so pathetically isolated in Paramaribo that he ran up to him crying "I knew at once it was you. I felt a sort of trembling." But in neighboring Guyana—possibly because English is the *lingua franca* of a literary world as formidable as that presided over by the Spanish-speaking poets—the writers return; or, if they do not, they at least write about the homeland with passionate concern. One such was Martin Carter, to whom we carried a letter from John Hearne—the Jamaican novelist who had already confessed to us that he feels as much at home in Georgetown as in Kingston. The following is from Carter's *Poems of the Resistance:*

> You come in warships terrible with death
> I know your hands are red with Korean blood
> I know your finger trembles on a trigger
> And yet I curse you—Stranger khaki clad.

> British soldier, man in khaki
> Careful how you walk

[2] For my talks with them, and Bill's drawings, see our book, *The Caribbean.* New York, Hawthorn Books, 1968.

My dead ancestor Accabreh
Is groaning in his grave

At night he wakes and watches
With fire in his eyes
Because you march upon his breast
And stamp upon his heart . . .

But this unsophisticated call to arms dates from 1953 when Negroes and East Indians in Guyana were briefly united in demanding independence from the British soldiery. Today Carter and the other rebel black bards may still pay homage romantically to Accabreh, Atta, Cuffy, and the other legendary leaders of the eighteenth century slave revolts, but the enemy is no longer the British. It is to the British, in fact, that Carter and his brethren now look for support in their struggle to keep imperialistic Venezuela at bay; and it is to the British they look when face to face with the more immediate challenge of the East Indian majority headed, as always, by former Prime Minister Cheddi Jagan, the communist Messiah.

More sophisticated Guyanese writers, like Wilson Harris, reflect this political confusion in the search for racial identity by retreating into a world of myth. Harris's elusive novel about ghost men in search of a mystic waterfall, *Palace of the Peacock*,[3] was written in England and has been published and highly praised there. In Guyana, where its scene is set, how many can fathom its wordy burden?

In the rooms of the palace where we firmly stood—free from the chains of illusion we had made without—the sound that filled us was unlike the link of memory itself. It was the inseparable moment within ourselves of all fulfilment and understanding. Idle now to dwell upon and recall anything one had ever responded to within the sense and sensibility that were our outward manner and vanity and conceit. One was what I am in the music—buoyed and supported above by the undivided soul and anima in the universe from whom the word of dance and creation first come, the command to the starred peacock who was instantly transported to know and to hug to himself his true alien spiritual love without cruelty and confusion in the blindness and frustration of desire.

What Harris has to say comes through in snatches—"We belong to a short-lived family and people. It's so easy to succumb and die." What the late Edgar Mittelholzer had to say about Guyana was not only comprehensible to everyone who read his novels, it was so obvious, and so turgid with sex and violence, that some critics made the mistake of dismissing the author as a mere sensationalist. What truly was sensational

[3] Wilson Harris, *Palace of the Peacock.* London, Faber and Faber, 1960.

was the energy and persistence of this boy from the sleepy hamlet of New Amsterdam on the Berbice. His assault by mail on the publishing houses of London had been relentless. He describes the campaign himself in his autobiographical *Swarthy Boy:* "Throw in more reserves. No retreat. Victory goes to the strong and persistent. Ignore the taunts on the home front. Keep on throwing in reserves. The enemy defenses must be smashed."

And smashed they were, as the torrent of novels from 1927 to 1963 began to pour out. Much could be written about the psychological clairvoyance of *Shadows Move Among Them*, the narrative skill, the impending sense of doom that keeps the reader feverishly alert, the capacity for sheer entertainment, in all the novels. But it is Mittelholzer's special genius to make that part of seventeenth century Guyana between the Berbice and the Essequibo more real than any nonfictional piece of geography:

> The mangoes were in blossom, and very faintly on the air drifted a turpentine aroma that of a sudden grew stronger as a breeze, audible a moment ago as a hissing far away, now came sizzling through the foliage . . . over the logies in the west.

The memorable novels—*Kaywana Blood, Children of Kaywana, Hubertus* —are the ones in which the van Groenwegel family holds that river bounded jungle, intermarries with Amerindians, and fights off the revolt of African slaves (the Great Rebellion of 1763) in which one of Mittelholzer's Swiss ancestors played a minor role. Perhaps it was because of that ancestral involvement that Edgar Mittelholzer—deeply concerned as all Guyanese (and all writers, for that matter) to discover his roots—wrote out of an obsession. The image of an emerging nation is projected, the unforgettable scene is caught, yet the author seems to identify more with the sturdy Dutch *patroens* than with their chattels who fathered the Guyanese:

> The family is what matters. The family must come before all other considerations. You must keep repeating to yourself: "I come from a great family. I must never let down the family name. I am proud that I am a van Groenwegel. The van Groenwegels never run." . . . Under their layers of culture and refinement, civilized men are animals, and it doesn't need much urging to have them flying at one another's throats. . . . In order that savagery may be kept in check, we must be strong, physically strong. Physical strength results in moral strength and peace follows. . . . In the easy way lies complacency—and weakness. Weakness is always bad. Strength is always good.

When the upright Hubertus talks mystically of the old blood and of the loyalty among God-fearing men that must unite all Dutch, English, German, Swiss, and French settlers, in the face of any threat from the African, who was created to work, and the Amerindian woman, who was created to satisfy his sexuality, it is a believable, not a self-serving or hypocritical racism; perhaps because Mittelholzer was enough of a Nietzschean himself to identify just a little with Hubertus' philosophy. What is most moving about Hubertus, however, and what endears him to the reader as he retains his fortitude through six disastrous changes of nationality in the beleaguered colony, is his lack of self-pity, his facing up to the moral problem of his conscience (however preposterously misdirected in our eyes), his effort to provide, against the immoral background of a colonial slavocracy, the character and continuity the times demand. "Because he has taken this area of our Guyana," writes the Guyanese critic A. J. Seymour of his friend Mittelholzer, "and invested it with the passion and holiness of his creative imagination, and peopled it with a gallery of speaking characters that are more real in one sense than the people we meet . . . there is constituted a world of reference and tradition upon which we will increasingly call as a nation." [4]

Mittelholzer's end was tragic. The death wish by fire was in his last novel. Much earlier he had anticipated it in the story of a man going slowly mad, with lightning seeming to flicker over his limbs. Mittelholzer set fire to himself in an English field. Out of guilt? Expiation for those ancestral sins of the old blood and of his own acquiescence in the renewed racial furies beginning to tear his homeland apart again? Who knows? I wasn't thinking of it, flying into Georgetown over the Berbice, but the hair rose on the back of my head at the thought of the poetry, the beauty and the mystery invested in that name and that place by that poet.

Arrival in Georgetown

Our entrance into this independent republic was as inauspicious as the Surinamese in their catty way had anticipated. There is no crime-in-the-streets—at least not yet; but legalized petty larceny and bureaucracy at its most irritating. No sooner had we disembarked from our half-hour jet flight from respectable Paramaribo than we were in the hands of rapacious customs officials reading us long mimeographed lists of new instructions. One had to do with exposed film. Did Bill have any? He surely did; it was in the nature of his mission to take pictures. He pulled out thirty-six cans of the stuff and his jaw dropped as they began un-

[4] A. J. Seymour, *Edgar Mittelholzer: The Man and His Work.* "The 1967 Edgar Mittelholzer Lectures." Georgetown, Guyana, Ministry of Education, 1968.

cheddi Jagan
georgetown GUYANA — 2.69

screwing the caps. Out popped the first roll—twenty-four shots ruined. Bill leaped the counter to save the others. "Over my dead body!" he shouted. "We're impounding them!" they shouted, as the scrimmage began. The only weapon I could think of was John Hearne's letter to Martin Carter which I began flourishing wildly. Reaching for a telephone, I handed the receiver to the Chief Inspector with the letter. "Call the Minister and see for yourself," I said, "before Customs is impounded!" This absurd threat, and the wholly unofficial letter, seemed to quiet them. Soon our film was returned to us, and we were exchanging vows of friendship.

All records for airport-to-capital taxi rides were broken by the hour-and-a-half it now took us to get to the Tower Hotel where we had reservations.

"Reservations? So sorry. None of your letters have been received." We showed them their letter. They were just as polite. "We have a new manager." The Tower is Georgetown's only hotel. We could use their pool, and their dining room, and meanwhile they'd call every boardinghouse in town for us. . . . No use: all full. "As a last resort," said the clerk, very chummy by now, "there's the Trent over there, but fair warning! Watch out for Mrs. Stafford. Some call her a Wasp but most just use the word Ogress. Want to try?"

We tried. And Mrs. Stafford more than lived up to her reputation. Twenty-five dollars apiece for two shabby rooms in a shed—"and I want all of it *now*, in advance, or get out!"

We cooled off with a swim in the Tower's pool—Georgetown has no beach, and the Atlantic is brown with the silt of the three great rivers—and walked around the multigabled white clapboard Cathedral and the light-blue balconied Municipal Building, as lyrical a piece of fantasy-Gothic as any fin-de-siècle extravaganza in Port-au-Prince or Port of Spain. And then we made a date to spend the evening with Kit Nascimento, Minister Carter's cultural attaché, to get our bearings in the Sargasso Sea of Guyanese politics. But first, armed with another letter from John Hearne, we took a cab to Cheddi Jagan's house.

The Indian leader (Hindustanis are called Indians here) lives with his American wife, Janet, in one of the split-levels of a new development called Bel Air on the outskirts of the capital. Cheddi met Janet while studying dentistry in Chicago in the thirties. Some say she made a Marxist of him, and others claim she is now a Maoist, but most admit that as Minister of Labor, Health, and Housing she administered her department fairly and ably. We talked in a very relaxed atmosphere over tea about Guyanese folklore and literature, and it wasn't until I mentioned the Surinamese description of Guyana as crime-ridden that the opposition leader delivered the harangue I'd been led to expect. Cheddi has a way, no matter what he is saying, of smiling like an angel—quite a young-looking angel whose innocence has been outraged but not destroyed.

"Yes," he said, leaning back in his chair, "there has been crime and violence here ever since the British-controlled police winked while hoodlums paid by the CIA took to the streets to force my government out. You see, after we'd won the 1961 elections, and Guyana was promised independence whoever won, the trouble began. You can read the genesis of it on page 668 of your friend Schlesinger's *A Thousand Days*[5]—how Kennedy was advised to back Forbes Burnham and to pressure Harold Macmillan into reneging on our independence. The CIA-inspired strikes and riots against us climaxed in 1963; the police didn't want it to stop. They had their orders from the British, who in turn had theirs from the Americans, that there would be no independence without proportional representation; and this shabby technical device was resorted to to give Burnham a huge block of votes from Guyanese supposedly living abroad —and thus to maneuver us out of power. Crime indeed! *The people were made to believe they could have anything they wanted if they overthrew me.*"

As we were leaving, I asked the Indian leader what he was doing to regain power, and he invited me to accompany him tomorrow night on a campaign swing through the countryside.

Kit Nascimento smiled knowingly when I told him at dinner about Jagan's charges that the CIA had financed Prime Minister Burnham's campaign. "Did he tell you how much Moscow has been paying him?" He was referring, he said, to a theft from Barclay's Bank here of a

---

[5] *A Thousand Days: John F. Kennedy in the White House.* New York, Houghton Mifflin, 1965. The passage on Jagan's October 1961 visit to Kennedy is on pp. 774-79 of Schlesinger's book. Schlesinger begins by observing that Jagan, though "his party lived by the clichés of an impassioned quasi-Marxist anti-colonialist socialism," was plainly "the most popular leader in British Guiana" and that at the time he was considered by the British "more responsible than his rival, the Negro leader Forbes Burnham." President Kennedy got his first view of Jagan watching him on the TV program "Meet the Press" where Jagan "resolutely refused to say anything critical of the Soviet Union and left an impression of either wooliness or fellow-traveling." At the White House the next day Jagan reinforced this impression, and Kennedy afterwards observed prophetically to Schlesinger: " 'I have a feeling that in a couple of years he will find ways to suspend his constitutional provisions and will cut his opposition off at the knees.' " When the race riots took place in Georgetown in February of 1962, Jagan, "forgetting his objection to imperialism," called in British troops to protect his government and his Indian following from the enraged blacks. That May, Burnham, whom the British still disliked, visited Washington and made an impression much more favorable than Jagan had, leading Schlesinger to advise Kennedy that " 'an independent Guiana under Burnham (*if* Burnham will commit himself to a multi-racial policy) would cause us many fewer problems than an independent British Guiana under Jagan.' " The way was open to bring this about, Schlesinger concludes, "because Jagan's parliamentary strength was larger than his popular strength. He had won 57% of the seats on the basis of 42.7% of the vote. An obvious solution would be to establish a system of proportional representation. This the British government finally did . . ."—with the result that Burnham's party defeated Jagan's at the polls, independence was achieved at last, and Guyana "seemed to have passed safely out of the communist orbit."

draft for several thousand dollars from the Norodny Bank in Moscow, made out to Jagan and endorsed by him when he cashed it. The thief was an employee of Barclay's who worked for Peter d'Aguiar's United Force, the third (and conservative) party in the elections. "The stolen draft was photographed for the newspapers before it was returned to Barclay's," Kit said, "but more serious than the question of who pays Jagan is the fact that he will never admit that he's been following Moscow's orders slavishly for years. Burnham admits quite frankly that he was a card-carrying communist back in 1953 when the two of them were political allies."

"What about Cheddi's charge that the British promised independence, and then used proportional representation to trick him out of achieving it for Guyana?" I asked.

"Not a word of truth in it," he replied. "In 1963 they said they'd grant independence after and only after proportional representation. The way Jagan controlled the country without a majority of the total vote was the unfairness that proportional representation did away with."

I asked him what proof of CIA help for Burnham Jagan had come up with.

"None, of course. But plenty of innuendo, including a phony East German book listing purported CIA agents all over the world, which included the Ambassadors and their staffs in every country in the world!"

"I've heard about that list," I said ruefully. "They say it also includes as 'agents' the names of every soldier who worked for the Office of Strategic Services during World War II—including mine."

"As for electoral fraud," Kit continued, "he has no evidence of that either. If he had, he'd have taken it to the Privy Council and won an automatic reelection."

"What effort is Burnham's government making," I asked, "to reach the Indian near-majority?"

"Last election," he said, "we actually won three of the predominantly Indian districts. Moreover, the Prime Minister has appointed Indians to four of the thirteen cabinet posts, including the Attorney Generalship, the most powerful. The leader of the House is also an Indian. More important still, consider what our government has done for the Indians. Rice is the biggest industry and employer of labor in Guyana, and ninety percent of rice production and distribution is in Indian hands. Our government has spent thirty million to rehabilitate this industry—our biggest single budget expenditure. As a result we're now self-sufficient and exporting fifty percent of the crop. Still more important are the radical self-help projects—unique in this part of the world, and these too help the Indian predominantly."

"Now that you're independent, Kit," I said, "how do you feel about the British?"

"Our party may not have affection for the British," he replied. "How could we, after the devastating neglect of the colonial period? But we respect their institutions, in which we propose to share, and there is considerable love for the Queen, and for the throne as a symbol."

"And Jagan—?"

"Jagan has no respect for democratic institutions in any form. When he was Prime Minister his bullies carried submachine guns and his police broke up legal strikes and demonstrations with tear gas. He placed barbed wire around the National Assembly building. He expelled two journalists (I myself was one of them, attached to Peter d'Aguiar's party at that time) who questioned him too critically. He tried to have the press muzzled by statutory edict, and he banned our papers. The curious thing was that although in power, Jagan, like a true Marxist perhaps, wasn't satisfied. He wanted absolute power. So he spent all his time attacking the bogeyman of British imperialism. He failed because the Guyanese are anti-communist; they want to be small proprietors. They simply refused to be anti-British or anti-American pawns in Jagan's chess game."

"Jagan told me that your party claims land reform but has actually only given title to the lands he'd already parceled out."

"Naturally we gave title! Jagan, like a good Marxist, opposed giving land to anyone. He was having the state lease it on a communal basis. What else did he tell you?"

"That Burnham exploits race and uses discriminatory racial devices to consolidate his Negro constituency in power. He said African names are being substituted for Anglican ones, for instance. And he added: 'We show the real difference between an Uncle Tom and a Black Panther.'"

Kit laughed. "Burnham has never gone along with that nonsense of adopting African names. If he did, he'd have changed his own. Speaking of names, did you know that the Jagans called their son 'Joseph Stalin Jagan'? Ask him about that when he takes you campaigning tomorrow. And ask him why, if he's so independent, he's the only communist leader abroad who has endorsed the Russian invasion of Czechoslovakia."

"On the grounds—?"

"—that the CIA was about to take over in Prague!"

On the Campaign Trail with Cheddi Jagan

Cheddi picked me up the next day about six and we drove—or rather were driven by an African chauffeur, the only Negro I was to see all evening—to the first of two speeches he was to deliver in the sugar plantations. The all-Indian audiences of three hundred were 90 percent barefoot. I estimated that 75 percent were under twenty-one, and 20 percent under ten—or is it that East Indians are so small and hairless that one can't properly estimate their ages? I had plenty of time to count heads because the speeches were long and I was seated in a singularly exposed position. The procedure at both speeches was the same. We'd drive up, Cheddi and the chauffeur would remove the loudspeaker equipment and batteries from the trunk, and the local PPP (People's Progressive Party) chief would hook them up. Then a reception committee would approach us with leis of flowers, placing one wreath around Cheddi's neck and one around mine (they didn't know who I was, but since I'd arrived with the chief I must be somebody). Then Cheddi would mount the soapbox and I'd be seated directly in front and below him, at a table with a bottle of iced Orange Crush and two straws. "Comrades!" the voice behind me would thunder, "the whole world is in revolt, and we must play our part! Everyone knows that Burnham is nothing but an American puppet!"

I felt like a puppet myself, sitting there in those garlands of flowers, and I wished I had eyes in the back of my wooden head to see whom Cheddi was pointing at as he concluded: "You know who they are, the people who rigged that election! You know what they look like, the ones that counted us out! You know who pays them! So long as Burnham's government controls the ballot boxes, you can't win. You must become a fighting party. You must make the unions strong and invincible. You must win over the Amerindians in the sugar and rice plantations— and the African workers too, if you can."

He got down off his perch, put his hand on my shoulder, and then stepped back up for this afterthought: "Work . . . and money. . . . It's up to you. I'll lead you as long as you want me. But remember: I don't have to. I can pull teeth, or lecture, or write books to make a living."

The applause was brisk but not deafening as we drove off in the hot dusty sweet-smelling darkness over the potholed roads.

"So you're through with the ballot box," I said, lighting my pipe.

"You'd understand why," he said, "if you'd seen the greasy lumps of votes tied with rubber bands in the suspicious boxes it took them two days to open."

"And you can't take it to the Privy Council?"

"It'll take at least another year to get it from the lowest court, where it still is, to the secondary court. The Privy Council is the final court of appeal."

By the time we got back to Georgetown, only one restaurant was still open, a cafeteria on the waterfront. "How would you like a native supper of rice and beans?" said the former Prime Minister as we queued up for trays.

"I'd like that," I said.

Looking around me to see how many recognized my companion in his work pants and pleated shirt, it was obvious that everyone recognized him, and looked at him, regardless of race, with some degree of respect and affection. How could anyone not like Cheddi Jagan? No matter how farfetched his charges are, he believes them, or believes he ought to believe them, or believes others ought to believe that he believes them, for the good of their souls—their Marxist souls. "You are a Marxist, Cheddi, aren't you?" I asked him.

"Yes. I tell the masses to oppose demagogic racism with an understanding for the only real differences separating people: class differences. I try to show exactly how this is done in Guyana."

I asked him if he thought the Dutch had only a moral stake in Surinam, Surinam being a loss to them financially according to all we had heard there.

"Some people," he said with a smile, "look at what goes into a colony or former colony, not at what is being taken out. I suspect that the Dutch get something out of Surinam, or will eventually. Just like the French, who found their slice very useful as a place for convicts, and today, very useful as a missile base. If it becomes useless, they'll get out, I suppose."

As we pulled up at the Trent, I asked him a last question: how did he become a radical?—and got a surprising answer.

"Attending Howard University in Washington," he said, "and seeing how badly Negroes were being treated."

The Prime Minister Points to Venezuela

Prime Minister Forbes Burnham has a charm as disarming as his opponent's. He is a powerfully built Negro with a resonant voice, handsome and humorous. As Bill and I took our seats in front of his desk, he looked at the white shirt with white embroidery I was wearing and said: "Beautiful! Where did you get it?"

"In Mexico, Mr. Prime Minister, in Morelia actually."

"You know the song about white-on-white? 'Two white houses, two white Cadillacs, and nowhere to go . . .' Tell me where you've been in our country."

I told him about last night's electioneering swing. He swallowed hard and assumed an expression of tolerance.

"Cheddi," he said, "to quote Shakespeare, is the kind of man who will seek out his proper reputation even in the cannon's mouth." Then he added, as sententiously: "A sufficient number of our Indian brethren, Mr. Rodman, are convinced that (a) at long last they are getting peace, and (b) that they are better off economically and getting some improvement in their lot all the time.

"My concept," he continued, "as a politician, is to see that unemployment is not only reduced—it was twenty-one percent of the work force, and is now sixteen percent—but done away with. I don't pretend to believe that this is easy, or even that it is possible, but I can try. I have until 1973 to make our work projects and truck-farm programs take up the slack. The results of the last election show that quite a large number of Indians are beginning to see it our way—unfortunately for Mr. Jagan."

"Unfortunately—?"

"He made his bid for the violent revolution he wants and needs, too

Premier Forbes Burnham Guyana

soon. The Guyanese had a taste of it and they don't want any repeat performances."

I asked him to what he ascribed Guyana's reputation for breeding thieves and other lawless elements.

"I can't fairly lay that at Mr. Jagan's door," he answered, "though some do. Of course crimes are exaggerated in the sensationalist press, and by such PPP adherents as the Reuters' stringer in Georgetown. But basically petty crime and the presence of pickpockets is a concomitant of unemployment. The youth, especially, become desperate enough to seize what they want. We're making a special effort to rehabilitate some of these youngsters through our self-help movement, like your CCC, which starts with three months' military training—"

"Good insurance against Venezuela?" I suggested.

He grinned.

"You're strong enough to defend yourselves?" I persisted.

He grinned again. "As the French say, ça dépend," and rising from his desk he drew a curtain aside revealing a large map of the area.

"If they should attack that way through the jungle," he said, using a pencil as pointer, "we'd be more than a match for them. But if they were to launch a full-scale invasion, with aircraft, landing on the coast—well, they're the most industrialized country on this continent, and the richest. They can buy all the equipment they need. We'd expect help from our friends—from Brazil, from Great Britain, perhaps from you—"

"And if your friends should not respond?"

He grinned a third time. "We could always turn Dr. Castro loose on Venezuela, couldn't we? The Venezuelans wouldn't like that, and neither would your country. We'd hate to have to, of course . . . It's interesting, isn't it, that when Britain was here Venezuela never misbehaved, never made such claims. Do you know that they now claim five eighths of our entire country? Everything north of here," he said, pointing to the Essequibo River, "which includes all our gold and silver and diamonds and zinc and iron antimony, most of our bauxite and hydroelectric power, most of our prospective oil on the continental shelf. Britain hadn't been out six months when they started after us. We have to spend twenty percent of our sixty-six-million-dollar annual budget on defense now." You saw what happened last month in Lethem." [6] The Venezuelans pay

---

[6] On January 2, 1969, the sons of Ben Hart, a South Dakota adventurer married to a half-breed Amerindian who had leased 185,000 rich acres near the Venezuelan border, staged a secessionist coup against Guyana with the help of Venezuelan border troops and planes. Fearing that the Burnham government, after its second electoral victory in December, 1968, would cancel their lease, they accepted arms and training from the eager Venezuelans and struck. Burnham threw everything he had into the area, routed the rebels, and burned the Harts' compound to the ground with flamethrowers. Then Guyana's ambassador to Venezuela, E. A. Braithwaite, author of the novel To Sir, With Love, handed the foreign ministry in Caracas a very loveless note. Venezuela handed the note back, but so far has responded with threatening words only.

our Amerindians—who were and are the best paid and best treated aboriginals on this continent—up to ten US dollars a day to work on their side. Then they train them, and send them back to engage in guerrilla warfare against us. Did you know that I have a full-blooded Amerindian as a junior minister in my cabinet?"

"I should think that would be most prudent," I said. "How many Indians are in the cabinet?"

Burnham counted on his fingers . . . "Four."

"The rest being Negroes?—or do you prefer the word African?"

He laughed. "Yes. African. But I don't really care what they call me, as long as they don't call me Black Sambo!"

I asked him if it was true that he'd been a card-carrying communist back in '53.

"Not card-carrying. But I was a sympathizer in those days—earlier actually. My disillusionment began in 1947 in Prague when I witnessed a certain incident, and then saw how completely distorted it became in the Party press—to serve Moscow's interests."

I asked him if it was true that Jagan's son was named Joe Stalin Jagan as indicated in his government's booklet on recent Guiana history. (Jagan had already told me it wasn't true.)

"No," the Prime Minister said, "He's Joe all right, but it's only a presumption that Cheddi named him Joe for Joe Stalin."

"Then don't you think you should have that corrected?" I asked.

"Yes, I do," he said.

Envoi

We had breakfast at 5:30 the following morning to catch our plane to Caracas, and while we were eating, our formidable hostess came over to the table and said to me: "I was in your friend's room yesterday. I always go in with the colored maids to make sure they don't steal. I couldn't help seeing the beautiful drawing Mr. Negron made of Cheddi Jagan. You know I was an old socialist—years and years before they saw the light—and Janet Jagan joined with me, after their marriage, to help me mobilize the women here. Cheddi could have gone so far! He could have had anything he'd wanted, if he hadn't been so crazy—sounding off that way about communism and the Revolution. All he had to do was wait, and he could have had that too. But he couldn't wait. He couldn't keep his mouth shut. He's an honest man, Cheddi is; and the present Prime Minister and his crew don't know the meaning of the word honesty. But you Americans would rather have a crook you can control, or rely on, in office here, than an honest man who proclaims from the housetops his intention of making a pro-Russian communist revolution, and who can blame you?"

7

VENEZUELA: THE LITERARY
NATIONALISTS—AND
CARLOS FUENTES

Wanting to get it all down from a distance: the festival
city as the counterpoint of musical fire would have it,
Noting the skills of the song, the Creoles
three days at their singing in a marathon without let-up
or faltering,
there comes to my mind the phrase about
"combative and passionate men," like a trademark
innate in the "typical Venezuelan family" announced
on the radio, with a whiff of the medicine chest.
The night shows three or four gashes
as rockets burst open, roller skates,
adolescent inductions in speed,
but the voice of the people vaults endlessly upward,
all that "great, happy heart" with its guitars, its
affirmative cadences, and its tear-jerking ballads—
"Mummy, where are my toys?"
                    —LUCIA UNGARO DE FOX, "Christmas in Caracas,"
                    translated by Ben Belitt

Look not in this chapter, O Reader, for the "great happy heart" of the
people, nor yet for the "typical Venezuelan family," nor even for the
night gashed open by "rockets," for it was not given to us to see any of
these. "Combative and passionate men," yes. But through a glass darkly,

154

the glass of literary fashion darkened by the smoke of nationalistic politics—a smoke from revolutionary fires long since banked, a smoke that
turns eyes red remembering the flames of idealism that once brought
every part of this abused landscape into focus.

We will recall as best we can the fire and the smoke, and we will
examine the dark glass, and those who look in it hopefully for clues to
the enemy's identity, but the well-rounded view we tried to give of other
countries by traveling far and wide as best we could, will not be here.
For it was not vouchsafed us to see the Andes from Mérida; nor Táchira
of the tyrants; nor the black gold of Maracaibo's bottomless basin; nor
Margarita's pearls and blue *piraguas;* nor the *llanos* of Apure and
Guárico; nor the jungled waterfalls of that vast hinterland stretching all
the way from Guyana and the Orinoco's spidery delta to the remotest
corners of Colombia and Brazil. In fact, the only well-rounded thing it
was given us to see with our own eyes was the cup of towering mountains
shielding Venezuela's heart from its traditionally neglected body.

Caracas does look like a heart, with its arterial elevated speedways,
and cable cars draped from sky hooks; and it throbs like one with the
power from its high-tension pylons and television transmitters. But if
that whole network of arteries is pumping blood and not oil, the pulse
is too feeble to reach even the festering *ranchos* that ring it like
Dejanira's shirt. And what is Caracas-born Simón Bolívar, mounted in
bronze at the heart's exact center, pointing at? At the republic they tore
from his grasp? At the continent they refused to let him unite? Or at
the exile's deathbed they drove him to, embittered and worn out at
forty-seven?

Caracas Cacophony

By an unhappy fate we arrived in Venezuela just as Carnival was
getting under way, and we had to leave without participating in its
climax. The Tourist Board, though informed of our date of arrival for
months, hadn't told us about this. They just had time to shake hands
with us cordially, tell us that every means of transportation within the
country was booked for a week, suggest we return next year, and then
lock the door for the duration. Worse still, everyone we had intended
talking to had fled the capital. Whether this was because Carnival is
better in the provinces, as some said, or because it is unbearable in
Caracas, as just as many insisted, we never found out. But the music—if
one can call it that—never left us for an instant. In its piped, canned,
or taped versions, it had been pursuing us all over the continent. And
we had rebelled only once. Maddened, during a short hop in Brazil, by
the tinkle of some such atrocity as "Liebestraum," "The Warsaw Concerto," or "The Dance of the Hours," we had asked if it could be shut
off, only to be told, "We're so sorry. We do it for the Brazilians who love

music." So our suspicion was confirmed that the public is never consulted; the captive audience in every country, including our own, is either too indifferent, or too cowed by what it accepts as culture, to protest.

This war of nerves climaxed in Caracas. It was assaulting our eardrums as we landed. It crescendoed in the airport. It rocked the taxi. It resumed in the Palas Hotel's lobby. It persisted in the dining room—though a cracked speaker there made "The Blue Danube" barely recognizable. It was on the telephone, for when you call the switchboard and are connected with your party, they leave the desk receiver off the hook so that your entire conversation is accompanied by the background music from the office radio and/or the lobby TV. We fled to the Tamanaco's gorgeous pool for a swim, and there it was in the locker room behind the pool. Bill had a brilliant idea: to escape it by riding the *teleférico* (cable car) that connects the deep set capital with its high northern rim, and from there dips to the Caribbean beaches at La Guaira. . . . Forget it! In the observation buckets, sound was supplied by Boy Scouts with portable transistors. At the mountain-top station it was leaking out of an ice-skating rink provided by the dictator of a decade ago, Pérez Jiménez, who had also supplied the multimillion-dollar cable cars and the multi-million-dollar superhighway outflanking them, to keep his people happy; and in the virtually empty Sheraton-Humboldt skyscraper (another Pérez Jiménez white elephant), it oozed from the automatic stainless steel elevator where we couldn't have gotten at its source with fire axes. When we got out onto the observation deck in the clouds, there was at last such a benison of silence that we reverted to childhood and spent

a whole hour making paper airplanes. How reassuring it was to skim them into that abyss that had swallowed all those sounds intended to assure us that emptiness and silence don't exist anymore . . .

At the risk of being called slaves to the basest American materialism, we had to admit that Caracas' nonauditory amenities were impressive. In no other South American city were there so many of the little luxuries that comfort tourists. The taxis are regulated to charge fixed fees, and tipping is discouraged. Though our hotel was so modest no driver could find it without a map, it was supplied with soapcakes large enough not to go down the drain. Cold water was in plentiful supply, and the milk (wonder of wonders!) was neither lukewarm nor sour. They picked up our laundry without being asked to, returning it the same day. And the cuisine was not only South America's most varied and delicious—as good as Surinam's plush Tororica—but was served with such dispatch that we suspected the chef of watching us on closed-circuit television.

Nor is the city without picturesque touches. The funeral parlor near us was called *La Populár*. A golden imagery pervades the signs: *Tio Rico*, *El Dorado*, *La Zapatilla de Oro*. The stone sculpture in the middle of the *Pulpo* (the truly octopus-like elevated highway that grasps the center of the city in its flying tentacles) is of a naked woman with huge breasts and bottom astride a wild boar; they say she is Maria Lionza, a folkloric *bruja*, though no one could tell us what it is the witch holds over her head with both hands. The immense circle of slums (called *ranchos* here) received Pérez Jiménez' stamp like almost everything else in Caracas. They are built out of brick, and almost every cluster is flanked with a modern housing complex or apartment skyscraper. One is even equipped with a poured-concrete shopping center so huge it fills the valley between two substantial hills. Yet after a decade of democracy it is unfinished and empty—reason enough, one driver assured us, for the hundreds of thousands of votes the absent dictator received in last month's election.

Poets and Politicians

It was on the plane from Guyana, picking up a copy of Caracas' *El Nacionál*, that I had my first taste of Venezuela's *farouche* literary scene. Venezuela's leading newspaper, published by the left-wing millionaire poet-novelist, Míguel Otero Silva, had just installed as editor an equally famous but less "political" leftist novelist, Arturo Uslar Pietri. This move, I learned later, was to restore the prestige of the paper, damaged, it seems, as a result of having played it safe in December's presidential elections; *El Nacionál* had supported *no* candidate.

The winning contender, Rafael Caldera, of the Christian Democrats (COPEI), had been anathema to Otero Silva and the other literati because of an early record of admiration for Mussolini's Corporate State, though actually COPEI's economic program was to the left of *Acción Democrática* (AD), the anti-communist but vigorously socialist party of democracy that had dominated Venezuela for a generation under such popular leaders as Rómulo Gallegos, the novelist, Rómulo Betancourt, and outgoing President Raúl Leoni. It was AD that had forced the state to share among the people, to some extent, Venezuela's vast riches in oil, thus making it the country with the highest per capita income ($745) in South America. The communists had fared badly in the election, with the Moscow-loyalists headed by Gustavo Machado (also a millionaire) throwing their support to an AD dissident, Luis Beltrán Prieto, a leading writer on education. Venezuela's traditionally rebellious students, who had spearheaded AD's victories over both of Venezuela's terrible military dictatorships of this century—the long one (1909-1935) headed by Juan Vicente Gómez and the shorter one (1948-58) headed by Marcos Pérez Jiménez—had no use for Machado's brand of communism, especially after Russia's imperialistic invasion of Czechoslovakia six months ago. But the big surprise of the election was the successful campaign of ex-dictator Pérez Jiménez to win a seat in the Senate, though he had not returned from exile to campaign for it and was not expected to occupy it in person.

What had surprised me in Otero Silva's paper was a double-page feature devoted to the opinions of leading poets, novelists, and educators on the subject of Venezuela's claim to what is called here "our Department of Essequibo." Perhaps because I had just come from the former British colony, five eighths of which consists of this department, and sympathized with the determination of its now-independent Negro and Indian people to hold on to their little country, I was shocked at the unanimity with which Venezuela's intellectuals demanded taking it away from them—by force if necessary. If it occurred to any of them that Venezuela, just beginning to colonize its own empty hinterlands in the vast Orinoco basin, had no need to expand, there was no mention of it. There was a sense, in many of the statements, that the United States must be behind Guyana's "illegal claim" to "Venezuelan territory" [1]—that this was somehow part of a traditional American conspiracy to rob its weaker Latin neighbors of what was theirs.

---

[1] The case was presumably settled in 1899 when an international arbitration board consisting of two British and two Venezuelan representatives and an impartial fifth member from Imperial Russia established the present boundaries. The government of Venezuela accepted this. But in 1945, when all five adjudicators were dead, an article appeared in a Caracas paper claiming that the British had made a secret deal with the Russian to award them the larger share of the disputed region —but supplying no evidence of such a deal. It was not until 1963, when Britain withdrew from Guyana, however, that Venezuela began to fortify the border, supply money and arms to Amerindians in Guyana, and move across the frontier into selected sites.

The Vision of Rómulo Gallegos

I was eager to talk about this literary nationalism and its implications with two distinguished Venezuelans, Rómulo Gallegos and Rafael Pineda.

Gallegos, author of the most famous and influential Latin-American novel of the century, *Doña Bárbara*, had the opportunity granted to few authors of putting his literary-social idealism into practice. It was he, along with Betancourt, who fathered the first phase of *Acción Democrática's* revolution. In the aftermath of the Gómez nightmare, these two, with help from the Army, seized the government in 1945. They then embarked upon a program of agrarian and industrial reform, using the taxes from oil to give the peasants and workers a share in the nation's wealth for the first time. Betancourt presided over the revolutionary AD regime from 1945 to 1948, and then turned over the power to Gallegos in a constitutional election. Gallegos' presidency lasted only nine months. The gentle novelist-president had failed to realize that the power-hungry Army officers would revert to type if given a chance. Betancourt had taken the wise precaution of sending Pérez Jiménez and others like him abroad on diplomatic missions. Gallegos hoped to tame the would-be dictator by making him Chief of Staff, but was promptly overthrown. Gallegos and Betancourt lived in exile during the nine-year dictatorship that followed—a dictatorship more ruthless, corrupt, and tyrannical than even Gómez', and a lot more efficient.

Gallegos, unhappily, was on his deathbed when we arrived in Venezuela. But rereading *Doña Bárbara* was an illuminating experience. The scene of this seminal novel is the *llano*, Venezuela's interior lowland, more specifically the cattle country bordered by jungles south of the Apure River. This tributary of the Orinoco is west of Venezuelan Guyana, but the countryside is similar in flora and fauna. And so is its character, a sort of unpoliced, unfenced frontier of boundless natural resources dominated by cowboys quick on the draw who are employed by *patróns* unconcerned about the methods by which their huge holdings are extended.

While the hero, Santos Luzardo, is getting a liberal education in Caracas and abroad, his family's estate is gradually being embezzled by Doña Bárbara, a woman of formidable ambitions, appetites, and superstitions. We are told that she appeared mysteriously out of the jungles to the east, determined to revenge herself for a terrible crime perpetrated upon her by some river boatmen when she was innocent and in love. The upright Santos Luzardo confronts this woman who has become an unscrupulous man-eater with missionary zeal. The very names of these two antithetical beings symbolize the struggle which Gallegos poses between civilization (blessed light) and barbarism. Santos Luzardo almost yields to the temptation to meet violence with violence, but is saved in the end from this regression by the earthy Bárbara's untarnished daughter. Bárbara herself then surrenders, redeemed by the very hopelessness of her passion for Santos Luzardo which brings back to her the lost love of her youthful innocence.

Old-fashioned? Naive? Idealistic? Polemical? Untrue in contrast to what we now think of as man's incapacity to know or confront his real motivations? Decidedly! Yet there is in this Tolstoyan epic, conceived as a primer of social action, something pristine and noble, something that has been lost and must be regained if literature and life are not to go their separate ways—to the enfeeblement of both.

It is true, as the heralds of the new Latin-American novel say,[2] that the social novel—the novel of Mexico's Martin Luis Guzmán, Brazil's Jorge Amado, Ecuador's Jorge Icaza, Venezuela's Rómulo Gallegos—"wore its heart on its sleeve," that it was a "cultural, not a visceral literature, intellectual rather than intuitive," and that Gallegos in particular "believed in the power of the word to move men to effective action," tending to see Venezuela as a "multiple whole capable of reconciling its differences, assimilating its various racial strains, integrating its teeming jungles, its open plains, its mines and its coastal mudflats." And it was also true that poor Gallegos, with his childish belief in man and his uplifting buoyancy, comforted himself with the hopeful thought that those who suffered defeat in one social revolution might triumph in the next "because 'with every young man the world in some sense is born again.' "

But it is also true that in *Doña Bárbara*, as in *The Purple Land*,[3] a sense of the country in all its virgin wildness and infinite possibility is conveyed:

> The swift dawn of the Plain was advancing. The fresh morning breeze came up with its smell of mint and cattle. The hens began to scramble down from the calabash and merecure trees; the insatiable rooster threw over them the golden mantle of his arched wings and made them, one by one, yield to his passion. Partridges piped in the grass. A *paraulata* on the fence of the sheepfold opened his silver throat. Noisy flocks of parakeets passed overhead, and higher up the wild ducks honked, and the red herons went by like a garnet rosary; higher still the wild cranes, serene, silent. And under the wild clamor of the birds dipping their wings in the gold of the soft daybreak the free rude life of the prairie beat out its full powerful rhythm over the broad land of wandering herds and studs of unbroken horses neighing a clarion call to the day.[4]

---

[2] Luis Harss and Barbara Dohmann, *Into the Mainstream: Conversations with Latin American Writers*. New York, Harper & Row, 1967.
[3] See Chapter 2.
[4] Rómulo Gallegos, *Doña Bárbara*. Translated by Robert Malloy. New York, Cape & Smith, 1931.

Optimism, the feeling that the future belongs to those possessed by such openness, rings through such passages. And the pervasive sense of people who enjoy being alive is expressed through their popular ballads:

> *If the Holy Father knew*
> *Of Chipola's flying-skirted*
> *Turns he'd take his cassock off*
> *And the Church would be deserted.*

And it is also true that all these deprecated novelists who believed in something larger than literature, larger even than themselves, conveyed their belief in the individual will beyond the confines of the literary salon. There are no scapegoats in *Doña Bárbara*. The enemies of Venezuela, those responsible for making it a retarded country, are home-grown. They have been so, Gallegos suggests, ever since the ancestral Spaniards, instead of acting as settlers, "turned into men of prey." Nor are there any illusions about why the descendants of the conquistadors spent all their energies fighting each other instead of developing the land:

> "And why did you join the rebels?" asked Carmelito.
> "Because I was tired of battling with stray cattle, and everybody's strongbox was full after all the peace we'd had, and it was time to divide up the coppers."

Nor is there any romanticism about the Plainsmen, as there had been about the Gauchos:

> The Plainsmen have done nothing to improve industry. Their ideal is to change everything that comes into their hands into money, put it in a pitcher, and bury it.

Nor is there any illusion that revolution of itself will solve anything:

> . . . because the minute the meat gets a little better, there'll be more revolutions, and other things that aren't war, but look a good deal like it—the authorities, for instance, that want everything for themselves. . .

Nor does Doña Bárbara feel any self-pity as she heads back to the Guyanese jungle murmuring:

> "All things return whence they came." [5]

[5] *Ibid.*

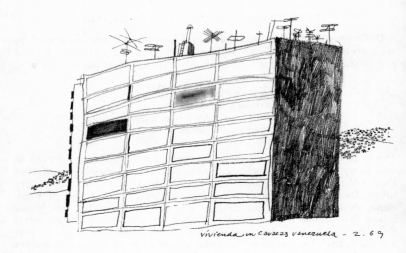

vivienda in caracas venezuela - 2. 69

Dialogue with Rafael Pineda

> *Streets parallel to the Orinoco end*
> *where once Sir Walter Raleigh must*
> *have glimpsed at the big river's bend*
> *his mother lode, or that fierce lust*
> *of lightning as the Conquerors told*
> *their sovereign or their sovereign's friend*
> *who slept from then on with one open ear*
> *and the other closed, as men less bold*
> *ravished the American Hemisphere . . .*

It was to the author of these paraphrased lines that I turned for clues
to the mood of the post-Gallegos generation—a generation not only in
search of scapegoats (Guyanese and American) for the intellectual frustration that seems a concomitant of affluence and responsible government, but a generation close to returning to the very aestheticism from
which Gallegos and his comrades had fought free. Rubén Darío, Nica-
ragua's great poet of the turn of the century, had initiated both attitudes.
It was Darío who had released poetry in the Spanish language from its
academic subjugation to Spain, inoculating it with the rarefied *modernismo* of French Symbolism, giving it the right to be happy. And it was
Darío, tiring around 1905 of the ivory tower of the Parnassians, who had
proclaimed a cult of the noble savage and sounded a battle cry to protect
Latin America's newfound heritage from that "terrible rifleman," Teddy

Roosevelt, personifying the aggressive materialism of the "Colossus of the North."

Rafael Pineda, one of Venezuela's best known contemporary poets and editor of the prestigious literary magazine, *Revista Nacionál de Cultura*, reflected both attitudes. At the moment he was publishing a set of polished tributes in verse to the cities, gardens, and Old Masters of Italy —a safe enough engagement with cultural internationalism—and at the same time exchanging acrimonious letters in the press with a poet named Juan Larrea who had evidently claimed to be more Venezuelan than Pineda. It seems that Pablo Neruda had once poked fun at this Larrea in a polemical ode that included complimentary allusions to Pineda. A friend of all three principals, who lives in Chile (and who wishes to remain anonymous), later summarized this literary pillow fight so amusingly that the reader will forgive the diversion, I hope, if I quote his comments on what he called "a barometer of the prevailing tastes and tendencies of the avant-garde in Venezuela."

> Larrea among his other charges had accused Pineda (who once interviewed Neruda in, of all places! New York) of serving as the communist poet's inquiring cat's-paw and political informer. Supposedly Pineda's reward was canonization in the Neruda ode. Larrea also claimed to be one of the faithful who attended the death agonies of César Vallejo in France, which he reported from a seat on the five-yard line until the equally demented and possessive *viuda* Vallejo threw everything she had at him including a murderous chronology of the life of her husband written for a nondescript edition of his works published somewhere in Peru. The whole *megillah* would amount to no more than a tedious exercise of internal vilification and South American ill will, except that it raises certain questions. Such as: Is all of literary South America a kind of embattled satrapy with its imperial seat in the fortress of Neruda's Isla Negra? Is South America *still* fighting its pitched battles over the grizzled New Americanism of Rubén Darío? Has anything really *happened* in South American poetry—anything but Whitman, Darío, Vallejo, and Neruda, that is? And is deracination the *only* problem South America's poets have to worry about?
>
> Of course deracination still remains Neruda's problem in a sense— the Neruda who asks "What can I do without roots?—but why must there always be a note of panic, or despair, in that question, ever since Darío's discovery of South America for the South Americans? Neruda, to be sure, has a record of honorable exile and political service on the other side of the Pacific; but is it the fate of South American poets to be either self-enclosed or self-exiled? Why have the best of them thrived in an anguish of deracination or reracination (Lautréamont, Darío, Vallejo, Neruda)? And what has happened in

the seventeen-year interval between Pineda's Venezuelan poems and his present deracinated love affair with Italy?

Since my dialogue with Pineda took place by letter—he, too, was escaping Carnival—I will summarize as fairly as I can his answers to My questions. (I omit our exchange on the subject of contemporary Venezuelan and American poetry, since nothing but conventional compliments resulted, but the poet's emotions were aroused as soon as I asked him to speak frankly on the reasons for the anti-Americanism of Venezuela's intellectuals, and on Guyana.)

S.R.: You mention some personal experiences that weigh for more than your admitted admiration for the "character, authority, and imaginative power of American society from Walt Whitman's time to the present." What were those experiences?

R.P.: On the day of my arrival in Caracas from Ciudad Bolívar, as a boy of 15, I was taken to a reception for President Franklin D. Roosevelt's wife. When her lighter failed, I was pushed forward by friends to light her cigarette with a match. . . . So now I ask myself in retrospect if the United States (like Mrs. Roosevelt), having everything it wants and needs, has no other function for Latin Americans than to light its cigarettes?

S.R.: If the wife or mistress of Venezuela's hero Simón Bolívar (neither of whom carried Eleanor Roosevelt's credentials as a humanitarian) had permitted me as a child to perform a similar service, I'd have felt honored for the rest of my life. But perhaps I'm being sentimental. Go on.

R.P.: Perhaps I should add that years later, at a Venezuelan literary ceremony honoring Walt Whitman, I felt obliged to contrast this only instance in which the United States can claim to approach glory with your government-by-business, choking, wounding, seizing from other countries, even erasing from the earth but not from the hearts of men those it disagrees with, merely by pushing a button.

S.R.: Though a poet myself, and yielding to none in my admiration for Walt Whitman's verse, I would have to concede greater "glory" in the service of humanity to Americans like Franklin, Jefferson, Jackson, Lincoln, and Kennedy. At least I should think that their achievements would be considered more worthy of emulation in Latin America.

R.P.: I'll try to cite less symbolic instances. Once, while working for an American oil company during the Pérez Jiménez dictatorship, I was asked not to attend a writers' conference that included among its organizers Miguel Otero Silva. I paid no attention and attended the conference anyway. After the fall of the dictatorship, the same oil company borrowed a painting from Otero Silva's collection and invited him to a cocktail party for the donors of the show.

s.r.: A poet who works for an oil company shouldn't expect an oil company to think like a poet. Or maybe Otero Silva should have defended his perfect right to be a communist sympathizer by refusing to loan his painting to an anti-communist company?

r.p.: During that same period, in a Venezuela dominated by dictatorial brutality, our tyrant was decorated by the United States. Your Eisenhower Government thus gave its support to the machinery of terror which Pérez Jiménez was applying to anyone in Venezuela who dissented even in thought.

s.r.: *Realpolitik* is ugly all over the world, whether it is Franklin Roosevelt giving a reception for Trujillo, Molotov embracing Von Ribbentrop, or Cárdenas and Neruda receiving peace awards from the butcher Stalin. I find my country's tolerance for criminals like Trujillo, Batista, Somoza, and Duvalier morally shameful and politically damaging. All that can be said in extenuation of Eisenhower's award to Pérez Jiménez is that (unlike those other misguided embraces) the award was probably made out of ignorance, or on the wrong-headed theory that since Venezuela had been governed by dictatorships during all but three of its one hundred twenty-five years of independence, one was obliged to treat this condition as normal.

r.p.: In Italy, quite recently, I encountered a Venezuelan boy of fifteen who had been educated in the United States. It wasn't long before I discovered that the boy had been indoctrinated with a virulent anti-Semitism.

s.r.: There are a handful of fanatical anti-Semites left in every sizeable country in the world, though the Soviet Union seems to be the only one in which Jews are still persecuted for their race. I've mentioned your shocking experience to a number of people in my prejudice-prone country, but not one of them has ever heard of a teacher *teaching* anti-Semitism. . . . You mention an earlier example of American bigotry—involving our first ambassador to Venezuela.

r.p.: Yes. His name was John G. A. Williamson and he was stationed in Caracas from 1935 on. He wrote a book making fun of our provincial society, its customs, and even its cooking. I translated this book into Spanish in 1955, in order to give Venezuelans an idea of your ambassador's lack of spirit and puritanical blindless. I was implored by an American diplomat not to publish it, lest it damage the good relations between Washington and Caracas. I published the book anyway, and after that your diplomat wouldn't speak to me.

s.r.: No doubt our diplomat thought he'd be contributing to better feeling between Venezuelans and Americans by keeping the offensive book out of circulation. But as a Venezuelan nationalist you had every right to bring it out in Spanish and make the United States look stupid. American publishers these days, who in contrast censor themselves when it comes to publishing anything that would offend Latin sensibilities, should perhaps be more concerned with the ugly truth. But I know you have more recent examples of American myopia.

R.P.: Only last January in New York a girl in a cable office on Columbus Circle asked me "Where is Caracas?" Naturally I was angered. Do you think it was an isolated case? There was the man who asked. "Do you have ice cream in Venezuela?" And the woman who thought our marriages were still arranged by the parents!

S.R.: Yes, it's deplorable that only the countries that "make the news" are widely known, but this is hardly peculiar to the United States. The clerk in question should be given a cram course in Spanish and transferred to the Caracas office for penance.

R.P.: Your intolerant consulates, I might add, have stirred up more enmity for the United States than any other single agency. Their denials of visas to Venezuelans should be compared to the ease with which we grant entry to your petroleum sharks, a majority of whom live in Caracas homes surrounded by wire fencing, never learn our language, and mentally never leave their rural communities in Arkansas or Texas.

S.R.: Touché, Rafael! Our consuls should be recalled and replaced with *aficionados* of the countries to which they are assigned. Public apologies should be made to writers like the Mexican novelist Carlos Fuentes, barred for political reasons; and all such should be given honorary dual American citizenship. All businessmen not officially invited to do business should be brought home forever. . . . But one more question. I was surprised in Caracas by the unanimity with which Venezuela's poets and educators demand the restitution of Guyana—and by their belligerency. Most of our poets and educators condemn our defense of South Vietnam. They call it imperialistic even though they know we have no intention of remaining there. Do you defend the proposed seizure of Guyana? and by arms if necessary?

R.P.: When I think about the border dispute between Venezuela and British Guiana (now Guyana) I feel I need ground under my feet. The fact is that the British Lion put his claws into what was rightfully ours. We have been trying to get it back for more then a century and a half. At the beginning of the nineteenth century Albert Schomburgk, a German explorer in the service of the Lion, incorporated into the map of Guiana the portions of

Venezuela seized by Great Britain simply by advancing the point of his pen. The arbitration settlement of 1899 favored England as a result of deceit and bribery. . . . The news chronicles of the time relate that even our women enlisted with the men to fight against it. The abundant and documented literature of the Venezuelans doesn't leave any doubt about our rights and the justification of our protest. . . . Recently in Ciudad Bolívar I visited the refugees of the Rupununi (Lethem[6]) rebellion whose leader, Valerie Hart, impressed me with her clear ideas and dedicated character, and I promised to negotiate with the authorities (which in fact I did) for the donation of musical instruments to supply the Rupununi musicians, "The Frontier Bandits," so that they could continue their work.

S.R.: Could you answer my question about whether you favor an armed invasion, if necessary?

R.P.: The independence of Guyana has now obliged us to exhaust our resources of diplomacy in order to recover what belongs to us. Venezuela is not a warlike nation—which explains our patience with the hostility of Guyana, which manifests itself on every occasion. But if Venezuela, in order to protect herself, must resort to the extreme of arms, then there can be no doubt that we will all enlist for the duration. I would not be worthy of being called a Venezuelan if I did not back up my country.

This surprising playback of the government's propaganda record could be partly accounted for by Pineda's revelation that he was born on the disputed border—"so that by a hair I was not a British subject." Perhaps it is human nature not to be struck by the irony of this accident of birth which decreed that only by chance was Pineda not a Guyanese citizen echoing Georgetown's condemnation of Caracas' imperialism. What seems surprising in an intellectual, however, is not to assume that the abundant and documented literature of the Venezuelans would ignore the claims of the other party, and not to be suspicious of the motives of ranchers like the Harts who had never given up their American citizenship and only invoked Venezuelan military help in their insurrection against their hosts when it seemed that the Guyanese might cancel the lease on their vast, tax-free spread.

Gringos on Guard

At the American Embassy, nestling suggestively between the gigantic peacock-green tower that houses Mobil Oil and the pristine headquarters of General Motors, we made our usual effort to find out whether the American support for dictators is as real as South Americans like to be-

[6] See p. 152.

Caracas View.

lieve. In a whisper barely audible above the hum of the air-conditioners, one spokesman said: "No matter what we say, the communists will use it against us; don't even mention our names in your general acknowledgments, for God's sake!" (What a situation! I thought, the communists warning everybody to beware of the aggressive Americans, and the Americans cowering in their embassy, afraid of offending the communists!) "They have a dozen techniques," he said leaning toward us, "to link us maliciously with any and every right-wing conspiracy in the Americas. Usually the connecting link is some character who came to the embassy to get our support and left empty-handed—but was seen. The classic case was the time Pérez Jiménez overthrew Gallegos. There was an uproar in the streets and our military attaché ran across to the Palace to find out what was going on. Presto! We had overthrown Gallegos!"

I asked him if he thought Pérez Jiménez had received his 375,000 votes in December from the *rancho* dwellers he'd rehoused.

"Only in part," was the reply. "His solution had been to move the migrants out of their shacks, bulldoze the area flat, and then erect a skyscraper or *multifamiliar*, as the Mexicans call them, and let it go at that. The result has been that even today the big government-owned units are half filled with low-paying tenants and the other half with squatters who don't pay anything and refuse to get out—and all around them are the same number of *rancho* dwellers as before! A better solution, perhaps, would be to admit the *ranchos* are here to stay, and supply them with services—drinking water, electricity, plumbing, and roads, letting private initiative take over from there."

None of the Embassy people took the vocal belligerency over Guyana seriously. "They're too proud of their peace tradition," one spokesman said. "They claim to be the only country that hasn't made war in over a century. No responsible Venezuelan has suggested military action to seize the disputed area. They're aware that Brazil is watching them closely. And finally, the military here seem to be taking very seriously their new-found role as guardians of democracy."

We had talks later in the day with Germán Arciniegas, the cultural historian who is Colombia's Ambassador to Venezuela, and with Miguel Otero Silva. I told Arciniegas that I was planning to spend my time in his country looking for the "Macondo" of Gabriel García Márquez' novels. I was pleasantly surprised to find that he shared my admiration for the young novelist. I asked Arciniegas why García Márquez lives abroad. "He is very shy," he replied. "He would be lionized to death in Colombia."

"In Macondo?" I suggested.

He smiled. "No, not in Macondo. But our writers are very civilized, you know. They would not be happy living anywhere but in a big city. . . . The publicity García Márquez has been getting since *Cien Años de Soledad* came out last year is fantastic. They're suggesting in Cuba that he present their big literary award this year. But he'd be crazy to get involved with Fidel. He is wholly nonpolitical himself."

Otera Silva was basking in the triumph of his election. He recalled that he and Gustavo Machado, the Moscow-communist leader who had also won a seat in the Chamber, were the last survivors of the Curaçao invasion against Gómez in the twenties. "I used to be a Senator," the portly millionaire publisher and poet said, "but now that I'm getting younger I'm a Deputy!" He spends half of every year in Italy, writing, he told me—

"and I shall continue to." Each member of the congress has a stand-in to take care of such contingencies, it seems. "Pérez Jiménez' stand-in will undoubtedly occupy his seat all year 'round," Otera Silva remarked scornfully. "Our ex-dictator is too cowardly to expose himself to the bullets of the fifteen thousand who survived his torture cells."

I told him that I'd read in his paper that the Mexican novelist, Carlos Fuentes, an old friend of mine, would be landing at La Guaira tomorrow. He said that Fuentes would be staying at his home and that I could visit him there tomorrow night.

Carlos Fuentes Speaks His Mind

Geography alone keeps Mexicans, like the noble poet Octavio Paz and the diabolic draftsman José Luis Cuevas, from walking in and out of the pages of this book, but Fuentes walked into it inadvertently, and through his close association with so many of the major South American novelists he belongs in it.

Fuentes is allied to his friend Julio Cortázar, the self-exiled Argentine, through his preoccupation with language, and by his own sense of sharing the growing isolation of Mexican artists ever since the Mexican Revolution shattered their ties with the Paris-oriented elite. "The epic choice," he has said, "that produced an epic literature—*Doña Bárbara, La Vorágine, Don Segundo Sombra*—has given way to a literature more equivocal, more critical, with a certain strain of anguish and ambiguity, produced by people displaced from their traditional positions, faced with the need to create forms that are more personal, more highly elaborated, and much more solitary," [7] and he cites Cortázar and Vargas Llosa as writers like himself who no longer look to the civilizing philosophies of the American and French Revolutions as foils to the feudal remnants of the Spanish inheritance. Similarly, Fuentes feels very close to his friend García Márquez, the self-exiled Colombian, since both write with pessimism as well as humor of "imaginary gardens with real toads in them," to borrow Marianne Moore's phrase.

Style is as important to Fuentes as to Cortázar and García Márquez, but the characters in the Mexican writer's novels think as well as feel. They are aware of the depths of their depravity, and to that extent have a tragic dimension. They worry about where they came from and where history is taking them. In *Where the Air Is Clear*,[8] for instance, the chief characters are a revolutionary turned financier and a desperate poet. "One does not explain Mexico," the poet remarks, "one believes in Mexico,

---

[7] Harss & Dohmann, *op. cit.* (*La Voragine* is José Eustácio Rivera's jungle saga of Colombia. *Don Segundo Sombra*, by the Argentine Ricardo Güiraldes, is the classic novel glorifying the gaucho.)

[8] Carlos Fuentes, *Where the Air Is Clear*. New York, Ivan Obolensky, 1960.

Carlos Fuentes

with fury, with passion, and in alienation. Mexico has never had a successful hero. To be heroes they had to fail. . . . Good may not be identified with victory, nor evil with defeat. For otherwise the United States would be good and Mexico evil." But when the poet tries to answer the question what Mexico is to do if it is to continue to search for material progress and at the same time escape the leprosy of Americanization, his thinking becomes vague. Fuentes himself is aware of this lack of concreteness. "We destroy ourselves," he notes, "in order to make and find ourselves in a desert no richer than our own skin and words." [9]

The home of Miguel Otero Silva where Fuentes was spending the night, en route from Europe to Mexico by ship, is in the Sebucán district of Caracas, out past swank Altamira Sur where the American Embassy squats, and then to the left up against the piney hills. Flanked by carports, there is a high white stucco wall with mahogany doors wide enough to drive a squad of cavalry through abreast. You ring a bell, there is a click, and you pass into an enclosed but roofless patio with a grand staircase leading to plate glass doors. There is no bell at this second portal. You wait. A curtain moves to one side and you know you are being scrutinized carefully. Then the inner doors open, revealing another staircase. There is a glimpse of a salon with an elegant, sophisticated painting, possibly a black-and-white Lam, from the Cuban artist's Paris period. . . . From a wing of the house to which I was not to gain access, floated the unmistakable sounds (tinkling ice and restrained hysteria) of a cocktail party. A secretary in striped trousers now approached to inform me that Señor Fuentes would receive me.

Fuentes, sprawled in an open-neck white shirt on a blue velvet divan, looked as out of place in this atmosphere of plush formality as a college freshman at a headmaster's tea. He leaped to his feet, gave me an *abrazo*, and started talking as if our last conversation in Mexico twelve years ago had never lapsed. Looking younger and more handsome, he had lost neither his infectious enthusiasm for ideas nor the colloquial English he'd picked up at the Mexican Embassy in Washington as a boy.

"And when will you be visiting us, Carlos?" I asked him, after we'd talked about mutual friends and how the passage of time had been kind to us.

"Probably never," he replied. "I spit on any government that won't let me enter a country unless I renounce my ideas and parrot theirs."

"It's asinine," I agreed. "If ideas, yours or anyone else's, could undermine our institutions, they deserve to be destroyed. . . . So you'll be going directly to Mexico?"

[9] These observations on Fuentes' novel are adapted from my conversations with him in *The Mexico Traveler*, 1969, and *Mexican Journal: The Conquerors Conquered*, 1957.

"By way of Puerto Rico. But if my wife and children weren't in Mexico, I mightn't. I expect trouble. They may not let me out."

"How could they stop you?"

"By denying me a visa, or an exit permit, in reprisal for what I've written in *Le Monde* and elsewhere about their massacre of the students. If they can shoot down four hundred innocent people in cold blood, denying me a passport won't be much of a feat."

I expressed surprise at his high figure for casualties in the riot that preceded the opening of the Olympic games. He said that Oriana Fallacci, the well-known Italian reporter, had been one of the few eyewitnesses to survive and had counted three hundred bodies. "She assumed in her *Paris Match* story that there must have been another hundred inside the buildings. But the worst part of President Díaz Ordas' criminal act was to reintroduce the Mexican Army into politics."

"I get the feeling that the massacre has changed your whole outlook," I said.

"Or confirmed it. The shooting down of those people gave me a very curious feeling, a feeling that my vision, and that of Octavio and others, had been *just!* The PRI[10] debacle had been intuited, of course, by writers like Georges Betailles. You know the general position, Selden. Aztec society consumed human lives on a monstrous scale, right? The price paid was the Conquest, no? Then, to enter the industrial-consumer society of today, post-Revolutionary Mexico has had to pay the same price, no? To achieve Western civilization's goals of waste and luxury, we are again sacrificing human lives on a monstrous scale!"

"And the effect of all this on the writer?" I asked.

"Subversive!" he answered. "Societies have made writing such a marginal activity that the very act of writing has become a revolutionary act. The traditional writings—including the texts by which our societies live, from the pronouncements of the conquistadors and Charles V's reforms for the Indians all the way down to the Alliance for Progress—have masked the truth and hidden us from ourselves. When you write outside those traditions, no matter how conservative your philosophy may be on the surface, you are being subversive. Borges, for instance—"

"Even Cortázar?"

"Even Cortázar. Before, there were novelists who specialized in social problems. Now the advanced writer uses the Spanish language as a weapon in itself, quite apart from national boundaries or party credentials. The old literature reflected reality, or was supposed to. We've gone beyond that. A work of art is not a reflection of reality but a complement to it, creating a new reality. Borges' stories, Cortázar's *Rayuela*, or Vargas

---

[10] *Partido Revolucionário Institucionál*, the monolithic party that has ruled Mexico since the Revolution of 1910-20.

Llosa's *La Casa Verde* are examples of literature that produced a new language. This fiction has an autonomous existence, and therefore confronts most unpleasantly an establishment that wants to regulate everything, and make hierarchical pronouncements on literature and every other form of expression."

"Vargas Llosa lives abroad," I said, "like all the novelists of your generation. Why?"

"Not to be controlled, not to be tamed—"

"If he felt controlled under the wide-open liberal regime of Belaúnde," I said, "he'll never come back now that the military he exposed in his first novel have taken over."

"I suppose not," said Fuentes, scratching his head reflectively, "but who knows? It's a military dictatorship, sure. But it's a collectivist militarism, isn't it?—a sort of new wave of Peronism that is sweeping over South America. Did you notice how quickly Velasco recognized the Soviet Union, and how quick Moscow was to support him? And to announce that they'd buy up Peru's sugar crop—the crop you left high and dry after they seized your refineries and fishing boats? My God! What are they going to do with all that sugar—Cuba's and now Peru's! They'll dump it all on the international market, I suppose, to drive down prices in the United States bloc. Then, as sugar prices fall in your poor satellites, you'll be forced to pour more and more money into them to head off riots and revolutions, no?"

I laughed. "Don't gloat yet, Carlos! Maybe you overestimate the importance of sugar. Like me, the world may turn to substitutes. And I don't think we have much stomach left for guarding the border-satrapies of the free world, after Vietnam; or pouring more billions into underdeveloped countries that only hate us for not giving them handouts. Besides, our rebellious youth is forcing us to think in terms of curing our own internal ills first."

"Youth," he said enthusiastically, "is waking up everywhere. In Mexico, in France, in England, in Italy . . ."

"In Cuba—? You've been in Cuba recently," I said. "Are they making the kind of cultural breakthrough there you've been talking about?"

"Not really," he said, "the writers and artists aren't being persecuted, as they were in Russia under Stalin, but it's far from being the kind of open society Czechoslovakia was becoming when the tanks rolled in. Mind you," he added guardedly, "I don't criticize the revolutionary process in Cuba."

"But you do criticize the party-line ideology that runs both Cuba and Russia, don't you?"

"The USSR and its communist parties abroad no longer have any appeal to this turned-on generation," he replied.

I told him of my talks with Pablo Neruda in Chile in December, and of

Petare - Caracas Venezuela - 2.69

how the Chilean poet had defended the Soviet invasion of Czechoslovakia as a preventive step against the reintroduction of capitalism.

He laughed contemptuously. "Now you know why the students booed Neruda when he visited Venezuela and Colombia in November! I was in Czechoslovakia after the invasion, with Cortázar and García Márquez. Brezhnev moved the tanks in for one reason only: to put a stop to the complete freedom, the total radicalization, the true communism being practiced there, and to keep this from spreading to his and the other police states. Do you know that eighty percent of the land in Moscow-dominated Poland is still in the hands of private landlords?"

"And in Czechoslovakia . . .?

"None. Not one acre!"

"Well, Carlos, I don't know whether that makes Czechoslovakia better off than Poland—worse off, probably—but I'm sure that what really alarmed Brezhnev and his gang was the way intellectual freedom and democratic practices were spreading like wildfire under Dubcek last year."

I told him, as I rose to go, that I would be in García Márquez' country tomorrow, and that he could write his friend that even the Colombian academy now accepts him. "Germán Arciniegas thinks *Cien Años de Soledad* is great."

"That will be bad news for Gabo," he shouted after me as I walked down the driveway. "He'll think he must have done something wrong!"

8

COLOMBIA: THE FOOTSTEPS OF THE POET

Sultry Sunday, noon
of shimmering
Sun, a policeman
as if embedded in the curb
profoundly asleep. A dog's
filth smeared on a fence. An abbot's
indigestion, the muffled
cacophony of a locust . . .
Solitude of the grave, complete
and sullen silence. But
suddenly in the ugly town,
the dominical hush is broken
as a raving drunkard screams
Hurray for the Liberal Party!
—LUIS CARLOS LÓPEZ, "Tropic Siesta"[1]

Reading these disillusioned lines by a forgotten Colombian poet as our Avianca flight carried us from Bogotá to Santa Marta, everything that I knew about this strange country of contrasting beauty and violence came suddenly into focus. "Satirical poets are hard to find in Latin America,"

[1] *Spanish-American Literature Since 1888.* Edited by Willis Knapp Jones. New York, Frederick Ungar, 1963.

read the introductory paragraph that accompanied the poem, "but Colombian López makes up for the lack . . . he railed at provincial life and poured out his contempt on politicians, priests, and bureaucrats. Bitter humor that is at times brutal, characterizes his verse. Parody of the sonnet, with uneven lines, faulty rhymes, and foreign words . . . López has influenced, and been influenced by, few poets of the hemisphere." In the United States, where the similarly raffish imagery of Pound, Williams, Cummings, Berryman, and Ginsberg comes close to being the typical poetic response to a bland or aesthetically warped environment, a poet who writes about rubbish, frying pans, barbers, "long-haired neurasthenic bards," and "lousy creatures who play dominoes" would be neither forgotten nor singular. But in Colombia, it suddenly occurred to me, López must have foreseen (or subtly shaken into motion?) everything that sets this country apart from its neighbors: in politics, the *bogotazo* and *la violencia* that led, like a great purge of the sick body, to the civilized alternating rule of Liberals and Conservatives under which the nation now flourishes; in art, the painting of Fernando Botero, unique in Latin America for creating a serene high style out of local pomposities and perversities; and in literature, the stories and novels of Gabriel García Márquez, "the South American Faulkner," who created "Macondo," that fantastic world of similar native plagues and humors, toward which we were now heading.

A Painter's and a Poet's World

The "*bogotazo*," sometimes called "Black Friday," was that April day in 1948 when all the contradictions that had been gathering momentum in Colombia since Simón Bolívar's death came to a boil. Bogotá was close to being burned to the ground by a citizenry out of control. The spark was fired when Jorge Gaitán, the most popular political figure in Colombia, was murdered. Gaitán had been narrowly defeated in the presidential election two years before when his majority party, the Liberals, split, giving the presidency to Ospina Pérez, a stand-in for the oligarchy, the land-owning aristocracy, business, and the immensely powerful Catholic Church. Gaitán, who had been Mayor of Bogotá, was the hero of the peasants. He was also a spell-binding orator, a foe of foreign developers (especially of United Fruit in the Santa Marta banana plantations, which had broken a strike in 1929 with the help of the Colombian Army), and, his enemies claimed, a front man for the communists. But just before his assassination, when the government was driving Liberals from their homes all over the country and putting the torch to their properties, Gaitán had made an impassioned plea for moderation. "All that we ask of you, Mr. President, is the guarantee of human life, which is the least a country can ask."

The first reaction to the crime was the lynching of the assassin. It took place two blocks from the Capitolio Nacional where the Ninth Inter-American Conference was being held, amid rumors of an attempt on the life of the United States Secretary of State, General Marshall. To cries of "Death to the assassins!" "Down with the Conference!" and "Foreigners go home!" a huge mob (which included, almost symbolically, the young Fidel Castro, then a student in Bogotá) marched on the palace. Not finding the Conservative leaders, they sacked the Capitolio, overturned cars and trolleys, burned down the newspaper offices, looted the hotels, the shops, and the churches. When the army arrived, a pitched battle took place. Hundreds, perhaps thousands, were killed, and only rain prevented the burning of the city. Foreign correspondents who covered the Conference compared the destruction to London at the height of the *luftwaffe blitz* during World War II. But the passions unleashed by the *bogotazo* were only the prelude to the widespread depredations of bandit gangs (*la violencia*) which have afflicted the countryside almost down to the present.

Christopher Isherwood, who was in Bogotá for a short visit in 1948, was as overwhelmed by the surface charm of the capital's society as he was depressed by the claustrophobic sense of family. He had heard that even the shoeshine boys quote Proust and he imagined one remarking ". . . there is in love a permanent strain of suffering which happiness neutralizes, makes conditional only, procrastinates but which may at any moment become what it would long since have been had we not obtained what we were seeking, sheer agony. . . ." He found that French culture was the ultimate criterion by which everything artistic was then judged, and he added "I suspect that Colombians follow the French in thinking that the U.S.A. would be better to stick to writing crime stories and making automobiles." And he quoted a student as saying that Gaitán was not a communist: " 'His models were Mussolini and Perón.' " [2]

But the background to the *bogotazo* is better conveyed by García Márquez [3] whose Colonel is told by a Macondo lawyer to forget his pension because "In the last fifteen years there have been seven Presidents, and each President changed his cabinet at least ten times, and each Minister changed his staff at least a hundred times." And by the Colonel's wife who tells him "You can't eat hope." Or by Big Mama, "absolute sovereign of the Kingdom of Macondo," whose phony apotheosis is attended by the President and the Pope: "Drowning in the pandemonium of abstract formulas which for two centuries had constituted the moral justification of the family's power, Big Mama emitted

[2] Christopher Isherwood, *The Condor and the Cows*. New York, Random House, 1949.

[3] See footnote on p. 181.

a loud belch and expired. She had guaranteed the social peace and political power of her empire by virtue of the three trunks full of forged
electoral certificates which formed part of her secret estate."

The visual symbolism of the old Colombia—which hasn't by any
means entirely vanished, despite the almost miraculous replacement of
the old order by responsible democratic government—is provided by the
paintings of Fernando Botero.

In a typical Botero painting, "The Presidential Family," a group
supremely unself-conscious of its bovine complacency is posing for its
portrait against a background of bulbous mountains that parody its
protuberances (one of the mountains, characteristically, is smoking—
but like a pipe rather than a volcano). As in all good matriarchies,
Mother is centered, one hand firmly grasping her shopping purse, the
other, a pair of useless white gloves; a fur boa, like a dead rat, is draped
limply over an arm. Papa, wearing thick rimless glasses and a battered
topper, is carrying something that might be a quill or a rubber
truncheon; his eyes are too stupid to focus. The nurse holds a baby girl
that looks a good ten years older than her mother; her fat fist grasps
a tiny jet bomber. The Chief of Staff is wearing a Nazi-type visored
garrison-hat, the chin strap of which won't fit under his double chin; his
left hand is cocked in a perfunctory salute. The priest, with a ceremonial
shepherd's crook in one hand and a diminutive rosary draped over the
other, is too fat even to see these obsolescent symbols of his trade or the
lapdog that sits on his foot, overfed and beady-eyed as the rest of the
family but a lot more alert-looking.

In another outstanding Botero, "Our Lady of Colombia," the typical
Renaissance Virgin and Child with donors à pied is deflated (or rather
inflated, like a rubber tire) to the dimensions of a peasant china doll.
Under her Nordic locks, the Virgin's face is sweet, sleepy, and mindless.
Colombian flags drape her overstuffed throne, "tastefully" studded with
wax roses. The pudgy Christ carries a miniature flag in one hand and
what looks like a toy bomb in the other. One slipper-sized donor is a
cardinal, the other, the kind of capitalist caricatured in the Marxist press.

It is the particular quality of the inhabitants of Botero's world, says
Stanton Catlin,[4]

> . . . to exude the blissful complacency of the 'Saved,' to feel no
> anguish, or complaint, to be permanently contented with their lot.
> Herein lies the good-humored twist of existentialist fate that is
> unique in his art. It is composed of a particularly subtle distillation
> of characteristic Latin elements from another era, aimed at what is
> essentially a Latin quality of decadence and seen from a wholly
> Latin American point of view. His world is essentially the Spanish

---

[4] Foreword to catalogue of the exhibition, "Fernando Botero March 27 – May 7,
1969 at the Center for Inter-American Relations, New York.

American's City of God after 400 years of worldly history, with only a fly here and there to mark its decline or a tiny cigarette modestly held to show a slight confession of indulgence. His compositions, figures and staffage are all projections of Colonial opulence. They are filled with the sweet aroma of the censer, the pale colors of institutionalized courtesy and piety, the swagger of spiral columns and festooned capitals and gilded surfaces piled high. This innocent satisfaction with exaggerated effulgence is at an apogee of social parody. The forms of social obsolescence, which Orozco destroys with overt force, Botero allows to fall from their own over-ripeness . . .

Not an heroic art, clearly! But then, neither is the fiction of García Márquez—or Fuentes' or Cortázar's—heroic. All four, in fact, are deliberately anti-heroic, concerned with stripping the masks off the graven images, the papier-mâché saints, the solemn rhetoric that has concealed for so long the rottenness that finally erupted in a *bogotazo*, an Olympic massacre, or a mass-canonization of the whore, Evita Perón. Once the Conquest's search for the City of God was shown in its true light as a search for the City of Gold, once what López in his poem called the dominical hush was broken by the drunkard's meaningless political war cry, the way was open to reassess all the provincialisms, subterfuges, and dreams of this society from the outside. For it is significant that all these artists live, or spend most of their time, abroad. Botero, after studying painting in Madrid, Florence, and Paris, lived for a year in Mexico City and now resides permanently in New York. And it was in Mexico and Barcelona, that García Márquez conceived Big Mama, Colonel Aureláno Buendía, and the Kingdom of Macondo.

Comedy, rather than tragedy, describes the worlds of both Botero and García Márquez, but black comedy. This is especially true of the novelist's dream kingdom of shattered expectations. There is no idealism, no vision of a better world, no call to arms, for even these attitudes are seen as part of the paraphernalia of the old order that must be stripped away to get at the long-concealed truth.

In his novella, *No One Writes to the Colonel*,[5] the colonel is waiting in Macondo for the pension that never comes. What he was fighting for, if anything, in the various revolutions in which he commanded Liberal Party forces, is purposefully unclear—and irrelevant. "For nearly sixty years," the story begins, "the colonel had done nothing else but wait.

---

[5] The American translation by J. S. Bernstein, of the 1961 book, published in the fall of 1968 by Harper & Row, New York, includes a number of short stories, including the hilarious title piece, *Los Funerales de la Mama Grande* (Big Mama's Funeral), from a collection published in Mexico in 1962. The big novel of Macondo, *Cien Años de Soledad*, was published by Harper & Row in 1970 under the title "100 Years of Solitude."

G. García Márquez from a photo

October was one of the few things which arrived." The colonel and his wife are slowly starving to death as they share a few grains of corn with a scrawny rooster, but the colonel sustains himself with the illusion that all their luck will change if the cock triumphs in just one problematical fight. The cock gets most of the grain, and when the grain is gone, the colonel's long-suffering wife asks him what they'll eat if the rooster loses. "It had taken the colonel seventy-five years—the seventy-five years of his life, minute by minute, to reach this moment. He felt pure, explicit, invincible at the moment when he replied: 'Shit.'" But the point is neither cynical nor sentimental. What matters is the spirit with which the colonel sings life and denies death. "If you feel like singing, sing," he says, "it's good for your spleen. . . . Life is the best thing that's ever been invented." "You can't eat hope," his wife reminds him. "You can't eat it, but it sustains you," he replies, and adds good-naturedly, "I'm taking care of myself so I can sell myself. I've already been hired by a clarinet factory."

The monumental *Cien Años de Soledad* is more poetic and more oblique. Latin Americans tend to see in it the long-awaited New World *Don Quixote* that embodies all their frustrations, fantasies, guilts, and hopes for identity. To be sure, there is no hero (or even anti-hero) like the sage of La Mancha; for this is a world of generations of hope-bemused Buendías and their more down-to-earth women, with even their names hopelessly repeating themselves in confusion, yet somehow so compulsively woven together by the author's genius for exact observation and psychological insight that the whole becomes greater than its parts. American readers, on the other hand, may find *Cien Años de Soledad* even harder to follow than the Faulkner of *The Sound and the Fury*—the author García Márquez appears to have learned most from, and most resembles in outlook and stature—and they may be put off by the extremely thin dividing line between fantasy and reality.

What is one to think of a village where it once rained for four years, eleven months, and two days—and another time rained flowers? Or Mauricio Babilonia, who is always followed about, indoors as well as out, by yellow butterflies. Or that village-wide loss of memory so great that one has to write on a cow: "This is a cow. She must be milked every morning so that she must produce milk, and the milk must be boiled in order to be mixed with coffee to make coffee and milk." Or the wife who wears a chastity belt lest she give birth to a child with a tail (in the end such a child is born anyway). Or of a young beauty taking a bath, so innocent that she warns the voyeur peeking through the roof that he may fall and injure himself. (He jumps down so quickly that he cracks his skull.) Or of the power of the dead in Macondo to live as perpetual visible but unspeaking residents in the houses of the living?

Colonel Auréliano Buendía is here shown in his youth making little gold fishes. Joining the Revolution, he rises to its command, becomes totally corrupted by its senseless demands, sells it out, gives an order out of pique to have his best friend shot, and finally returns to make little gold fishes—but no longer for profit, only to keep himself busy in his solitude. The gringos of the encroaching banana boom—never clearly characterized—kill off Auréliano's seventeen sons, thanks to the Church which conveniently identifies them for their pursuers with crosses of ashes on their foreheads. Buendía's sister, Amaranta, announces that she will die when the shroud she is embroidering for her funeral is finished—and does just that:

> It was then that she understood the vicious circle of Colonel Auré-liano Buendía's little gold fishes. The world was reduced to the sur-face of her skin and her inner self was safe from all bitterness. It pained her not to have had that revelation many years before when it had still been possible to have purified memories and reconstruct the universe under a new light and evoke without trembling Pietro Crespi's smell of lavender at dusk and to have rescued Rebeca from her slough of misery, not out of hatred or out of love but because of the measureless understanding of solitude . . . and she announced without the least bit of dramatics that she was going to die at dusk. She not only told the family but the whole town, because Amaranta had conceived of the idea that she could make up for a life of mean-ness with one last favor to the world, and she thought that no one was in a better position to take letters to the dead.

At the end of the novel a parchment document is translated, written a hundred years before, predicting everything that has happened. Is the moral that everything that happens is inevitable? or that by the way we evade love and truth we make it so? It is the way of the artist of García Márquez' "cool" generation to raise questions but never to answer them, to represent the age-old ambivalence and tragedy of Man with tongue in cheek—or seem to! And it may be argued that the great artists, from Shakespeare to Brueghel, from Goya to Melville, have done no less.

A Day in Macondo

Santa Marta is on the Caribbean, plentifully supplied with small but comfortable hotels, good beaches, and beautiful girls. The Colombian Tourist Board—which offers to put us up indefinitely if we'll promise to see everything from the Amazonian alligators of Letícia to the Nicaraguan gulls of San Andrés—was nonplussed by our opening gambit, as I had expected.

"So which would you gentlemen like to see first," said the local repre-sentative in the Hotel Irotama's lobby, "the beaches or the house where Bolívar died?"

"Neither, thanks just the same. We only have a day here, not counting the day we fly through on our way out, so we'd like to spend it all in Aracataca."

"Aracataca! No one in the world has ever asked to visit Aracataca. . . . Why?"

"Because García Márquez was born and grew up there."

"García Márquez? Ah, yes, García Márquez . . . Macondo? But you'll see nothing of that in Aracataca. It's a run-down village far off the main road, left to go to sleep after the banana companies moved out thirty years ago."

"I know," I said, "but it was asleep then, too, so it must have something. Anyway, until we see for ourselves we won't be happy."

"Very well. It might make an interesting story, at that! We'll have a car for you in half an hour, and the two girls who are training to work with us here might like to go along, if you want them?"

We did. And in half an hour Bill, Marie-Teresa, Myriam, and I were off.

There is a paved road part of the way now, because cotton has taken the curse of unemployment off this terribly parched and cactus-studded region, but the village itself, at first sight entirely depopulated, can't have changed much from the time the novelist lived in it, except perhaps that there is a touch of hope in the air—or did we only falsely deduce this later on from the naturalness, hospitality, and infectious good humor that emanates from any Latin American village untouched by tourism and modernity?

Who could have blamed these simple people had they received us sullenly as the well-heeled snoopers (with cameras and writing pads) we were, and sent us packing? How foolish we felt—and must have looked—getting out of our comfortable car in the unpaved, dusty main street of this still poverty-stricken village, asking one passerby after another if he or she might be familiar with their famous native son and his books. Could they direct us to the house he lived in as a boy, and find people who might remember him? Yet in a matter of minutes we were surrounded by a crowd of friendly well-wishers of all ages who accepted our bizarre mission as though it was the most natural thing in the world—natural and flattering to them! Everyone had a friend or acquaintance who might help, and ran to get him. And everyone—except one old crone who had vowed to the Blessed Mother not to be photographed—was delighted to pose for pictures. Marie-Teresa was sure that the Buendía family, perhaps even the redoubtable colonel himself, really existed and might be found here still living—such is the power of the novelist's pen! And there was, amazingly, a Buendía; but he had never heard of the author or his books—"regretfully, *señoritas y caballeros.*" But one of our troop scoffed at the idea of a man of eighty still being alive. "Only women live to be that old in this town!"

In the house where the novelist was born, which still exists behind a modern front two doors beyond Calle 7 on Carrera 5, we did find a very old man, the present owner of the whole collection of wooden shacks with thatched roofs, who, standing among his pigs with great dignity, told us the little he remembered of García Márquez' childhood, and pointed with considerable pride to the gnarled stump of an almond tree which (he had been told) "figures in that big book about us, the name of which slips my mind, and was planted by the writer's grandfather." He suggested that we talk with García Márquez' nurse, Tomasa.

Tomasa, a white-haired Negress bent with age, came out to receive us graciously and revealed a ready wit. When Myriam asked her age, she replied: "Three hundred!" She would not only be glad to help us any way she could—she was understandably vague about her charge of forty years ago, one of many, no doubt—but she would be glad to go for a ride in our car—"anywhere you care to take me, and for as long as possible. I have plenty of time!"

A schoolmate of García Márquez, who is principal of the village school, joined us. When he told us that Tomasa had been photographed for hours some months ago by a magazine called *Flash!* without receiving a cent for her trouble, we made up for that discourtesy. The novelist's friend also told us that García Márquez frequently revisits Aracataca, and that when he does he gives a traditional feast of *sancochos* for his friends, who are legion, and stays up all night dancing with them to the music of the guitar and accordion. His wife and children came with him once, and apparently he feels as comfortable with these people—perhaps more comfortable—than when he was a serious lad of twelve about to go forth into the world to seek his fortune. At the pharmacy where the novelist used to help his father—after his father shifted to this profession from his old one as telegraph operator—we secured the address of the parents in Cartagena and made plans to call on them when in that city the following week. Then we inspected the two modest memorial markers in the village square, both so worn by wind or touch that the lettering could not be read.

García Márquez may be the South American Faulkner, but a key to the difference between the worlds of the two writers was Aracataca. It is not a sick place, though it may be as poor as any village in Mississippi. There are no neurotic aristocrats with antebellum memories of lost grandeur, no victims of racial bigotry. As the sun went down, we saw blacks and whites playing together happily in the street with bits of framed cardboard on strings and their elders on the porches shaking *dados* or moving dominoes. And in Santa Marta, we discovered that night, Aracataca is as famous for its superstitions as for its poverty, and the latest evidence of its credulity, quoted in *El Informador*, was that a pig had been heard to talk and that it was going from house to house grunting *"Mírame mi zapatillas rojas!"* (Look at my little red shoes)—a likely enough situation and title for García Márquez' next story.

Architectural Interlude: Popayán, Guatavita, Zipaquirá

The Orenoque lieth even from the sea unto Quito, in Peru. This river is navigable with barks little less than 1000 miles; and from the place where we entered may be sailed up in small pinnaces to many of the best parts of Nuevo Reyno de Granada and of Popayán. And from no place may the cities of these parts of the Indies be so easily taken and invaded as from hence.

—SIR WALTER RALEIGH to Queen Elizabeth in his report of his journey in search of El Dorado in 1595

Raleigh was a better poet than a geographer; though he was correct in assuming that tributaries (navigable?) of the Orinoco do rise not far from Bogotá in Colombia, he forgot about the Andes. Bogotá, and Quito, the capital of what is now Ecuador, are in their midst, 10,000 feet high, and Popayán is on the other side.

Waiting for a car to get to Popayán, we relaxed by the pool of Cali's principal hotel, a pool ingeniously sunk into the roof of the sky-scraper—one of many in this Pacific slope city of 800,000. There we listened to the conversation of three overripe Cali belles who were hanging over the parapet watching the wind tear off huge chunks of the tin roof of the building next door and betting on whether a passerby in the street thirteen stories below would be decapitated. "I love violence without blood," was the philosophy one of these girls was imparting to her friends, after explaining how bored she was at nineteen to be expecting her fifth child. "I was married at fourteen," she told us later, "but my mother was only thirteen when I was born." They all laughed when we told them that we had heard that the population explosion was Colombia's biggest problem, and that now we knew that it was true.

The road to Popayán passes the eighteen-hole championship golf course of the Club Campestre and then follows the banks of the Cauca River for the first forty of its one hundred and forty kilometres. The pastures are filled with herds of humpbacked Brahmas and set apart by clumps of bamboo. After Santander de Chiquichao, the road begins to climb into the foothills of the Andes. The houses are beautifully spotless: white adobe with cut-in verandas supported by slim wooden posts. The roofs are of tile with a very long overhang. One house called Cartagena—which we visited on the way back and which turned out to be a candy factory, with two horses turning the press into which the canes of sugar are slipped—was painted yellow, with posts of red and green like barbers' poles, and another had satiny yellow and black doors. Another, Villa Hermosa, had red doors with blue diamonds. No two are alike.

Popayán would be a thrilling revelation of Colonial architectural homogeneity to anyone who hadn't visited Sucre or Ouro Preto. It is a great sight anyway, with its marshmallow-white houses, black grills, and red tiled roofs, and especially for its unique feature, those immensely wide overhanging cornices painted the same cumulus-white as the walls and belfries. A small church, La Eremita, demonstrates this feature most spectacularly, and its walls are additionally an object-lesson in simplicity—the miracle that can be accomplished by spacing windows widely apart and letting a plain wall speak for itself.

After a lunch introduced by *lulo* juice (strained from a plum-size orange with a flesh like a pomegranate) and concluded with glasses of ice-cold chopped mangoes, sapodillas, melons, and something called locally a *níspero*, we went to see the city's two considerable pieces of sculpture. The large equestrian bronze of Colombia's conqueror, Belalcázar, overlooking the city, is impressive in the commanding tradition of Verrochio and Donatello. But Simón Bolivar's so-called hitching post in the Museo de Arte Colonial is something else again—a windblown, hand-smoothed rock shaped vaguely like a human being which would fit easily into any retrospective of Henry Moore.

La Eremita in Popayán, and an even more eloquent work of art, the primitive thatched-roof church of San Andrés de Pisimbalá between Neiva and Popayán, set me to thinking about Guatavita. In New York I'd seen models of this government showpiece—a made-to-order Indian village designed by Colombia's best modern architect in the Indian style—and was impressed. In principle, perhaps, it was all wrong. You work in the style of your own time or you're an antiquarian. As an undergraduate at Yale I had helped to launch an offensive against "girder-Gothic" that eventually led to the most avant-garde building program on any campus in the world. To build a neo-Colonial marketplace, church, bullring, and dwellings for a displaced Indian community was just as anachronistic as surrounding a gymnasium with ogives, finials, and flying buttresses—or was it? Did it make more sense to give peasants split-levels with picture windows, and pen their pigs in accordion-pleated aluminum? The test should be: were the Indians at home in their new home? And did the architects exhaust every other solution? I wanted to visit Guatavita and talk to its architect.

The Guatavita Reservoir that had flooded out the original Indian village is at Sesquilé, a little more than an hour's drive north of Bogotá. The surrounding fields of the Chibcha Indians are enclosed with walls (*tapia*)—huge blocks of pressed dirt and manure that make an interesting pattern and blend perfectly with the dun landscape. The resettlement village soon appeared over the crest of a hill. It was built in 1962-66—a laudable social experiment, perhaps unique in South America, where little or nothing has ever been done to make the aboriginal feel he has a place in his own land. The homes are of adobe with tile roofs. The walls and the columns of the larger structures are of a handsome locally-made cooked brick, volcanic reddish-black. There are many

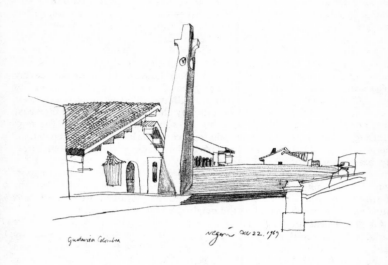

Guatavita Colombia   negun dec 22. 1969

shallow arches, and the church, with its elongated bell-tower and
cornices supported by beams of gaily painted wood, is striking.

Somehow, though, an atmosphere of phoniness pervades Guatavita.
For one thing, the overall effect is neo-Mission, like the worst of the
California and Texas campuses. In other words, it looks like what it
isn't—a university or a tourist hotel—instead of what it's supposed to
be, a peasant village. And the forty-five hundred peasants, who still walk
around in rags, with bare feet and dirty faces, look as out of place as
cowpokes on a Long Island "ranch" or Congo savages in Disneyland. In
fact the Guatavita Gift Shoppe is already selling peasant dolls that are
beginning to acquire the arch expressions of Disney's dwarves; and cute
neo-pre-Columbian ashtrays and vases. The "keynote" fountain at the
entrance, with a fake idol in the reflecting pool and a legend spelled
out behind it in block letters, is another disturbing touch. And still another is the model jail across from the fountain, with jailbirds behind
antique iron grills in lunettes (I thought of old movies of the Middle
Ages, like "When Knighthood Was in Flower"), making plastic-tape
wrappers for ballpoint pens to sell to the tourists, or being fed (while
being photographed) out of GI-chow-pans by their free relatives.

On the way back to the capital we stopped at Zipaquirá to see the so-called Salt Cathedral—a church converted out of an abandoned section of a salt mine that both of us expected to be in worse taste than Guatavita. For one thing, a friend of García Márquez in Bogotá had already tipped us off that the novelist prided himself on having gone to school for years in this town without seeing it. He had made a great mistake. The entrance is spectacular and rather frightening. Our driver made a sudden turn and shot into a black hole in the mountain barely large enough to receive our car. For several minutes we were rocketing through a tunnel hardly illuminated at all and filled with an overpowering stench of sulphur. Almost as suddenly the tunnel gives way to a vast chamber. You park and get out and are soon walking through the one-hundred-foot-high nave of a stupendous cathedral. It was hacked out of the gray-black salt by generations of Indian miners who had been working here even before the Conquest, it seems, with no sense of what a church should look like but with a very good sense of the proper proportions to make piers and vaulting in order to support the crushing weight of three hundred feet of rock salt. No doubt primitive machinery and later dynamite were used, but the original shape remained.

An organ was playing Tchaikovsky's "1812 Overture"—improved by the sepulchral acoustics. The eerie Piranesi-like lighting was supplied by banks of white fluorescent tubes, concealed to back light the stone cross in the apse, the chapels, and the sacristy. This particular kind of lighting is as stunningly effective as the candles and torches in the catacombs. And it does wonders for the occasional sculpture—an angel on a column, a Virgin with barnyard animals in the Baptistry, a monumental unfinished Pietà in the manner of Michelangelo's Rondanini group—all, no doubt, hardly superior to garden-sculpture if exposed to glaring light, but in this murky atmosphere wondrously evocative.

I thought about it on the way back to Bogotá. Is it the crudeness, the sense of being underground, that gives the Salt Cathedral its awesome otherworldliness, its aura of persecuted Christian martyrs at a time when Christianity bore some resemblance to the religion of the underdog which Christ preached? . . . And Guatavita? Wouldn't a better solution have been to let the peasants build their own village, with whatever materials and accessories they might want, financed by the government, of course?

I asked one of Guatavita's architects this question the following morning. "Mightn't they," I said, "have built houses as handsome as those between Cali and Popayán?"

Jaime Ponce de Leon is no journeyman in his profession. His office overflows with masterworks from his collection of pre-Columbian sculpture. He speaks so familiarly of the stylistic breakthroughs of Wright, Mies, Le Corbusier, Gropius, Saarinen, Johnson, and the other inventors of modernism that they sound like family matters. He pushed back his chair, rolled up his pink shirt-sleeves, and offered me some of his own pipe-tobacco.

"Fifty years ago," he answered, in perfect English, "they might have. But those skills and that sure touch for simplicity have gone. They've seen the comic books, and TV. They'd build—you know what! They knew it themselves. There were three solutions open to us and we posed all of them to the villagers we'd been asked to rehouse. One was: to move them to the two nearest villages that wouldn't be flooded out. 'No,' they said. Two: a wall could be erected to protect the original village, which was dying anyway. They were skeptical, and besides the wall would have been astronomically expensive and not earthquake-proof. Then we proposed modern architecture. 'We don't want it,' the peasants replied, 'and if you give us anything but white walls and tile roofs we won't move in!' Personally," the young architect added with a smile, "I think they were quite right to reject modernism of the Ciudad Kennedy variety, which reduces its inmates to the status of rats in a trap. 'You build something for us,' the peasant spokesman said, 'and then we'll move in and tell you whether we like it,' so we built the first fifteen units of Guatavita, and they did move in, and they liked it. Then we built the rest of the one hundred and sixty-two, not using any steel or concrete at all, for these are prohibitively priced in Colombia. The arch was a better solution anyway. . . . Why the little sticks in the cornices instead of the planes they used in the much wider ones at Popayán? Because in those days wood was cheap so the beams could be wide and deep enough to support such overhangs without propping."

"And now?" I asked.

"They love it. And I love them. And they love me. In fact, they've just elected me president of their council for the second time!"

I asked him if it was true that peasants had attended a harpsichord concert in Guatavita recently.

"Clavicembalo," he corrected me. "Performed by my friend Rafael Puyana, the master of this instrument."

"They went for it?"

"Enthusiastically. It's very close to their traditional instruments, like the guitar and the zither."

Was Ponce kidding himself? Or was I underestimating the peasants? The only peasant music we'd heard thus far had come from their transistor sets, but of course we hadn't spent the night in Aracataca or Popayán—and those towns are not exactly primitive. Ponce insists that the tourist gift shop, bullring, theater, etc. were added to Guatavita only in order to give the peasants additional sources of revenue, to make the well-heeled Bogotá citizens and tourists come here to spend their money. Ponce's answers are unanswerable. Yet the phoniness of Guatavita remains. . . . Peasants-on-display at Guatavita. . . . Rats-in-a-trap at the Alliance for Progress' showcase, Ciudad Kennedy. . . . Perhaps the whole idea of doing things for people, like the *Alianza* itself, will have to be discarded. . . . Perhaps the citizens of Aracataca, like the citizens of Macondo, should be left alone, to join the twentieth century on their own terms—if they want to at all. Isn't that what García Márquez is saying?

The Footsteps of the Poet

> Sister of light, first unawakened breath
> of a life to put this life of ours in shade;
> Season where hunger is delayed
> to hide its rendezvous with death;
>
> Bride of my song, ear of wheat, knowing
> that your great weakness is your strength,
> that luck in love will go to any length
> to make the dawn go where it's going;
>
> Highway of drought, way of the wind,
> I look (and catch) your image in my mind
> and by your shadow measure what you'll be;
>
> but to surprise you in this verse
> would be in vain, and to detain you worse,
> in the first flour of your infancy.

Before leaving for Cartagena, I was shown this somewhat labored conceit by the young García Márquez and a second poem (below) that may very well constitute the complete poetical works of the poet-novelist. Both poems were written in 1943 during the school days in Zipaquirá, when García Márquez was seventeen. My informant and benefactor was the novelist's friend Daniel Samper, the young assistant director of Bogotá's influential *El Tiempo*. The second poem, which Samper's secretary dredged from a back file of the daily newspaper, I translate as follows:

Elegy for Marisola

You have not died.
You have begun your late afternoon journey.
At two in the afternoon
you will find San Isidro
with his two gentle oxen
ploughing the limpid sky
in order to sow the lights
and the stars in their clusters.
At six in the afternoon
the Angel of the Service
will come out to hang the moon.

Samper, who had just come back from Barcelona, was full of revealing sidelights on the personality, methods and hang-ups of his friend. "He needed to live in Mexico," he began, "and now in Spain, in order to feel homesickness. But when he finishes his next novel, which will be his last, he says, he will come back to Colombia for good, settling down with Mercedes, and the two boys, Rodrigo and Gonzalo."

"What will the final book be about?" I asked curiously.

"A tropical dictator, one hundred and nineteen years old, who has been in the saddle so long he's forgotten when he seized power."

"Sounds like Venezuela's Gómez," I said, "and a far cry from the apolitical *Cien Años de Soledad*. Does everybody in South America love that book?"

"Almost everybody. But not Gabo's father—ask him about it tomorrow in Cartagena! The old man told Gabo, according to Gabo: 'Don't write any more of that shit.' "

"Was the novelist offended?" I asked.

"Of course not. He was amused. He is very fond of his parents. He told me his letters to his mother would make a fine book. In fact, a Spanish publisher heard about them and offered him a house in Palma de Majorca for the publication rights."

"And—?"

"Gabo said: 'Go to hell! What you think I am, a *puta?*' "

One out of every three words the novelist uses is foul, Samper said. "Even in front of his wife and children. After all, he was born on *La Costa* where everybody talks that way."

"And he'll live on *La Costa* when he retires?" I asked.

"Yes. In Barranquilla. Since Aracataca, he's always lived in cities."

"But what will he do?"

"He says he'll study classical music, and compose a concerto for full orchestra and triangle."

"Triangle—?"

"He calls it the most neglected instrument. To illustrate he sings a series of ascending notes concluding with a PING!"

"He must be pulling your leg?"

"You never can tell. Maybe he'll do exactly what he says. It would be more like him than not to do it!"

"I've heard that he's very upset by publicity and reporters. Is that true?"

"Very. He went to Barcelona to escape from it. But since *Cien Años* came out, it's worse than ever. He told me about one girl reporter who wanted him to answer two hundred and fifty typed questions. He glanced at them and said: 'In *Cien Años* I've written three hundred and fifty pages of opinions. There's all the material reporters could wish for.' While I was there an editor came to propose a prologue for the diary Ché kept in the Sierra Maestra. Gabo said to him with a straight face— as straight as he can manage with that sly low-browed peasant's face of his—that he'd need eight years. 'After all,' he said, 'I'd want you to have a well-done piece of work.' He thinks Colombian literature has a bleak future because the young writers write to get published instead of just for the sake of writing, and that the old song-and-dance about editors not being willing to publish them is for the birds, because, as he puts it, 'They're sweeping around under the beds with a broom looking for authors.' He himself never brought a book to an editor. He calls all editors parasites who live off writers and readers, and he says that he and Fuentes and Cortázar and Vargas Llosa are preparing a deadly remedy to shield writers from editors."

"Did he tell what he did all those years in Zipaquirá, besides not see the Salt Cathedral?"

"He said he avoided the sadness and cold of this area by staying shut up in his house and reading the books of Jules Verne and Emilio Salgari. Evidently, after the hot climate of Aracataca and Barranquilla, Bogotá's altitude got to him. Here is something I quoted from him in an article for *El Tiempo*:

I was a little boy when I came for the first time to Bogotá. I had left Aracataca with a scholarship for the National College at Zipaquirá. The trip was cursed by the river and by the train's ferocious climbing of the mountains. When we finally reached the capital, that railroad station was like another world. I remembered immediately that those who came here from La Costa died of pneumonia. But I climbed into a cart with the "aide" they furnish distant students and had my first view of that cold and gray city at six in the afternoon. Miles and miles of ruins. No sound of the familiar joy of the *barran-quilleros*. The buses passing with their dead weight of human freight. When I crossed in front of the governor's mansion, all the *cachacos* were walking in black, under their umbrellas and hats and mous-taches, and I couldn't resist it: I sat down and cried for hours. And from then on Bogotá has been for me apprehension and mourning. The *cachacos* are dark people. And for years I choked in the at-mosphere one has to breathe in that dark city, only learning three points and the shortest distances between them, never climbing to Monserrate, never visiting the Quinta de Bolívar, and having no idea to this day where the Park of the Martyrs is.

"And in Barcelona—?" I asked Samper. "Is your friend a changed person?"

"Transcendentally! He never wears a tie. He always has the same black woolen shirt on, and horrible red socks. On the avenue of the department stores he looks everywhere for a shirt with a long collar and fine stitch-ing, but not finding it he settles for orange-colored stockings which Mercedes has to pay for because he never handles money. The family lives on the steep street called Lucano. There's a fifteen-year-old recep-tionist, a few flights of stairs, a Carmelite door. The living room has three chairs, a tape recorder for classical music, and a very modern electric typewriter; the typewriter writes so fluently, Gabito says, that it writes the novels by itself. At four in the afternoon the boys are back from school, either looking at the monkeys before Mercedes sets them to doing their chores, or covering the black sofa with comic strips of Tarzan, Mickey Mouse, and Donald Duck. There are very few books in the house and for a simple reason. Gabo throws out every book he's finished read-ing. Once, when his wife asked him to finish one so she could start it, he tore it in two and gave her the part he'd already read."

Cartagena: The Shoes of López and the Parents of García Márquez

Cartagena is a swinging Negro port, like Colón in Panamá or Bahia in Brazil, and if they don't restore its Old City to death (as they're threaten-ing to do), straightening out those crazy crooked triple-decker balconies, burying the knots of black wires strung between the streets as narrow as angel fish, cleaning up the pock-marked palazzos and moldering churches, and lift its seamy pink-and-lavender face—what a treasure they'll go on having!

It's just blowsy enough now not to be cloyingly picturesque, so they want to scrub the charm off it. But for now, the gray-green, garbage-greasy Caribbean lapping the rotted hulls of gas-powered fishing smacks, the hot sun and the howling wind, the pungent smells of rickety side-walk kitchens on wheels, and the crowds of exuberant blacks were the perfect backdrop to the grade C pirate movie some Hollywood crew was shooting in the massive citadel that looms over the sack-prone sixteenth century city.

The scenic route by which they taxi you in from the airport is perfect too. The road is the beach! One wheel is in the angry surf and the other in a waterlogged mangrove swamp. What makes it even sweeter is that it's the shortest, cheapest airport-to-hotel ride in all South America.

On a leisurely walk through the shopping district, we were suddenly confronted in a traffic circle by the world's most derisive memorial in bronze: two gigantic battered shoes, the high kind of the turn of the century that you need a button-hook to put on, with children clambering all over them. A memorial to what? We crossed over and read the marker. Too perfect! I translated it on the spot:

To My Native City

Noble corner of my forefathers: Nothing
Evokes like crossing narrow alleys
The times of the cross and the sword,
The smoking candle and the sulphur match.

Gone utterly . . . City of massive walls,
Age of chivalric tales, your caravels
Have sailed through the neck of the bay for the last time,
And oil is no longer stored in leathern bottles.

You were heroic in those colonial days
When your sons had the shape of well-heeled eagles
Before becoming a swarm of swifts . . .

But today, crumbling in rancid disorder,
You inspire only in the tolerant heart
The affection one feels for a pair of old shoes.

—LUIS CARLOS LÓPEZ

Gabriel Elígio García and his wife, Luisa Márquez, have eleven children, of whom the oldest, the novelist, was born in 1927, and the youngest, a son just twenty, is beginning to publish papers on physics. Señorita Margot, the only unmarried child, works in the local treasury office, and it was she who guided us to the house of her parents in the suburb of Cartagena called Manga.

In a matter of seconds we were in an (enclosed) mirror-image of the Aracataca scene. The same innate dignity and hospitality of adults; the same happy proliferation and racial integration of children. For though the Señora is as white as samite, and the Señor quite dark but square-jawed with Spanish features, the nineteen grandchildren milling around us ran the gamut from African to Indian and even Oriental. Or so it seemed, though some of the children in this indoor-street-scene could have been friends from the street. There was a constant circulation, curious but respectful, during the hour we stayed. Every time I looked up I saw a new face, or faces—the *nieta* on Grandmother's lap, falling asleep and being quickly replaced by another three- or four-year-old—a boy looking over Grandfather's shoulder at the scrap-book with the clippings about the famous uncle in Barcelona—far down the corridor, a knot of children, appearing and disappearing—a boy of seven with big round eyes, stretched out on the floor, his chin cupped in his hands, regarding us unblinkingly. Nor was it easy to ask questions and get coherent answers, for everybody over twelve was eager to help and sometimes four or five voices were answering at once.

I felt sure enough of the Buendía hoax of Aracataca to want to scotch that one first. "Of course there was no such name," the novelist's father said. "It was invented. But my wife's father was a colonel, and he gave Gabriel some of the features of the portrait. You want to see him?"

He gave orders to a youngster who rushed out of the room and back with an outsize tinted photograph in an oval frame. The picture, taken in 1916, was of a very proper old gentleman with pince-nez.

"How does he look?"

"Prosperous," I said, "and more like a small-town banker or mayor than a colonel—and certainly not the commander who ordered his best friend hanged for insubordination."

Gabriel Elígio García smiled and said: "My son added many, many features, but his grandfather did see action in the Thousand Day War of 1899."

Luisa Márquez smiled as proudly and said nothing. She said nothing all evening, and yet her presence, contented and assured, held the family together as masterfully as her husband's, I felt sure.

The house is spacious but sparsely furnished. The principal decoration is a large store-bought mural of Spanish galleons setting fire to one another in Cartagena Bay. On the table in front of it was a vase with three feathers in it and a china figure of a peasant girl stroking the back of a goose. At the far end of the corridor off which the bedrooms open was a color print of Christ, and a phonograph on which the proud parents played for us a recording of their son reciting a part of *El Coronel*.

A picture of the novelist's development was beginning to take shape.

As a child in Aracataca—they left the village in 1937, about the time of his tenth birthday [6]—Gabriel had been quiet, curious, all-absorbing. "He liked to be with other people," his father said, "but in his first year of high school he won eleven medals for excellence. Cien Años de Soledad proves that he never forgot anything he saw or heard."

"When did he start to write?" I asked.

"Later, when we moved to Barranquilla and he went to school there, he began writing poems."

"Which of his books do you like best?" I asked.

He misunderstood me and said that Cien Años had sold two hundred thousand copies to date, twenty thousand in Argentina on publication day, but that it was not easy to find in Colombia—"because they can't keep up with the demand, I guess." Then, correcting his answer, he added that he preferred the earlier El Coronel No Tiene Quien Le Escriba to all the others.

"Why does Gabriel live in Spain?"

"Because he likes to travel. He knows six languages."

"And has success changed him?"

"Not at all. He visits home often—most recently in August of 1966— and I think he will live in Colombia one day, in Barranquilla probably, because he grew up there, though he loves Aracataca too."

"Who is your son's favorite writer?"

"Faulkner."

"And among the South Americans?"

"I don't know. Borges and Neruda perhaps."

"And his closest friends?"

"Fuentes and Vargas Llosa. But in Barranquilla it was Alvaro Cepeda Samudio, who now edits Barranquilla's leading newspaper."

I asked Gabriel Elígio when the United Fruit Company had pulled out of the Santa Marta-Barranquilla region, and how this had affected Gabriel —if indeed it did. He said that there had been a bloody strike in 1928, in which many Colombian workers on the plantations had been killed, and that it had been as a result of this that the American company had decided to liquidate its holdings; it had bought directly from the growers for a while but finally moved its big base of operations to Ecuador. "The whole novel Cien Años is about that strike, which my son remembers in every detail though he was only two at the time. I'll give you another example of his memory. When he was in Aracataca in 1966 he encountered an old man who had been very friendly to him in 1928. Gabriel addressed him instantly by his nickname, Hebilla (belt-buckle)."

I asked the father how many grandchildren he had. He counted to himself. "Thirty-eight," he replied, "including the offspring of my four legiti-

[6] In Aracataca they had said twelfth. In Barranquilla a boyhood friend, now editor of that city's Diario de Caribe, told me the family moved to Cienaga when the novelist was two. I felt sure this was the way García Márquez would like it—elusive.

mate children and the seven illegitimate ones." (I hoped that unlike the *Cien Años* Buendías, they all knew they belonged to the clan.)

With the novelist's sisters and older nieces and nephews answering every question at once with a different answer, this was about as much as I could take in. We had a second round of whiskeys and Coca-Colas and went out to quiet the taxi driver who was ringing the bell impatiently.

The whole family accompanied us onto the porch and were still waving as we turned the corner on the way back to our hotel.

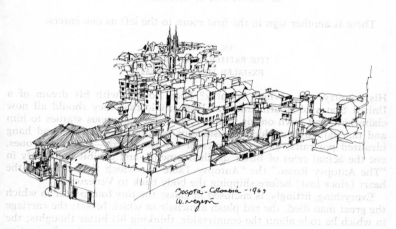

Envoi: Bolívar Died Here

If only because we would be off to Ecuador tomorrow, and I was looking forward to seeing the place in Guayaquil where the two great liberators had their strange meeting, I was glad to return to Santa Marta with enough time to visit the scene of Bolívar's death. Marie-Teresa and Myriam were our companions again as we drove to San Pedro Alejandrino. "They say," Teresita said, "that he died because there was nothing else to do in Santa Marta—then as now. Some call it Santa Muerta." Bolívar had come to this hacienda at the invitation of his friend, the Marqués Don Joaquín de Mier, who owned it. What supreme irony, that after being vilified and cast out by every country he had liberated from "tyrannical Spain," the only person who would give the Liberator a house to die in was a Spanish grandee!

The quadrangle of white-plastered bungalows is surrounded by huge shade trees that must have been ancient even in 1830, a noble *campaño* and several tamarinds almost as ample. One of the latter, by the gateway, had recently been cut down and the stump bore the following sign:

UNDER THE SHADE
OF THIS TREE
ENRIQUE OLAYA HERRERA AND GUILLERMO VALENCIA
PRODUCED SUBLIME ORATIONS
ON THE HUNDREDTH ANNIVERSARY
OF THE DEATH OF THE LIBERATOR

There is another sign in the first room to the left as one enters:

IN THIS ROOM
THE FATHER OF HIS COUNTRY
EXHALED HIS LAST BREATH

His country? . . . Which country? Poor Bolívar with his dream of a United States of South America! How ironic that they should all now claim him, and fawn on his memory; and erect pompous statues to him and martial, eagle-studded mausoleums of imported marble; and hang idealized portraits; and sell copies of his last words—the official ones, not the actual cries of bitter disillusionment—and exhibit tastelessly in "The Autopsy Room" the "Autopsy Table" at which they removed the heart (since lost) before shipping the body back to Venezuela.

Everything, fittingly, is enclosed in glass: the tiny four-poster in which the great man died; the red plush armchair in which he sat; the carriage in which he rode about the countryside, thinking his bitter thoughts; the table at which he ate, with three unmatched glasses and a diminutive stein; the decanters, labeled in English "Brandy" and "Sherry"—from which he presumably poured his last drinks; the desk, with a few yellowing letters and documents; an engraving, which looks like a bad photograph of the happy marriage that terminated so quickly and tragically.

In keeping with the unreality of the whole display, there is no suggestion of the brilliant equestrian Manuela Sáenz, Bolívar's Ecuadorean mistress, who alone was faithful to his ideals and his memory—or of anything that would lead one to suspect that here died one of the most complex, humanly-flawed heroes in history, a man who recognized his own incorrigible Bonapartism when he said "I want to fight for my glory even at the cost of the whole world." Supremely gifted, mercurial, idealistic, neurotic, and lovable, Bolívar spent the last and best years of his life trying far-sightedly to save South America from the ruinous nationalisms closing in on it and at the same time by his actions and example insuring that the very *caudillismo* he hoped to send packing with the Spaniards would be perpetuated in exaggerated form.

Both liberators, Bolívar and San Martín, died in bitter exile. But in the aftermath of their rejection, when it came to selecting a hero for the continent, it was significant that San Martín, who resembled Washington in seriousness and puritan rectitude (qualities feared by the Hispanic temperament) was decisively rejected in favor of the egocentric Bolívar whose only enduring creation was his life: the life of a romantic poet.

If self-recognition of what one biographer calls "the secret insincerity of his life" [7] ever came to Simón Bolívar in those last defeated days at San Pedro Alejandrino, it must have taken the form described by García Márquez in *Cien Años* when Colonel Buendía is given the terms for his armistice:

> They asked first that he renounce the revision of property titles in order to get back the support of the Liberal landowners. They asked, secondly, that he renounce the fight against clerical influence, in order to obtain the support of the Catholic masses. They asked finally that he renounce the aim of equal rights for natural and illegitimate children, in order to preserve the integrity of the home.

Buendía accepted the sellout fatalistically, but with despair in his heart. Like Bolívar, he had had "to start thirty-two wars and violate all his pacts with death and wallow like a hog in the dungheap of glory, to discover the privileges of simplicity almost forty years late." Had Bolívar, like the Colonel, kept his trunkful of early poems, would not he also have recognized that it was too late to become "a nameless artisan, a happy animal," and burned them? And was the cause and manner of his death here in San Pedro any different from that which Buendía intended when he aimed the pistol at his accusing heart and pulled the trigger?

[7] Salvador de Madariaga, *Bolivar*. University of Miami Press, 1952.

9

FIVE DAYS IN ECUADOR

For several reasons I present the Ecuador chapter of this book as no more than the raw, undigested journal out of which the other chapters grew. Ecuador is a raw, undigested country, a country of extremes. To draw any conclusions from its semi-feudal society and the failure of its ruling classes to even begin the country's unfinished business would be premature and unkind. Has one of its many talented poets and novelists ever come to grips with what gives Ecuador its unique personality? The glittering fragments are all there—waiting to be put together.

Never having experienced a socialist revolution like Bolivia's, or a democratic one like Uruguay's or Venezuela's; never having had a ruling class with a national sense of responsibility, like Colombia's or Chile's; never even having had a militarists' house-cleaning like Argentina's or Paraguay's or Peru's—Ecuador survives in limbo, in a state of permanent cultural and political crisis that is best described piecemeal. Its Indians remain as isolated in their windswept mountains as in Peru, and its low-land Negroes and Colorados could be compared to the blacks and Orientals of the Guyanese coast—if anything were being done to help them develop leadership of their own. Ecuador's city slums are even grislier and more neglected than Brazil's. And its current strong man is a political chameleon with so many lives and disguises that no one can say with any certainty whether he is Left or Right, benevolent or tyrannical, good or bad. Nor can Ecuadorean culture be conveniently summarized around the towering figure of some creative synthesizer, for such there has never been in Ecuador, though there is as lively an interest in the arts as in any of the other countries, and as rich a heritage of colonial and folk crafts. So the diary of five days in Ecuador which follows is presented in the hope that it will (by the very intensity of its pursuit of a portrait) throw some light on all the diversity, vitality, and confusion.

Quito I

March 1, 1969: Iberia was only an hour late so we arrived at 11:30 A.M. and were whisked to the Hotel Intercontinental where we had a swim. Neither on the flight in, nor at the pool, was there so much as a glimpse of those snowcapped volcanoes that are said to be Quito's glory, Chimborazo, Cotopaxi. . . . On a trip like this there's no time to waste, but without exercise and relaxation we'd be flat on our backs half the time. By great good fortune we ran into the Embassy's Cultural Attaché at the pool. William Pugh took us across the street to his house for lunch. I asked him if he knew Osvaldo Guayasamín, the Ecuadorean painter I'd met in Mexico City last winter, and he proceeded to relate last week's contretemps between Guayasamín and Marta Traba, the Colombian art critic, whom I'd also met in Mexico.

Marta Traba was then and still is the *doyenne* (or demon) of Latin American art critics: cold, brilliant, scathing, incorruptible. The day she arrived, Quito was plastered with posters advertising a big exhibit of Guayasamín's work in the Feria de la Fruta y de las Flores at Ambató. "Guayasamín," Pugh said, "actually dislikes publicity and is something of a recluse, but Marta was infuriated by what she took to be his self-advertising and sailed into him, pouring it on until the day she left in interviews, newspaper articles, radio and TV appearances, and private conversations. The gist of it was that Ecuador's best-known painter is a mere poster artist, an aesthetic reactionary for sticking to human imagery, and by implication a time-serving tool of both the Moscow-communists to whom he adheres and the rich Americans who buy his pictures at high prices." I recalled that Marta detests the propaganda art of Rivera and Siqueiros, and suspects any styles realistic enough to convey a social message. I gathered the Guayasamín, like so many other communist artists and intellectuals, lives well; he owns a palatial studio overlooking Quito, drives a Mercedes-Benz, and is married to a rich French wife. It seems that Guayasamín was present at Marta Traba's first savage assault on him and held his tongue. But after she'd left, he mentioned casually to a friend or two that he'd jilted her some years ago when she was his mistress—and this was quickly reported in the Quito press as the true motivation for the art critic's attack. We must get Guayasamín's side of this.

Some friends of the Pughs dropped in and the talk shifted to politics. There is no leader here to correspond to such great public servants as Colombia's President Carlos Lleras Restrepo, or his predecessor, Alberto Lleras Camargo. But Ecuador's present ruler, José María Velasco Ibarra, is a more colorful figure than either. In his seventies and still going strong, Velasco is having his fifth fling at the presidency. One guest described him as a great demagogue-orator in the Getulio Vargas tradition who loves and is loved by the peasants—though he is an intellectual who doesn't speak any of their dialects. His genius, it seems, consists in keeping the four power blocs of Ecuador, the landed oligarchy, the Church, the Army, and the Guayaquil export-import merchants, off balance. By appointing Marxists to his cabinet and threatening to give the oil exploration and pipe-line contracts to the Russians, he also keeps the American Embassy off balance. We made a date to talk this evening to Bob Norris, who is reputed to be working on a no-holds-barred biography of the President.

At 2:30 Tony García of the Tourist Department picked us up and gave us a three-hour tour of the ancient colonial city. We began with Guyasamín's mosaic mural at the University's Law School: stylized figures weak in draftsmanship and imagination symbolizing Ecuador, under the worthy motto "While you are free, you can live to dream." (A state no one in Ecuador but the elite has ever known). On the way, we passed the Plaza Indo-Americana with a rotunda around which runs a circular bench bearing academic portrait-busts of the outstanding Indians in each country. The American entry, in this corny display of racism from a country that still treats its own Indian majority as serfs, is labeled "Sequoian."

There were many Indians to be seen in La Compañia (first of the triad of famous churches we visited): cripples, mutilated beggars, lepers, under an incongruous explosion of gold décor. They follow one even up to the high altar with outstretched hands murmuring "gringo . . ." (Even more than in La Paz an air of sorrowful hopelessness hangs over Quito—so much natural and architectural wealth as a background for such grinding and fawning poverty.)

San Francisco, behind an extremely ugly facade that looks more Victorian than sixteenth century as our guide insisted it was, has several features of interest. One is a pulpit supported by three life-size, stooped, polychromed, and moustachioed conquistadors—perhaps the only Spaniards of colonial times ever represented doing an honest piece of work. But no! They're not doing an honest piece of work after all: a column concealed by their gesticulating hands supports the pulpit; they're only pretending to be lifting and groaning under the weight of God's platform. Almost as wild was the monk we encountered in the flower-and-bird-filled cloister of Doric-columned arches; he was doing a crossword puzzle as

monk working on crossword puzzle

he walked back and forth. There was also a huge smoky painting, a Franciscan family tree, with St. Francis at the bottom and the Virgin at the top, and a thousand lesser functionaries like robins on the branches—"just like an IBM chart," was Bill's comment.

We walked over to La Merced next, a vision of surpassing beauty with its immaculate white walls separating the cluster of domes with their moss-green caps from the crenelated square tower with green bells in the belfry. As in the other churches, however, there are too many blood-spattered images of the saints depicting death, too many Buchenwald-like scenes of torture and damnation. There is also a painting of Marshal Sucre at Junín, charging on horseback at the head of his brigade with his eyes riveted on a vision of the Virgin of the Andes. . . . La Merced, I recalled, was also the scene of the Quiteños' premature revolt against Spain in 1809 when the president of the Audiencia was dragged from the sacristy, mutilated, and beaten to death in the streets.

In the square behind La Merced a huge crowd was gathered, shouting and waving its arms. We approached, expecting at the very least a food riot. The focus of attention turned out to be an easel bearing an intricate heart-shaped design in reds and yellows. Slithering closer still, we discovered that the heart was composed of hundreds of packs of chewing gum and that the crowd was paying for the privilege of shooting them off the easel with a popgun.

While I was photographing this sideshow, a file of Indian women passed in their dark blue skirts and embroidered white blouses, wearing ropes of gold beads that formed a glittering truncated pyramid from shoulders to chin—just like the waitresses at the Intercontinental. "Yes," said our guide, "these Otovalos do our weaving for us. They are our cleanest Indians. But the gold beads are made in Czechoslovakia and are terribly expensive." Too expensive for us, at any rate, at twenty dollars a rope; so we settled for some pretty one-dollar brooches of armadillos and flowers which the Indians make out of baked waxed bread and returned to the hotel.

Still no sight of those volcanoes . . .

After a couple of sets of tennis with Bill Pugh and his son on the Ambassador's court near the hotel, we had dinner and were driven by the Pughs to a party being given by the Projecto de Estudios Andinos. Bob Norris, the organization's Catedratico de Historia (out of the University of New Mexico), was there, and he and I managed to slip upstairs away from the din for an hour's talk about Velasco. Norris is a YMCA-type American married to an Ecuadorean girl and has a very firm grasp of his complex subject. I began by asking him who the Velasquistas really are. "Are they the Indian masses? The peasants?"

"No," he said. "The peasants, the pure Indians who make up forty to forty-five percent of Ecuador, are mostly illiterate and take no part in politics. The so-called *huasipungo*, a hateful law which entitled them to work their plot of land on the master's *hacienda* as long as they performed certain services for him, was abolished by the military junta in 1963-66, making the peasants *minifundistas*, with title to their tiny holdings, as in Bolivia. Velasco, a city intellectual who has lectured on his specialty, international law, all over Latin America, doesn't speak their language (Quechua, the Inca dialect) and neither do any of the other politicians, though of course the big landowners and priests do to keep control of their constituencies."

"Then it's the *cholos* who support him," I asked. "You call the mestizo ex-peasants that here, as in Peru?"

"Yes—but don't call anyone here by that name to his face unless you know him well enough to joke with him! Velasco is supported by the urban masses, the poor in the *suburbios*, the slums like the *barriadas* in Lima that ring Quito and Guayaquil. Close to a million of Ecuador's estimated 5.5 million live there, and they're the hard core of the voters."

"What does Velasco offer them?" I asked.

"That's a good question," he said, smiling. "Velasco himself once answered it to me this way: 'Why should I offer them a program? What this country needs is a government of action.' The first two times he came to power, in 1934 and 1944, he talked radically and was overthrown by the military, though he'd won by such a landslide the second time that they didn't dare oust him until 1947. In the 1952 elections everyone thought him dead and his campaign a bad joke; but he won and lasted

out his term. In 1960 a military junta suspected he was playing a com
munist game and making deals with Castro, so they threw him out, an
were in turn thrown out by the very Army from which they had sprung
This fifth time Velasco barely squeaked by with twenty thousand vote
more than the other two parties of the moderate center, each of whom
got about one-third of the vote, as he did."

"Why did the military lose power," I asked, "after reputedly doing s
much for the Indians?"

"Perhaps for that very reason," he replied. "Those who benefite
had neither votes nor guns. The brass was momentarily popular fo
having ousted the alcoholic interim president, but they lost it with th
powerful Guayaquil merchants by their decrees restricting imports an
exports. What finally finished them, though, was the ruthless way the
cracked down on the protesting University students. You just don't bea
up students in Latin America; psychologically they hold the key to an
regime's survival."

"Has Velasco ever been a communist?" I asked Norris.

"No. But the conservatives think he is one, or call him one—and th
doesn't hurt him a bit in a country where almost everybody has nothing
In the fifties, when regimes in Latin America were supposed to line u
pro-US or pro-USSR, he took a neutralist position and this was the ke
to his strength; the Right and Left always attacked him.

"Has he been anti-Yanqui?" I asked.

"He's been careful to draw a distinction between the American peop
and the State Department. Nobody can be pro-US and be a successf
politician in Latin America. Distrust of our power and wealth is to
deep-seated. It's always good politics to rap the U.S. So the prejudice
anti-Yanquiism is self-pepetuating and is exacerbated by this sure-fi
political ploy."

"Would you ask Velasco when you see him tomorrow what he thin
of the new regime in Peru and its expropriation of Standard Oil?"

"I couldn't. Unless he brings it up himself. I'd be playing into th
hands of those who suspect me (or would like to prove me) a CIA age
or at least a spy who is relaying the President's thoughts to our Embass
Velasco himself might misinterpret my motives if I asked him such
question. I stick strictly to history. Of course, when he wasn't Preside
that was different. I spent a month talking to him when he was in exile
Buenos Aires, and then I could ask him anything."

"What are the demands on Texaco that Velasco is currently making

"First he asked them to return four hundred thousand of the almc
two million hectares they now hold for exploration and developme
They agreed. Four hundred thousand hectares had already proved i
operable. Then Velasco asked for almost a million. Was it only a pok
move, raising the ante? No one knows. But Texaco claims that returni
that many hectares will in effect wipe out the two hundred and fif

million dollars it has already invested in pipelines, rigs, feeders, etc. Besides, if they agree, he can raise the ante again; or so they figure."

"Is there an income tax in Ecuador?" I asked.

"On the books. But those with wealth get around it. An industrialist from Guayaquil, one of the nation's richest men, paid a tax of five thousand *sucres* in 1967—about two hundred and fifty dollars."

"Does a liberal democrat like former President Galo Plaza Lasso [now OAS chief] have any following in Ecuador, or did that book he wrote giving United Fruit a fairly clean bill of health rise to haunt him?"

"Galo Plaza," Norris answered, "has always been the white hope of the Americans. He was President from 1948 to 1952. Velasco smashed him beyond local repair in 1960. Not only for whitewashing United Fruit, but even more for speaking slightingly of the Ecuadorean banana, which Plaza called inferior in quality. That was unforgivable!"

March 2, 1969—Quito: I awoke with a slight touch of *soroche*, probably caused less by the capital's 9,236 feet, almost straddling the equator, than by the extra two hours' effort it took me to make the last journal entry after the party broke up at 2 A.M. So I've skipped the country market and the *tienta* of bulls that Bill is taking in, and instead am stretched out by the pool, watching the sun appear and disappear behind the gray-black clouds that settle over Quito from about 11 A.M. I'm still hoping for a glimpse of those volcanoes with the spine-tingling names that Humboldt climbed. I'm also reading a back number of *Time* that quotes retiring interim President Otto Arosemena: "A rich man here is poorer than a porter on Wall Street." The two percent of the population the government considers rich, he adds, has an annual per capita income of $1,167; and the rest of the 5.4 million live either in the rock-strewn Andes or the scabrous slums—victims of the time-honored policy of exporting bananas, coffee, and cacao to a price-crazy international market, and of unpredictable, irresponsible politicians.

Among the Poets

> I was born in the century of the death of the rose
> when the motor had already driven out the angels.
> Quito watched the last stagecoach roll . . .
> All has gone now in sequent waves,
> like the futile cyphers of the foam.
> The years go leisurely entangling their lichens,
> and memory is scarcely a water-lily
> showing on the surface timidly
> its drowned face.
> The guitar is only a coffin for songs,
> and the head-wounded cock laments.

All the angels of the earth have emigrated,
even the dark angel of the cacao tree.

—JORGE CARRERA ANDRADE [1]

[1] From "Biography for the Use of the Birds" in *An Anthology of Contemporary Latin American Poetry.* Edited by Dudley Fitts. New York, New Directions, 1942.

Filoteo Samaniega, a poet to whom Daniel Samper had given me a letter of introduction, picked me up in his delivery truck—which indicated that the number of his occupations is at least four, for he had already told me that he teaches the history of art in the morning and works on *El Comercio* afternoons. We talked very little about his poetical profession because the girl to whose house he took me was a painter and opened up on Guayasamín with both barrels. But in the truck I did have a few minutes to sound him out about a field with which I was more familiar, the Ecuadorean novel. I'd read stories by Diez Canseco, and more recently Jorge Icaza's *Huasipungo.*[2] Filoteo thinks this book, pub-

[2] One of the first of the regional-social genre that included the novels of Ciro Alegría, Rómulo Gallegos, and Jorge Amado, Icaza's *Huasipungo* (1934) is lacking in the spring-like zest for life and pantheistic identification with natural beauty that redeems the message fiction of the other writers. It has been translated into a dozen languages, and is said to be immensely popular in Russia and China. Icaza's militant Marxism, which reduces his characters to stereotypes and their speech to clichés, seems ludicrously oversimplified to anyone who has ever seen an exploited peasant laugh, an exploiting landlord get drunk and laugh with him, or an overbearing American give way to the equally ubiquitous type who helps others help themselves. The tone is set from the opening pages:
" 'The native huts, the *huasipungos,* must be cleared on both sides of the river so that the gringos can erect their comfortable villas there.'
" 'But how can that be done quickly?'
" '. . . What do the Indians matter to us? We come first . . . The accursed Indians have seized the two most fertile strips. They can put their huts higher up the mountain.' "
Yes, says the Evil Landlord, there are plenty of precedents for calling in the troops to mow down the recalcitrant peasants: "Don Jorge had been thrown into a cauldron full of honey and boiled alive, simply because the man had been accustomed to rape small Indian girls between six and eight years old. Yes, they were real savages!"
Andrés, the brutalized Indian hero whose wife, Cunshi, has been done to death, appeals to the village priest for a loan for a burial plot. The priest, who extorts their last pennies out of the superstitious peasants with the threat that those buried furthest from the altar will have the least chance of getting to heaven, shakes his head. But there was another solution for Andrés: "He could steal a cow so that he could send his Cunshi to heaven with a first class ticket. In this way he was following the examples of the white masters who worked on their haciendas so they could send their sons to Europe."
But of course it doesn't work, and inevitably the Indians rebel, and are machine-gunned as they try to save their plots. " 'We're only interested in making money,' " says the Evil Gringo, and "with the greed of vultures the white *señores* fell upon the *huasipungos* until only their remains lay like bones on the ground."
A true story, no doubt; and for another true one, told with more understanding, compassion, and humor, and also set in the Ecuador of the peasants, read the Peace Corps classic, Moritz Thomsen's *Living Poor,* Seattle, Washington, University of Washington Press, 1969.

lished in 1934, is still his country's major novel. Icaza is still alive, and so is Diez Canseco, his contemporary, whose fiction deals with the mestizos of the coast. Diez Canseco (related to the Peruvian presidential family, from which Belaúnde sprang) is also a leftish socialist, though he manages a bank these days and is a close friend of Galo Plaza. Filoteo finds Ecuador's younger novelists much less committed.

No one denied that Guayasamín was committed—at least committed to the Marxist program of exhibiting the workers as victims and heroic rebels in the class war with the bosses—but here again the report was negative. Filoteo's painter friend charged him with commercialism not only for cultivating the Americans ("He ridicules them behind their backs, but not when they come to buy his pictures.") but for allegedly charging four *sucres* each for his autograph on the Ambató catalogues. "When Marta arrived for the fateful lecture, he hung a gold chain with

Osvaldo Guayasamín
Quito Ecuador March 69

one of his jewels around her neck. She refused to accept it. Later on he actually proposed marriage to her—and was rejected again!"

"But isn't he already married?" I asked in surprise.

"Not really," the painter said. "But the real reason the other artists dislike Guayasamín is that he's lost touch with his times. Marta thinks artists should travel abroad, absorb the new styles, and then return to apply what they've learned to their own milieu. She attacks revolutionary artists who paint the revolution without living it—as Siqueiros and Orozco did."

"What are her own politics?" I asked.

"She's for communism with freedom" [—the contradictory Fuentes position]. "But she's married to a member of the party, Jorge Zalamea Borda, one of Colombia's leading poets."

Filoteo drove me back to the hotel where Bill Pugh was waiting to take me to meet another poet, Alfonso Barrera, who is Deputy Foreign Minister. I prevailed on him to stop at Guayasamín's on the way.

Guayasamín and his pretty wife—who turns out to be Belgian, not French, and a poet in her own right—were entertaining a host of potential buyers when we arrived. We spoke to them only long enough to make a lunch date. The artist was wearing Levi's and a plaid shirt. He is short, with hunched shoulders and a bull neck. His features are very Indian, and in the self-portrait that stood on his easel he had accentuated the shaggy lock of hair which hangs over one eye. The portrait (in black and white) is monumental and tragic in the Siqueiros manner, but too stylized to really get beneath the surface. Silvery lines cutting into the surface to accentuate the eyes, nose, and mouth seem to say: this far and no farther. The large, elegantly appointed house is divided into living quarters, a two-story studio, and a workshop where Guayasamín designs jewelry and has it executed and sold by assistants.

Barrera didn't agree with Samaniega about the Ecuadorean novel. "Our biggest names today are Angel Felicissimo Rójas, whose *El Exedo de Yangana* deals with the forced evacuation of a peasant village, and Demétrio Aguilera-Malta whose *La Isla Virgen* is set in the Guayaquil-Esmeraldas region; I find the latter a less civilized writer than Diez Canseco but a more natural one. . . . Of all Latin American novelists I still like Ciro Alegría best."

"Better than García Márquez?" I asked.

"I don't like *Cien Años* half as well as *El Colonel;* it's too hoked up: I've lived in a poor village and I don't see it that way at all. . . . *Doña Bárbara?* Yes! Miguel Otero Silva's novels, definitely no. . . . I prefer not to be a friend of writers like these intellectuals, though of course in Ecuador itself I can hardly avoid it."

The Ecuadorean poet Barrera regards most highly is Jorge Carrera Andrade who deals with social issues obliquely, through an Oriental ambience. "He lived in the Far East for many years and doesn't believe that the world was made for man, as we do in the Christian West."

Among younger poets his favorites are Cesar Davila Andrade, who just died, and Jorge Enrique Adoum, a communist who has lived in Paris since the military exiled him years ago. "Adoum writes colloquially, like the Afro-Cuban Nicolás Guillen, and his popular style uses Indian historical figures, like the Aztec general Rominaqui, as symbols. When he was only eighteen, Neruda called Adoum the greatest poet of Latin America.[3] I wonder whether he'd still think so. . . . But we have at least twenty good poets. This art is more developed in Ecuador than any other."

"Including Guayasamín's?"

"Guayasamín was a great painter eight years ago. He still paints a great picture occasionally."

"You think he was corrupted by success?"

"I just don't know. I fear to go that deeply into another man's soul. I do think he tries too hard and too self-consciously to be Indian. But if I had been at that lecture, I would have defended him."

"I think I would have, too."

"He's an artisan of the Middle Ages," Barrera went on, "in the best sense, with his apprentices and all. I admire that."

"And Marta Traba?" I asked.

"She's unique. Apart from her, we don't have any art criticism. We have indulgence. She tells the truth. But sometimes her purity carries her too far and she becomes self-righteous, a cultural fanatic. But she is necessary!"

The poets are necessary, too, and unlike the critics, they recognize their vulnerability and speak with humility. Adoum, for instance:

> *Here I begin, emerging from resentment*
> *as from the mother, dressed in my bones. I leave*
> *this hotel of sadnesses without delay,*
> *prepared to learn hope like an archaic language*
> *forgotten in the rubble of so much falling*
> *into failure. But I have good listeners! those who have died*
> *by letter, beyond belief, on their way to prove*
> *their credentials: the receipts torn up*
> *by the century's savagery and the year's caprice . . .*

Among the Colorados

March 3, 1969—Quito: I had wanted to visit the villages of the Colorado Indians ever since reading of their jungle-river paradise two thousand feet above the port of Esmeraldas in Von Hagen's book.[4] When Von

---

[3] Adoum as a very young man served his apprenticeship in Chile as Neruda's secretary.

[4] Victor Wolfgang Von Hagen, *Ecuador and the Gallapagos Islands.* (Based on *Ecuador the Unknown*, 1940). University of Oklahoma Press, 1949.

Hagen was here, in 1936, only thirty-three families were believed to have survived the smallpox and pulmonary diseases of the missionaries, but by the time Earl Parker Hansen's researcher visited Santo Domingo ten years later[5] the number had risen to two hundred and fifty. I had heard that the Colorados received their name (red) from their manner of painting themselves with balsam and gold dust—one of the many explanations for the El Dorado myth; and I knew that their traditional affability was in sharp contrast to the laughterless Jivaros, those formidable headhunters and headshrinkers of Ecuador's Amazonic provinces.

We drove toward Ilinizas volcano (without seeing it, as usual) in a light rain. The fields pyramid toward hilltops, the surfaces rippled and humped here and there as if a body were buried under the emerald coverlet. The town of Santo Domingo reminded me unpleasantly of Escuintla in Guatemala, that depressing boomville of the defrocked Indians (*ladinos*) who have sacrificed the beauty of their heritage for the tawdriest commercialism. The *ladinos* here are the *cholos*, of course, and in the similar unpaved, muddy streets they were buying and selling the same debased products of our civilization while being blasted at by the same jukeboxes and radios.

Federico Arturo Ehlers, the MC of the Intercontinental's folklore show which we are going to see tonight, was our companion as we drove into the Colorado reservation. He thinks that these Indians may be descendants of Orientals—possibly Japanese, shipwrecked off Esmeraldas, just as the Negroes who populate that port were descendants of a capsized slaver whose African cargo took to the blessedly familiar jungle before the Spaniards could round them up. At any rate, the Colorados were not disturbed by the invading Incas, who had been established in Quito only fifty years when Pizarro's lieutenant, Belalcázar, drove them out. The colonial regime, after a futile attempt to destroy them, made a pact that left them relatively undisturbed. The Colorados were always unwarlike. They respected their sorcerers who taught them to paint black lines on their reddened skin when worried—many lines, many anxieties. The tribesmen we encountered had very few black lines. They draw them with indelible *guito*, a nut which they also chew. It blackens their teeth but prevents cavities, so they told us. The *achiote* seed has long since replaced gold dust as the reddening agent for basic skin painting. The Colorado's topknot of hair, around which he shaves, and which looks like a sliced, red inner tube, used to be slicked with vegetable oils. He has now switched to Brylcreem—one of the few Colorado concessions to modernity.

The Colorados are relatively prosperous. Their chief, traditionally rich

[5] *The New World Guides to the Latin American Republics*. Edited by Earl Parker Hansen. New York, Duell, Sloan & Pearce, 1943, 1950.

Colorado Indian
Santo Domingo de los
Colorados - ECUADOR 2.69

and a big drinker, is privileged to deal directly with the President of
Ecuador. Catholic nuns have converted them, but we could discover no
sign of their conversion—unless it is the fact that the women now feel
obliged to wear brassieres (but not blouses) when visiting Santo
Domingo. Their music and dance is monotonously repetitious, with none
of the exuberance of the Esmeraldas Negroes from whom they borrowed the marimba. This instrument, which the Guatemala Mayas like-
wise took over from the coastal blacks, consists of *chonta* wood keys
over bamboo tubes of varying lengths. It gives a plaintive, atonal sound
when pinked by the musicians' two little hammers. Ehlers told us that
the tourist ministry pays this village a retainer to keep a complement
of tribesmen always available to pose at their marimbas. There is no
fee for photographing them.

"What would they be doing otherwise?" I asked

"Cultivating their yams, or hunting guinea pig and wild boar in the
bush yonder."

We saw only two women in each of the two villages we visited, but
were assured that the Colorado population has now risen to almost

two thousand, thanks to modern medicine. Some of the men were chopping up balsa logs with their machetes, or policing the yard, a leisurely occupation that consists of picking up an occasional leaf on a spiked stick. They seemed quite unself-conscious as they went about their chores, and unresentful of our intrusion. The elders and chiefs wear a circlet of cotton, banded with orange thread, on top of their bizarre hairdos. One of them, with a necklace of a dozen or two vanity-case mirrors strung around his neck, and two Swiss watches on Speidel bands on each wrist, informed us that he was about to be married. We asked him his fiancée's name.

"A girl," he replied.

"You don't know her name?"

"No."

Strips of balsa bark cover the muddy paths through the jungle to the various settlements. The houses in the clearings are very much like those of the Amerindian village we had visited in Surinam: spacious and thatched and half walled, with fires on the earthen floors. The Colorados weave their own cloth on ancient looms. The marimbas hang from the roof, two feet off the floor, on ropes decorated with the shells of snails and the skins of pythons. The men laughed at us and with us. The women, breast-feeding their babies, smiled but said nothing. It seemed a good life in a passive sort of way—just the sort the dropouts from our affluent society are looking for. With the government as *patrón* and the tourists as audience, they have it made. I thought of a complaint a young Brazilian revolutionary had made to us at the restaurant last night— "We'll never have a revolution in Brazil . . . Why? Because our government gives the people two soccer games a week and that keeps even the poorest perfectly happy."

On the way back to Quito, Ehlers filled us in on President Velasco and his legend. An old joke against him goes: Who is the father of the United States and what is the American aspiration? Answer: George Washington; world peace. And the USSR? Lenin; to make men economically free. And Ecuador? Velasco; to be an orphan. But at least in his present fifth incarnation, Ehlers thinks, Velasco has been a good president. His salary is a modest six hundred dollars a month. No one questions his personal honesty and frugality—in exile he always supported himself by teaching and lecturing. He was the first to crack down on the sugar barons of Guayaquil—even jailing one—because they were refusing to pay his tax on what they were getting from the U.S. for their sugar quota. He had given the rebellious students what they asked for—easier examinations and no entrance requirements at all—even though there are no funds to pay for the resulting doubled enrollment. Ecuador was the "only country in South America" with complete freedom of press and assembly—"even in Colombia and Venezuela there is a 'state of siege' to enable police to cope with guerrillas." There were no "oligarchs" in the cabinet. In this year's Latin American edition of the World Almanac,

Velasco is listed as one of the three men of the year, the other two being Galo Plaza and Miguel Angel Asturias, the Guatemalan novelist who won the Nobel Prize for Literature. Ehlers' mention of Galo Plaza reminded him of two more points Velasco scored off the present OAS chief in the 1961 election: the fact that Galo Plaza had been born in Washington (his father had been Ecuador's ambassador to the U.S.), and that he had once referred to the supposed wealth of the Amazon jungles as a myth.

Ehlers calls Velasco a moderate Marxist. He thinks that the invitations just extended to Jean-Paul Sartre and Daniel Cohn-Bendit to join Bishop Camara of Recife as the principal speakers at this summer's student conference reflect Velasco's Sorbonne background rather than any special sympathy for communists.

I told him I was still trying to find out whether it was true that the Army junta had abolished the *huasipungo* system. He said yes, but that there had been an escape clause stating that any owner could substitute for the acreage being deeded to the Indian any plot of land of the same acreage, with the result that the Indians had only been driven higher into the Andes to rockier, less productive land.

"Here's the tip-off on the Army's good deeds for the Indian," he said: "An Army horse gets twenty-five cents a day for food. Do you know what the average daily income of a peasant is? Seven and a half cents."

Quito II

We were back in Quito by five o'clock, in time for an appointment I had with one of our economists at the Embassy. I was eager to get our side of Velasco, and especially of his present imbroglio with Texaco-Gulf and the 1.4 million-hectare concession the military junta had given them in 1964 to explore for oil across the Andes. The situation was this, he said: The old British oil fields on the coast west of Guayaquil are virtually exhausted, forcing Ecuador to import its crude oil from Venezuela. Texaco-Gulf has already tapped eleven new wells south of the Amazon tributary, the Putumayo, and these eleven have a greater potential yield than all the hundreds in the Anglo-Ecuadorean concession, but they've been capped, pending the construction of a pipeline. "Obviously if Velasco retracts nine hundred thousand of the hectares in their concession, as he now threatens, they're going to think twice about spending one hundred and fifty million dollars more on a pipeline. The Ecuadoreans err in comparing their situation to Venezuela's where the government takes seventy percent in taxes; the wells have been operating under American management for fifty years in Venezuela. Here, not a single drop has been taken out to repay the investors. But of course Velasco's demands make him very popular since it is naturally felt that the highest possible price must be obtained for Ecuador's oil. He's now dropped a hint that he may open the oil concession to international bidding."

The dance put on tonight by the Ecuadorean Folklore Troupe was so-so, but the costumes were sensational. Especially those worn by the *danzantes* from Sequisili, a village fifty miles south of Quito. They wear sets of placards or billboards, a big one covering the back, two or three in front, one on the head, sometimes another in each hand, each a different color and shape, with dolls, bells, mirrors, jewels, and sequins pinned to them—under the spotlights a dazzling fragmentation.

Guayaquil, the Damned

March 4, 1969: Airborne from Quito—the snow volcanoes are still lost in the clouds. But I've never seen anything to compare with the richness and beauty of the land over which we've been flying. The patterning of fields covering all but the steepest slopes with those emerald pile carpets is fantastic. Variation is provided by the ploughed fields with their lavender-brown loam, the planted ones with checkerboards of tender shoots. Then there are the herds of Holsteins in this corner or that; the clusters of white houses with orange tiled roofs; the walled gardens; and the hedgerows of poplars and *super rosa*, that unbelievable bush that bears pink and yellow flowers at the same time. Beyond Cotopaxi, the world's highest active volcano, whose lower slopes were visible, the terrain becomes too rugged for cultivation and the deep, proximate clefts are dense with virgin jungle, scored at the low points by silvery streams as with an etcher's pencil. For a hundred miles or more everything is jungle, jungle, jungle, with hardly a bright green farm chopped out of the darker viridian, when suddenly the coastal lowlands unfold, cultivated in long swathes of sugarcane or banana along the valley floors, the rivers widening and perceptibly darkening with silt, the plain becoming enveloped in the equatorial sea-level heat, as we glided down swiftly through a thick blanket of clouds, our ears protesting agonizingly, to the flooded rice paddies and cow pastures of the tidal estuary of the Guayas, settling at last (sight unseen) into Guayaquil.

And what a sight it is when you do see it!

Either in desperation, seeking tourist points of interest which don't exist, or by some prescient sixth sense that guided him to an accurate symbol as surely as an iron filing to a magnet, our taxi driver drove to a hilltop cemetery and suggested we feast our eyes on the view. Was he being sarcastic? There was no trace of it in his voice or eyes.

Avoiding the immediate foreground, Guayaquil lay at our feet in its crapulous gray pall, the festering mass of undifferentiated buildings stretching along the waterfront from the port-estuary to the rock quarry

on the horizon. Downtown is distinguished from the *suburbios* (Remember the *miserias*, the *favelas*, the *callampas*, the *barriadas*, the *ranchos*?) only by its taller buildings. The poorer you are in Guayaquil the further away from the port you are and the nearer to the rock quarry, till finally you are in El Salado. There, where the tide withdraws every six hours, the feet of your hovel, its stilts, emerge from the black water and you look down into that quagmire of oozing sewage which even the crabs and rats avoid.

"How many dead are here?" I asked our driver, pointing to the graves in the immediate foreground. He threw up his hands. "Two hundred enter every day, the day of their death," he said. "Only the rich in their mausoleums at the bottom can afford to be embalmed, and no one bothers to unless they made a flight to the United States for a medical checkup and happened to die there."

We drove down the hill and looked at the part of the graveyard in which the rich rest. I walked outside the gate and took a photograph through the iron picket fence of a marble businessman with an arrogant expression. Behind him was Christ in benediction; on either side, an avenue of marble mortuaries, like frozen-meat lockers, as far as the eye could see; and directly above, the hill of the poor with its thousands of decaying, weatherbeaten, cockeyed crosses. Who was better off? The living?

It was only with the greatest difficulty that we persuaded the driver to take us into the *suburbios*. "Well," he said finally, "O.K., seeing as how it's day—but at night, never!"

"Why not at night?" Bill asked him.

"Supposing I have a flat tire? That's the end of my car, for sure; and perhaps of me personally too."

I recalled our friend at the Embassy warning us yesterday to avoid Eighteenth Street. It seems an American recently had his wristwatch snapped off entering that notorious street, and as he lunged to retrieve it got a knife in the ribs. Long before the police found him, he'd bled to death. The police, in fact, avoid this whole area of three hundred and fifty thousand pariahs like the plague—the plague for which Guayaquil was famous in its palmier days. There are only eight hundred policemen for the whole city of eight hundred thousand, and the few assigned to El Salado are rarely seen in it even in their badly battered prowl cars. "No cop would ever enter on foot at night," our driver said. The present tenants, he added, have squatters' rights to their shacks, but the city is doing everything it can to discourage a further influx. There is no sewage system, of course, and no water supply. Water is sold in tin cans at five *sucres* a can.

As we penetrated deeper and deeper into the maze of squalid streets, we saw a man selling water, and more luridly colored drinks, on a corner of the famous street of the whores, under a sign HIGIENE Y SABOR. An almost indecipherable second line translated NO CREDIT. The *putas*, even at eleven in the morning when we drove by their numbered booths, were seated in front in bright print dresses, or bikinis, or gaudy nightgowns; or walking back and forth provocatively in their war paint; or even in one instance, sprawled naked on the bed, the one piece of furniture, with legs drawn up.

"They won't let customers stay longer than ten minutes maximum," said our driver, who had professed a few minutes ago never to have been in El Salado. "Those little items," he said, pointing to a row of little black boxes on a corner stall, "wouldn't be any help here." "Aphrodisiac," the label said, "guaranteed to provide an all-day erection." We stopped and asked one of the black girls if she owned her stall. "We rent them," she said. "They make us pay twenty *sucres* [one dollar] a day, thirty on Saturdays, Sundays, and Saints' Days." We drove on, past piles of waste and garbage, to an improved area where the best houses are double-deckers of bamboo and every now and then there's a TV aerial—the sets bought on the installment plan at twelve percent interest —and unmatched teams of bony burros carry loads of cooking charcoal from shack to shack. Small pieces of almost black, stringy meat were hanging in unshaded butchers' stalls in the one-hundred-degree heat.

In less than five minutes we were driving through the richest part of Guayaquil, where every house is surrounded by a bottle-spiked wall and most of them have swimming pools. "The thing about this country," said our driver apologetically, "is that you have to know people. You get nowhere without connections. And the connections are no good unless they lead to Quito." He was making a desperate effort to show us one of his city's "good things," a "tourist attraction" as he put it. There was a fort, being restored out of "antiqued stone," and a street leading nowhere named after the man who wrote the words to the national anthem, Calle Numa Pompilio Llona, its houses badly cracked by the earthquake of May 13, 1942; it actually leads to Ecuador's biggest beer factory. We asked him to show us the building where San Martín and Bolívar held their famous meeting. He took us to a colonnade on the waterfront enclosing two heroic bronzes of English make. We insisted that it was the *building* we wanted to see. He drove back into town and pointed to a huge baroque structure with a sign LA PREVISORA BANCO NACIONAL DE CREDITO. Under one of the arcades was a modest marker: "On this site July 26, 1822, the Generals San Martín and Bolívar met." The original building, like every other of colonial vintage, was destroyed in a fire that leveled the city in 1896.

Farewell to Guayaquil

We had two interesting talks late in the afternoon, one with a USIS man, Donald Besom, the other with an ex-USIS man disillusioned with American policy, Vic Canby.

Besom thinks that the military and the Guayaquil sugar barons, if they get together, have more than enough strength to topple Velasco. The masses of the poor who elected Velasco couldn't do anything about it because they have no cohesion, no arms, and no money.

I asked him what was being done about the *suburbios*, if anything. He said that the thirty-five Peace Corps volunteers assigned to Guayaquil tried organizing the slum dwellers, or at least giving them some spirit to make demands in their own behalf. They were promptly removed, for causing political problems, and shifted to the rice and coffee co-ops that AID is trying to develop out of town.

"Do the slum dwellers work in the fields?" I asked Besom.

"No," he replied. "The sugar barons bring the pig-tailed peasants down from the Andes to harvest their crops, because the Indians are willing to work for less than the urban poor. Then they bus them back to the Andes. These city folk are not revolution-minded because, believe it or not, their move to the *suburbios* was a step up from the coastal *campo!*"

From our window at the Humboldt Hotel where Canby came to have a drink with us, there is a view of the river that is hypnotic and perhaps symbolic. Flotsam floats by downstream for six hours, then upstream for six. In the foreground a foundered windjammer and a rusty destroyer are stuck in the mud. In the background endless green fields, apparently uninhabited, stretch as far as the eye can see. The hotel is designed, of course, not to give a view of the endless *suburbios* in the other direction.

I asked Canby, who headed the Bi-National Center in Cuenca for several years, what he would do about the *suburbios* if he were president. He threw up his hands.

"I'd try to face up to the three basic problems first," he said finally, "without which nothing can be accomplished. Take bananas. Ecuador has lost its huge American market because it failed to shift over to the improved Cavendish variety. Central America took over. The Iron Curtain countries will buy the inferior Gros Michel brand, but at lower prices. Ecuador can't make up its mind which market to shoot for.

"Or take oil. You've seen in today's paper that Velasco is washing his hands of the crisis he's created by turning it over to the Senate. This is his usually successful way of getting off the hook. He'll reenter the picture when they've exhausted themselves, reshuffle his cabinet, and be off again. Texaco—which would have been producing oil by 1972, thereby giving the government fifty million extra dollars a year with which to deal with the *suburbios*—will probably not pull out, yet. The Russians? They could try, but they'd lose a hell of a lot of money, and besides their entry into Ecuador on such a scale would create political problems. So—stalling, no decision.

"Or take education. There are no textbooks for the primary schools—none at all. The University of New Mexico gave scholarships, under a contract between the Ecuadorean government and AID, to young Ecuadoreans to be trained in the United States. They returned and wrote the needed textbooks—without guidelines from us. But now the appropriation to print and distribute these desperately needed books has been blocked in the higher circles of the Ministry of Education, or in the cabinet, where every minister must sign the bill, by a campaign of passive resistance subtly organized by the Left—"Who? Me?" they say, "I've never even heard about signing it! As a matter of fact my telephone has been out of order for a week . . ."—and the President himself is probably quite unaware of this! Especially in the field of education, the power of the Left is out of all proportion to their actual numbers and is bound to influence the next generation profoundly.

"So to answer your question, I'd first settle the oil business, one way or another. Then I'd push through the teacher-training and textbook programs to insure some proper education for the years ahead. And with the fifty million additional annual revenue from oil I'd tackle the *suburbios*, beginning with potable water and sewage systems, and then moving on to vocational training and jobs in a diversified agriculture. This would have an additional advantage; it would reverse the age-old malaise of Ecuador—highland Quito's political stranglehold on lowland Guayaquil, where the real economic power is. The point was reinforced by the energetic, able Mayor of this city, Assad Bucaram, a Fiorello La Guardia–type who is honest and vocally concerned about the *suburbios*, but blocked for funds by Quito."

"Sounds exactly like Mayor Lindsay in New York," I said. "And what's our role?"

"I can only speak from my experience in Cuenca," he replied. "All our energy—at least all USIS's energy—seems to go into telling Ecuadoreans about the success of Apollo 9. We aren't pushing hard for anything that concerns them. We back off. We refuse to take risks. I'm not saying that we should make a big noise about what we are doing, but that we should establish closer human ties with the Ecuadorean family—where things are actually accomplished in this country. Here's a case in point: Suppose you want to interview the President. I had a friend from the States who wanted to. He got nowhere through the Embassy or the Ecuadorean government. Then I put him in touch with a woman who is a friend of the President's wife. The next day Velasco gave him two hours of his time.

"The Bi-National Center," he concluded, "wastes its time teaching English. We teach English to those who want to get out of Ecuador! Instead we should be building a community center and library in the *suburbios* with night classes in primary literacy, adult education, vocational training, cultural exchanges, etc. Forget the middle class and go after the poor! Recognize the fact that Guayaquil is one vast slum. This is the only practical way to arrest the drift to communism in Ecuador, to identify with the future revolutionaries before they become storm troopers of the extreme Left or Right."

March 5, 1969: An American businessman who travels widely through-out South America chatted with us at the airport as we waited for the early morning flight to Quito. He thinks Texaco-Gulf is paying the piper for the sins of Standard Oil in Peru. "IPC acted with complete arrogance there just like United Fruit did the generation before here—doing only what was minimally required in labor relations and paying taxes."

Our driver had some last words, too. He had heard Mayor Bucaram's talk on TV last night and pronounced it pure demagoguery.

"How so?" we asked him.

"Because he denounces the rich and makes demands for the poor."

"Is that unfair? Do the rich do anything for the poor here?"

"No. That's the trouble. They're not like your rich. They don't give money to foundations or charities."

"What do they do with it?"

"They put it in Swiss banks or invest it."

"In Ecuador?"

"No. Abroad."

"And it's demagoguery to criticize them for that?"

"Half of what he says is true, perhaps—"

"And the false half—?"

He hemmed and hawed and then when I'd repeated the question several times he said:

"They say he's lying about his birth. That he wasn't born in Ambató at all, but in Lebanon."

"Is that bad, to be born abroad? Galo Plaza—"

"Ah, but Galo Plaza's parents were Ecuadorean."

"So Bucaram has no birth certificate to prove he was born here—?"

"I suppose he has. But what would that prove? You can buy any kind of a document in Ecuador. A forged birth certificate wouldn't cost five *sucres*."

Quito III

Paradox—the airport in Quito is the cleanest and most efficient we've seen in South America. Its public toilets put ours to shame. Its cold milk is bottled, pasteurized, and dated. Its information girls knock themselves out to be helpful. But while one of them was making a complicated series of phone calls for us, we stepped outside to see whether the car the Tourist Ministry had promised an hour ago had come. A team of Indian women where shovelling rock and cement. One had a *guagua* on her back. We asked the foreman what the women were doing and why they were doing it in such a hurry. They were building a sidewalk, and are contracted for as a family for eighty cents a day. They're working like mad, he told us, because they're paid for the whole job, and have to finish quickly to be ready for another.

The information girl now told us that there'd be no car. "*Turismo* got three hundred unexpected visitors on an earlier flight, and is jamming them into your hotel."

"What shall we do if our room is gone?" Bill mused.

"Force our way in, of course," I said jokingly.

"Forced entry? Hoteloptomy?"

Guayasamín and his wife took us to lunch at a typical Quito restaurant: cheese-stuffed potato pancakes of the consistency of celluloid, chunks of rock-hard kidneys in piquant sauce, semifermented corn *chicha.* But our hosts couldn't have been more charming. Far from conforming to the art critic's image of a money-mad publicity hound, I found the artist soft-spoken and humble about his own work. He was also genuinely enthusiastic about Bill's. "Now I know how people suffer when I'm doing their portraits," he sighed, as Bill maneuvered him into the light to get a drawing for our book.

Two other things, perhaps, prejudiced me in Guayasamín's favor: the fact that Orozco was his hero among modern artists; and the fact that he'd been badly treated by our Embassy. He had worked with the great Mexican muralist, assisting him with the frescoes in the Templo de Jesús Nazareno in the forties, and then returning to paint his first mural in the Casa de la Cultura here. We'd seen this mural earlier in the morning and found it much stronger and simpler than the "Guernica"-inspired one we'd seen the day we arrived. Guayasamín, nevertheless, described it as "derivative in every sense, not only of Orozco but of Rivera as well."

Apparently an edict had been issued by our present Ambassador's predecessor, requesting members of the Embassy staff, Point 4, AID, etc., to avoid Guayasamín's studio and person. Only the Ambassador's wife, it seems, rebelled against this order—so typical of our genius for alienating foreign artists and intellectuals; she had put on dark glasses and slipped in with a group of visiting tourists. Whether Guayasamín is or isn't a card-carrying communist—he denied that he was, though not concealing his sympathy for the Moscow line—it's as idiotic to refuse him a visa as to ask Carlos Fuentes to sign a loyalty pledge that no self-respecting artist would sign.

Was Guayasamín being a good actor, showing no emotion or resentment when discussing Marta Traba's assault on him? It all started in Bogotá ten years ago during an exhibition of his paintings, he said. He had publicly taken issue with her championship of abstraction to the exclusion of other modes. He had thought no more about it. In fact, he said, he had been the one who had invited her to come and speak at Ambató. He had chosen to hold the retrospective there, he added, because this was the poorest branch of the Casa de la Cultura and they needed the money. By the same token he had made the posters at his own expense, and signed as many catalogs as possible to raise additional funds. "Each of the speakers and judges was presented with one of my necklaces."

"Why did she reject hers?" I asked.

"I should have known better," he answered, shaking his head glumly. "That's the way she operates. All over the continent she creates personal crises to advertise her independence and incorruptibility. I've never doubted that Marta is independent and incorruptible, but somehow this insistence upon her virtue becomes an end in itself. It's a way of advertising her particular aesthetic which I frankly find reactionary. She wants painting to be up to date, pure, uninvolved in politics or even in human misery. I want mine to be based on a humane tradition, impure, involved in politics and human misery. I fight with my paintings. She fights with her invective. It's hardly surprising that when our paths cross, the sparks fly."

Since I was flying back to Chile in the morning and Bill to the blizzards of New York, we decided to have another set or two of tennis in the late afternoon. Our friends, the Pughs, couldn't make it but suggested we play on the Ambassador's court anyway. We walked across the square with our racquets, wearing long pants over our shorts, and just as we arrived at the gate the Ambassador and his wife drove in. Sitting stiff as ramrods in the back of their air-conditioned limousine, they gave us a disdainful sidewise glance. The gatekeeper picked up the phone and then shook his head regretfully. "The Ambassador says you may not play."

"We're now full-fledged members of the not-so-exclusive club," I said, as we walked away laughing, "along with Guayasamín, Jorge Icaza, Fuentes, Siqueiros, and the rest. But imagine what the repercussions would be if we turned out to be brothers of the new Secretary of State!"

"The Ambassador would be out in twenty-four hours—with his escutcheons flung after him . . . and reassigned as Second Secretary of the Maldive Islands Consulate," added Bill, completing our fantasy.

But it turned out to be a fortunate snub because in half an hour we were in sole possession of the eight magnificent red clay courts of the Ecuador Tennis and Golf Club, which refused to let two gringos even pay for the privilege, and in dazzling view (at long last!) of all eight of those snowcapped volcanoes, glowing with an unearthly orange-lavender light in the last rays of the setting sun.

Bill Pugh drove us to the airport. We had a parting cup of coffee (a lottery ticket attached to the fifteen percent tax), and he showed us a cabled copy of an editorial that had just appeared in *The New York*

Times expressing indignation over our latest diplomatic gaffe. Carlos Fuentes, it seems, had passed through Puerto Rico on his way back to Mexico from Caracas, and in the San Juan airport our customs official had torn up his transit card, refusing to let him step on Puerto Rican soil even for an hour. This must have infuriated Puerto Ricans as much as Fuentes—the prize of the Spanish American War and our principal reservoir of cheap labor being told that a leading novelist in their language (and an anti-Moscow one at that) was too hot for them to handle.

I asked Pugh why he thought the Alliance for Progress had failed, and I liked his answer: "Because basically it's an attempt to get land reform, social benefits, and a meaningful tax structure accepted in Latin America, and most if not all of the governments we're asking to do these things are made up of those elements of society who would have to give up something. So they find lots of ways of not complying—attacking us, seizing our investments in their countries, denouncing us for humiliating their intellectuals, and so on. How can we argue them into adopting an income tax without loopholes, when it's constantly being revealed that some of our biggest millionaires find ways of paying little or no tax themselves?"

I looked for the volcanoes as I flew south, but they'd disappeared again. I didn't care. I'd seen them. The memory would last a lifetime. Surely a country with its head always reaching above the clouds couldn't be held down in the mud forever.

10

PABLO NERUDA'S CHILE

Chile may not have Ecuador's churches, Peru's ruins, Brazil's beaches, or Bolivia's jungles to lay before the jaded foreign traveler, but it is a land of great beauty notwithstanding; and it has one great advantage over all the other South American lands: It has a poet who sings of its contrasting enchantments in accents so majesterial that all Spanish-speaking lands (and little by little the rest of the world) have begun to take notice.

Were Pablo Neruda appealing mainly to students, intellectuals, and politicians throughout South America, who habitually read poems or dabble in poetry, this would be extraordinary enough. The barriers of nationalism separating, say, even such close neighbors as Colombia and Venezuela have always been sufficiently formidable to insure indifference. Few if any Argentinians have the foggiest notion what Ecuador is about, because few if any care; and the same is true of Ecuador's indifference to Argentina—and of the almost complete ignorance of every other South American country to be found in any given nation of the continent. One is tempted to say, in fact, that these nations have only three things in common: a nostalgia for Iberia, a distrust of the United States government, and the poetry of Pablo Neruda.

The fact that Neruda has been an active member of the communist party through most of his mature life has nothing to do with the popularity of his poetry. Those who think the Soviet Union is a paradise may like the poetry better on that account; but those who don't, shrug

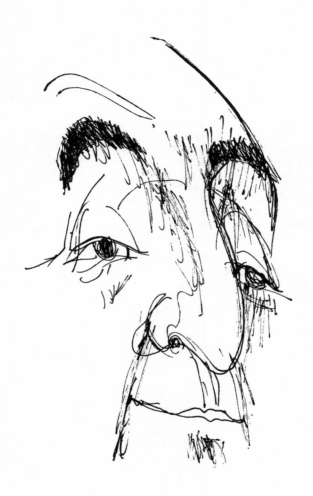

their shoulders, ignore the five percent of overtly political poems, and
happily go on devouring the rest of Neruda's stupendous *oeuvre*. One of
the most popular of his books has always been *Veinte Poemas de Amor y
una Canción Desesperada* (*Twenty Love Poems and a Desperate Song*),
written when Neruda had no political convictions of any kind; but no one
would contend that this is his best book, or even that the startlingly
original surrealist poems of *Residencia en la Tierra* (*Residence on Earth*),
that also preceded his political conversion, are the whole Neruda; or
even that his politics have not contributed substantially to the zeal with
which he identifies himself with the common man.

But what makes Pablo Neruda's poetry uniquely universal in the world
today is neither the youthful ardor, nor the surrealism, nor the Marxist
philosophy, important though these have been in shaping it. Rather it is
Neruda's capacity to project his own personality, unflaggingly over the
years, as a particular person who feels, sees, eats, drinks, suffers, enjoys,
loves, dreams, laughs, dawdles, gossips—one who invites his soul as his
idol Walt Whitman put it and rarely lacks the magic (as Walt often did)
to make his most inconsequential thought seem important. As, for instance, in the opening of the "Ode to the Socks":

> *Maru Mori brought me*
> *a pair of socks, knitted*
> *with her hands*
> *of a shepherdess,*
> *socks soft as hares.*
> *My feet slipped in*
> *as in two jewel boxes*
> *woven out of twilight*
> *on the skin of a sheep.*
> *Violent socks: my feet became*
> *two long sharks*
> *of ultramarine blue*
> *flecked with gold, two gigantic*
> *lovebirds, two cannon.*
> *My feet became so honored*
> *by those celestial socks*
> *that they seemed unacceptable:*
> *two decrepit firemen*
> *unworthy of the fire*
> *of incandescent socks . . .*

But there was another reason why Neruda hardly ever succumbed to
abstraction or mere windiness: he constantly renewed his inspiration by
identifying himself with a particular place in a particular time—Chile.

There is nothing quaintly regionalist about Neruda's love affair with
Chile. Nor is he possessive about it, as Gabriela Mistral often was, identi-

fying Chile with her sexual frustrations. Were that so, Neruda's poetry would appeal mainly to Chileans. On the contrary he has always conducted his affair on such a plane that every reader tends to see his own country in the poet's intimate concern—sometimes brotherly, sometimes indulgent, sometimes chiding, sometimes even despairing. Moreover, Neruda ranges over the whole of Latin America in his search for meaningful referents to what is common (and universal) in the Iberian experience; and sometimes even to Europe, North America, and the Orient, being at pains to point out that he is no flag-waver:

> They have talked to me of Venezuelas,
> of Paraguays and Chiles.
> I don't know what it is they say.
> I only know the skin of earth
> and that it has no name.

But it is to Chile, nevertheless, that Pablo Neruda always returns, to his roots and for his substance:

> . . . In this time of the swollen grape,
> the wine begins to come to life
> between the sea and the mountain ranges.
> In Chile now, cherries are dancing,
> the dark mysterious girls are singing,
> and in guitars, water is shining.
> The sun is touching every door
> and making wonder of the wheat . . .
> My house has both the sea and the earth;
> my woman has great eyes
> the color of wild hazelnut;
> when night comes down, the sea
> puts on a dress of white and green,
> and later the moon in the spindrift foam
> dreams like a sea-green girl.
> I have no wish to change my planet.[1]

Santiago

Neruda was a little apologetic about the capital in 1966, when I visited it for the first time, in his company. He told me that I was not seeing Chile, and that even among Chilean cities Santiago could not hold a candle to Valparaiso, either in architecture or downright character. He

---

[1] Conclusion to the poem "Lazybones," translated by Alastair Reid. All poems throughout this book are my own translation, unless otherwise noted.

knew that I was then living in Lima, and he explained to me why Santiago had none of the rich colonial monuments of the Peruvian capital: it had not been the seat of the Viceroyalty, its importance under Spain had been more mercantile than ecclesiastical, and finally most of what little colonial architecture Santiago could boast had been leveled by earthquakes. We drove past the Senate ("Where I spent the two dullest years of my life," the onetime communist senator remarked); past La Moneda, the French-style presidential palace flanked by parks with impressive statues of Diego Portales and Arturo Alessandri, Chile's great statesmen; and to the house where the poet then lived, halfway up Cerro de San Cristóbal, one of the two wooded buttes that poke up out of the plain in which the metropolis sprawls. Magnificent views of the city and the nearby Andes are afforded on clear days from both of these rocky extrusions.

I was impressed then, and I was more impressed two years later when I got to know Santiago well, by two things about the Chilean capital. It has a visual character of its own, black and a little grimy perhaps, but exuding solidity and power. Residents of Brussels or Madrid might not be awed by this concentration of squat columnar facades, frowning arcades, minatory cornices, and dignified politicians in bronze—but in South America it is unique. Furthermore there is an element of intriguing mystery in the way Santiago's dozens of squares were put together eclectically in the century of Chile's imperial growth to give it a Victorian bearing consonant with its almost forgotten Spanish past. In the Plaza de Armas, for instance, they criticize the equestrian bronze of Pedro de Valdivia for lacking reins; one explanation is that the conquistador's hands are too full of documents—documents establishing his tenuous legal claim to Chile—to hold them. And in the same square with this oddly Pickwickian burgher is a curious marble goddess, raising a feathered Indian to his feet, and surrounded by reliefs of battle scenes clearly depicting Napoleonic triumphs. Found in a cellar circa 1850, no one could remember where it came from, who ordered it, or what it was intended to memorialize.

The city's outskirts are surrounded with similar period pieces, and a description of one may serve to convey their peculiar charms.

Viña Concho y Toro, Chile's largest winery with twenty-four hundred acres of grapes surrounding its huge vats and subterranean storage chambers, is a half-hour's drive from the city. It belongs to a family of French origin that has long been a pillar of the oligarchy. The manor house next to the winery, although built in Victorian times like most substantial structures in Chile except office skyscrapers and factories, is neo-Colonial (the oligarchs looked back mystically to pre-Independence times as a Golden Age). Its pediments and colonnades are of wood smothered in bougainvillea. Greek nymphs leap from the shrubbery. And there are marble busts of Roman emperors on the spacious veranda that girdles the house. But the curious thing about this lordly villa is that it is kept under lock and key by the family which owns but never uses it—and that no effort is made to keep it up. The rose gardens are choked with weeds. The lawns are uncut. No one feeds the two surviving black swans on the hidden lake. The house hasn't been painted in decades. The stuffing is coming out of the chaise lounges and ottomans. The velvet drapes are in tatters. The Sargentesque family portraits of fin-de-siècle beauties in satin evening gowns are cracking in their sumptuous frames. A folio edition of La Fontaine's *Fables* (which I unhinged furtively, for this visit under guard had been preceded by weeks of protocol) contained a backgammon set. I might have assumed from this symbol that the family had succumbed to hedonistic sloth, but a glimpse of the library itself suggested that this family, along with the rest of the oligarchs (in eclipse lately), had been politically misguided in the thirties. Among the French classics and the hundreds of bound volumes on theology and wine culture, I could find only one title of contemporary vintage, Hitler's *Mein Kampf.*

Northern Chile

Northern Chile, as everyone knows, is a desert, part of the same coastal desert that runs the whole length of Peru. Neruda has described it often:

> . . . *the nitrous plain,*
> *the wastes, the stains of alkali,*
> *desert without a leaf,*
> *without a scarab, a chip, without a shadow,*
> *without time . . .*

Some think that this desert will one day creep all the way to southernmost Chile—a gloomy view reinforced by the drought that has desiccated the Santiago area for the past two years. But deserts can be beautiful, and the Atacama Desert of northern Chile is filled with awesome landscapes, surprising oases, and tenacious ports.

My favorite among the latter is Iquique, architecturally a close rival to Valparaiso as the most interesting Chilean city. It was built at the time of the War of the Pacific (1879-83) and it was the Peruvians who had put up, before their defeat, most of the spindly-columned wooden buildings that are painted in such subtle pinks and blues. Iquique has a classically styled opera house and a neo-Gothic clock tower, relics of the nitrate boom that touched off the war between Chile and her northern neighbors; and the city is precious to Chilean nationalists (what Chilean is not a nationalist?) for the exploit of Arturo Prat who gave his life leaping aboard a Peruvian ironclad in the harbor.

But Neruda seems more drawn to Tocapilla, the cliffhanging nitrate port to the south with its

> . . . *sand billowing north and south,*
> *fallen limestone, barges, broken planks*
> *and twisted iron,*
> *which, to the planet's pure line, golden and baked*
> *out of dreams, salt, and gunpowder, adds*
> *the rusted tool, the silt of nothingness . . .*

and Antofagasta—Bolivia's lost avenue to the ocean, through which Chilean copper now flows, with reluctantly tolerated American know-how.

This great desert city by the sea was no more than a boomtown village ninety years ago when the Chilean nitrate prospectors pushed the Bolivians out. There were no roads and the nitrate had to travel overland by mule and afoot across these burning flats where it hasn't rained for a thousand years. (There is a shower at Antofagasta itself every seven years, they say, "except when it forgets.") I drove inland to visit Anaconda's open pit copper mine at Chuquicamata, and the oasis of San Pedro de Atacama beyond, stopping along the way to inspect the ghost towns of the nitrate days in this driest region on earth. When you step on the spongy white sand, you leave a footprint that will be there "forever" if untouched. And yet the mining engineer who drove me had seen a map of 1879 that showed water holes (long since covered and forgotten) that had enabled the Chilean Army to survive that year and win this nitrate bonanza that turned unexpectedly into a copper one. The spoon-shaped pit with its contoured shelves that make it look like an abandoned Roman amphitheater employs close to thirty thousand Chileans, but at diminishing wages as the machines take over and prices on the world market drop—an enterprise the American imperialists will be lucky to get out of solvently if their phase-out agreement with the moderate Chilean President, Eduardo Frei Montalva, isn't repudiated by radical successors.

> . . . blind moon, by mourning corridors of copper
> with nothing but the nights and days of man,
> but close to the thirst of the thistle: there
> where a sunken scrap of paper, abandoned stone,
> marks the deep cradles of the spade and cup:
> the sleeping feet of calcium . . .

An enterprising foreigner "runs" the oasis of San Pedro de Atacama too, but with no hard feelings since what he takes from the surrounding sands he places in a local museum he has built himself. This is Padre Le Page, a Belgian Jesuit-archaeologist who has resurrected the pre-Columbian desert dwellers from their shallow graves, placing them with their perfectly preserved textiles and surgical instruments in display cases ingeniously arranged like the spokes of a wheel. By desalinating the sand, and planting trees whose leaves drink the moisture in the air, this lovely garden spot in the desert is being constantly enlarged.

A Poet in Arica

I had an encounter with a young poet in Arica, Chile's northernmost city, that illuminates the younger generation's ambivalent feelings toward Neruda, and its idolization of Nicanor Parra, Neruda's friendly rival for the Chilean laurel sprig. Neruda had taken me to lunch the week before with Gabriel Valdez, Chile's Foreign Minister, and during the meal one of the guests had brought out a copy of a new book, *Manos Arriba!* and prevailed on Neruda to read some of it aloud. I was intrigued by the lines

> *I am tired of thinking*
> *that Neruda is a genius*
> *(when I consider a genius*
> *anyone capable*
> *of telling me anything) . . .*

I ferreted out Nana Gutiérrez, who wrote them, by following a clerk of the Gutiérrez hardware store through a maze of streets to the studio, papered with art show posters, in which Nana takes refuge from her bourgeois family. She is wraithlike, with shingled hair, and a wit so compulsively eccentric I suspected it disguised a basically conventional woman. Her thing is to be against the expected, and to generalize grandly:

"I love flowers and hate babies. I love Peruvians but hate Bolivians. . . "

"You wouldn't give them back Antofagasta?" I baited her.

"Of course not! Why don't you give them California?"

"The Mexicans might not like that," I said, with a smile.

"Mexicans—? Ah, but I'm not a political person. Of course I know enough to know that Lyndon Johnson is a monster . . ."

"So the intellectuals tell me," I chided her, but she wasn't listening.

"Shall I tell you how I started writing poems? I didn't have any program like Neruda. I just got tired of writing horizontally—my prose stories—and began to write vertically. Parra gave me my title."

Parra, the physicist whose *Poems and Antipoems* is the cool manifesto of the younger generation (Parra himself has abandoned this position, I was soon to find out), is Nana Gutiérrez' favorite poet, along with Vallejo, Cortázar, García Márquez, Marco Denevi, and Carlos Germán Belli—the last two young writers of Argentina and Peru respectively. We were sitting in the cafeteria milk bar, El Pinguino, where Nana writes her poems and meets her friends, sipping mango milk shakes and discussing another of her heroes, Ché Guevara. Eugenia Concha, a painter who is a friend of Nana's came over to speak to us but couldn't show us any of her pictures. "They're all in Moscow," she explained. When she left, I asked Nana whether her style was figurative or abstract.

"Neither," Nana said. "They're only Eugenia. Just as my poems are pure Nana. I am an anti-person," she added, "because I am an anti-poet. What does that mean? It means that they are Nana-poems—all me. But I am very anti-Nana, too!"

When I told her that Neruda had read her poems aloud at the Foreign

Minister's luncheon, her defiance melted, she gave herself a little pat on the back, and looked up to the ceiling in ecstasy. She wouldn't let me leave two *escudo* notes (ten cents) on the table for a tip, stuffing one of them back in my pocket firmly—one mustn't spoil the *inquilinos domesticos* by overtipping.

We stood on the sidewalk outside looking for a taxi. Bolivian *cholo* women in their derbies were carrying on a brisk trade. One step ahead of the police, they come down the artificially-watered valley of olive trees called Azapa after crossing the fifteen-hundred-foot mountains. A fifth of Arica's eighty thousand population is estimated to be Bolivians without papers. Though the Chileans complain that they are undependable and surly, there is a great demand for them as domestics. They can be had for two hundred *escudos* (twenty dollars) a month, tax-free, whereas a Chilean servant gets seven hundred and fifty *escudos* plus three hundred and fifteen for social security.

We took a taxi to the top of the high bluff with its fort that the Chileans took by storm in 1879 and from which the Peruvian hero, Alfonso Ugarte, made his fabled leap on horseback rather than surrender. Then I took a second look at the little iron church Eiffel designed in Paris in 1870 and sent to the Peruvians prefabricated; it is almost dwarfed by the twelve-foot banana trees that flank it, and the interior is visibly rusting, even in the diffused red and blue light of the cheap stained glass.

But there was never a dull moment with Nana. As we were leaving an uninteresting exhibit of local painting at the University, she looked around furtively, snatched the poster advertising the show from the bulletin board, and stuffed it in her shopping bag. "For my poster collection," she explained in a whisper, giving herself another of those little pats on the back.

Valparaiso

> *Valparaiso, what a blunder!*
> *How mad you are, mad port*
> *with your uncombed hills,*
> *combing yourself but never finishing it,*
> *dressing yourself, surprised*
> *by life, wakened*
> *by death, wearing*
> *long underwear*
> *with rags of color;*
> *naked*
> *with a name*
> *tattooed on your belly . . .*

Plaza Bilbao, Valparaíso, Chile

Driving to it the morning of the last day of the year with Neruda and his wife Matilde—they commute back and forth between their home in Isla Negra and an apartment perched on top of a movie house above the city—the car broke down. We were within walking distance of a gigantic tree root, like a sectioned airplane engine, that the poet had tried in vain to get hauled to his home. He collects things like that: driftwood, an out-size shoe, an ancient steam engine, bottles, bells. I photographed him standing covetously beside the root. "I love to pose like Mussolini," he chuckled.

"How about that chain over there?" I said, pointing to some huge links across the road, fastened to a post. He walked over and hammed at pulling the chain loose. But when the car was fixed and we moved on he found a better place: an itinerant photographer's vividly painted backdrop, with a wooden horse to which he lifted his wife, holding the bridle for her as I snapped again. The photographer recognized him, and so did a passing *carabiniero*. Soon everybody was posing, and collecting autographs. But in the street outside his apartment where I took one more shot, Neruda wasn't posing, but doing what comes naturally to him, talking to people—in this case a little girl dressed in white for her first communion who had no idea who he was but was flattered to be addressed by such a democratic *don*.

The house, Neruda told me, was built by a mad, bird-loving bricklayer of execrable taste. But Valparaiso is like that: if you put so many bad tastes together you get, somehow, good taste—or at least something highly flavorful. I already knew how Neruda had found it:

> To Valparaiso the workers of the sea
> invited me: hard and small they were
> with sun-baked faces out of
> Pacific geography:
> a current within huge waters,
> muscular waves,
> wings of the sea in torment . . .

The whole city is built around a horseshoe harbor with an eighty-degree slope—shack piled on shack, buttressed, warped, cramped, and crippled to fit the ornery terrain. There is only one level street and that one doesn't go far. There are alleys of stone steps, ladders, cable cars, even an elevator one gets to by groping through a quarter-mile tunnel in the dripping, solid rock. In the gorges too steep to build on, roses and yellowbells dispute the slope with wind-blown paper and excrement. "Garlic and sapphires in the mud . . ."

The city is an architectural wonder of spontaneous growth, disturbing proof that poverty best generates poetry; and of course they talk of tearing it down. "It's too ugly, too filthy . . . it's a firetrap . . . the cable cars and *ascensores* lose money . . . it distracts from the tourist's delight in nearby Viña del Mar. . . . But then, progress, for some reason, is always identified by non-poets with sterility, beauty with uniformity and clean-

liness. Valparaiso, *rosa inmunda* (filthy rose) as Neruda called it once, survives only thanks to the inertia of those who would improve it. Its builders, without knowing it, are primitive artists, profoundly sensitive to form and color in a folk tradition that is self-perpetuating. Necessity is the mother of invention here, necessity and joie de vivre; these artists don't invent to exalt their egos or shock their contemporaries. So almost every part of the city is visually surprising—a Bavarian onion dome, a triangular baroque office building, a Wild West saloon, a Tudor castle, an Italianate fountain, a Moslem minaret—all combined perfectly in one style (or no style, if you prefer).

Neruda in his Olympian glacis atop all this reflects something of the ambivalance. At the New Year's Eve party, I couldn't find him among the elegantly attired guests and tables groaning with king crab, lobster claws, turkey, and vitage wines. Finally the bartender, in his silk topper and shirt-sleeves, said "Sel-den," and it was Pablo shaking Pisco sours and holding forth with animation to his enthralled (and perhaps not overly bright) guests.

"Now," he said, squeezing out from behind the bar, "it is time to put more champagne in the punch."

"Champagne—?" I said in the tone of a mock accuser.

"—is the cheapest Chilean wine," he responded without batting an eye, ambling through the crowd to a small table by the picture window on which reposed a porcelain cow with a fitted lid in its back. There was about an inch of fruit punch in the bottom of this unwieldy receptacle, and when he added a bottle of champagne, about three inches. "Come, let me help you," he said, but though I held out my cup hopefully for the ladle which he was sloshing around, he had turned to other guests with quips that delighted them, and five minutes later I served myself.

Behind Neruda, the spectacular scene revealed itself: Valparaiso at night, glimmering with fairy lights and firecrackers, a house or two burning in the distance, and in the great arc of harbor the training ship *Esmeralda* and several Chilean destroyers lighted from bowsprit to mast with loops of electric bulbs, their foghorns booming, while streams of multicolored rockets turned the full moon dead center into a pale period.

"Pablo has always been like that," said one of the guests with whom I prowled the waterfront after leaving the party about 3 A.M. "He has made the world revolve around him. That is one of the secrets of his success, his health, his longevity, his undiminished creativity. You notice he wouldn't commit himself about tomorrow or the day after? It has to happen at his rhythm. When it's siesta time he retires from the rest of the world totally—wherever he is. You've noticed that Matilde is the policeman. When he gives the word to her, the traffic in the world outside is permitted to move again, and intrude—just a little. He didn't like it at all in New York when the poets didn't come to him, as they do here;

that wasn't Pablo's style. And his poetry unfolds at the same pace as his life: deliberate, fecund, jovial, all-embracing, with Pablo at the center of it pointing out the places and things to be savored, the philosophical implications to be drawn."

Sentimental Journey: Parrál and Temuco

> *The first thing I saw were trees, and barrancas*
> *ornamented with flowers . . . Jungles dripping,*
> *forests on fire, winter encroaching . . .*

It would be remarkable if Neruda were referring to the town of Parrál where he was born, for he left there about the age of one. I spent the

Oné

Birgida
Reyes
Parral

better part of a day in Parrál looking for the house. Everybody knew about Neruda but nobody knew the house. Finally it was suggested that I call on his aunt. We drove past the dusty, chestnut-shaded square to her house and knocked on the door.

"Excuse me, but could you tell me where Pablo Neruda's birthplace is? I am writing . . ."

I was talking to a little old lady of seventy-five or so quite elegantly dressed in a wool skirt, a white ruffled blouse with a diamond brooch at the throat. Her face, with the same hooked nose and sleepy eyes as Pablo's, lit up:

"I am a communist, too! So I will be happy to help you write about my nephew."

"I'm writing about his poems, not his politics," I explained. "You know his poems—?"

"I read one once, many years ago. . . . But I can take you to where he was born. You know he was here last month," Brigida Reyes confided as we drove to the site, "making election speeches for the party. . . . No, I am not a member myself, but I have always been a militant."

We knocked on the gate at Calle San Diego 765, just off Calle Urrutia. A large family of very poor people were living in an adobe bungalow along one side of the empty lot.

"That is where my nephew was born," said Señorita Reyes, pointing to an empty space at one corner. "Pablo's mother died when he was two months old, of a pulmonary disease. Soon after, my brother took the eight children to Temuco. This house collapsed in an earthquake later on . . ."

Parrál is the name
for
what winter brought forth.
The house and the street
no longer stand.
The mountain untethered
its horses,
power
massed
in the depths,
the ranges
kicked upward
and a village fell
gutted by earthquake.
The mud walls, the portraits nailed to the walls,
the tatterdemalion furniture
in shadowy parlors,

> *the silence crosscut by the flies*
> *sank back*
> *into dust . . .*[2]

Temuco, where the poet spent his formative years, was still in the early 1900's a frontier post facing the wild country of the Araucanian Indians to the south, and terminus of the railroad that now continues on to Puerto Montt. With the young Chilean novelist, Jorge Edwards, who knows Neruda well, I visited the house where the poet spent his boyhood while his father worked on the railroad, and we talked to Neruda's nephew, Raúl Reyes, a baker.

Here, happily, nothing seemed to have changed. The fishwives and shrimp girls were still brawling in the streets. The shops were still selling carved wooden stirrups and *huaso* ponchos. Even the rain, that piano of his childhood, as Neruda called it, was still banging away at the tin roof of the room where he had lived until he was sixteen:

> *My boyhood was wet shoes,*
> *broken tree trunks fallen in the forest,*
> *devoured by lianas and beetles; sweet days*
> *over the oat fields, and the golden beard*
> *of my father going out*
> *toward the majesty of the rails . . .*

Even the station around the corner, with its arched shed, was just as he had known it, with the wooden boxcars and caboose waiting to be coupled, and the Mapuches on the platform loaded with silver bangles, hawking their woolen belts.

We climbed the hill called Nielól, high over Temuco and still dotted with Araucaria pine, that

> *. . . tower of Chile, point*
> *of the green land,*
> *pavilion of winter,*
> *ship of fragrance . . .*

It was of this hill that Neruda must have been thinking, that day in Veracruz, Mexico, in 1941, when he recalled

> *. . . a day of the South, my land, a silver day*
> *like a swift fish in the water of the sky,*
> *Loncoche, Lonquimay, Carahue, from above*

[2] "Memorial de Isla Negra" (1964), translated by Ben Belitt in *Pablo Neruda: A New Decade: Poems 1958–1967*. New York, Grove Press, 1969.

scattered, surrounded by silence and roots,
sitting in their thrones of leather and wood . . .

—and how he became one with the dogs of Saavedra to the west, when the girl who had inspired *Veinte Poemas de Amor* abandoned him to his sweet sorrow.

Southern Chile

Oh yes, imprecise snow,
oh yes, trembling full flower of snow,
boreal eyelid, small icy blast—
who called you to the ashen valley?
who dragged you from the eagle's beak
to where your pure waters touch
the terrible rags of my fatherland?

I continued on south, Edwards joining me later in Puerto Montt for the flight to the Straits of Magellan and Cape Horn.

Concepción, Chile's third city and its most important industrially, boasts a major university but has few natural attractions. Every Chilean with an interest in history and the arts, however, has visited it at least once, if only to drive inland to Chillán

. . . the heartland of Chile that matters, where
green hair grows dense in the vineyards,
the grape lives on light
and under the feet of a people, wine is born.[3]

This town (before the earthquake of 1833 that shifted its site—there was another in 1939 that shook it down a second time) saw the birth of Bernardo O'Higgins, the Independence hero, and more recently of Nicanor Parra, the anti-poet mathematician and his sister, Violeta, the folk singer. And here is the great folk market that displays the finest pottery and ceramic sculpture to be found south of Peru. In Chillán, too, may be seen one of the two outstanding mural paintings in Chile, both by Mexicans. Siqueiros painted his barbaric tribute to Indian *guerrilleros* in Chillán in 1941. Gonzales Camareña, in a more sophisticated but less original vein, painted his gigantic "Presencia de America Latino" in 1960-65 at the University of Concepción, attempting to synthesize the whole Hispanic experience out of the same Marxist philosophy.

Valdivia's beauties and pleasures are wholly pastoral. Like all the rich farmland from Temuco south to Puerto Montt, it was settled by German

[3] Translated by Ben Belitt, *ibid.*

immigrants after 1848. They prospered and built tidy frame houses and neat fences, but seem to have contributed nothing to Chile culturally— or even politically, for they have kept out of politics except for an indiscreet enthusiasm for Hitler in the thirties. Here was the Andwanter's grave plot, that Neruda describes, with its

> *founding cadavers: the towheaded gentleman,*
> *his wife with a flair for fine cookery, his sons whom the winter*
> *devoured . . .*
> *Could this teacup of water and oblivion, this secretive*
> *rumble of darkness have nurtured the terror*
> *that paces the solitude, with soaked clothes, in Valdivia?*
> *Was it here the volcano licked out its tongue,*
> *the inexhaustible waters intent upon murder,*
> *the outcry thinned to a scream, ocean's cry against all oblivion?* [4]

There were earthquakes in 1936 and 1960, the latter so severe that it changed the course of the two rivers at whose confluence Valdivia is situated. A local poet who witnessed it told me that he thought Chile's laissez-faire mood is conditioned to some extent by these convulsions. "I saw the richest man in this city become in one second the poorest," he said. "It makes you think twice about spending a life making money— or making anything. Doesn't it make more sense to live for the pleasures of the moment?"

Almost the only sound to be heard in this city of one hundred thousand is the occasional clop-clop of a small horse pulling a grocery cart. And the most pleasurable way to spend a day—or a week, or a month—is to sit in the shade of the arched bridge watching the fishing dories unload their Pacific catch, or drift down the placid river, past the ruined Spanish forts that Lord Cochrane outflanked in 1810, to Corral, and then chug back again. The river fishing is good, and the lakes, from Villarrica in the north to Llanquihue in the south, reflecting adjacent volcanoes, are very beautiful.

Puerto Montt, 675 miles from Santiago, and the southern terminus of the state railways, is gateway not only to the lake district that stretches eastward over the border into Argentina, but to the large offshore island of Chiloe, and to the wilderness extending another thousand miles south through the provinces of Aïsen and Magallenas to Cape Horn. That poet of stony integrity, Gabriela Mistral, made much of her sorrowful song in this region, and Neruda quotes her as saying, "In Chile, it is the skeletal one sees first of all, the profusion of rock in the mountains and sand. . . ."

In her "Sonnets of Death," Gabriela, from Aïsen and Chiloe, dreamed of the hot lands far to the north, and identified them with the love she had lost there:

---

[4] Translated by Ben Belitt, *ibid.*

From the cold niche where men put you
I will take you down to the sun-drenched land.
Men did not know that I would go there to sleep
and that we would dream on the same warm pillow.
In that sun-drenched earth I will bed you down
with the sweetness of a mother for her sleeping child,
and the hard earth will become cradle-smooth
to touch your body of a sleeping boy.
Then I'll go scattering earth and rose-dust
and in the powdery blue of the moon
those weightless spoils will remain forever.
I will go away singing my vengeful song
because to that depth the hand of no woman
will descend to contend for your handful of bones.

Edwards and I took a ferry to Chiloe, that delectable isle whose local mythology had so enraptured Gabriela. It is as unspoiled, and as fiercely independent of the mainland as in the years when it held out alone against independence, preferring to take orders from Madrid as the more distant of despotisms. The villages of Chonchi and Huillinco are pure Chilean Cape Cod, and Ancud's Hotel Prat, with five double beds to a room and no running water, is the perfect antidote to Lake Villarrica's Antumalal where Queen Elizabeth II slept and reputedly found that the running water had tired of running.

Puerto Montt itself is a picturesque fishing port, with its multicolored clapboard shanties running downhill to the docks, and its wooden Parthenon of a cathedral capped with a silver dome; and the town would be handsome indeed if they'd plant a few trees and a little grass along the naked waterfront. At a French restaurant called (improbably) "Stop!" all the wonderful varieties of Chilean seafood were to be found, and a specialty of the Araucanian Indians called *curanto:* shellfish, urchins, roast pork, and potatoes baked together over a pit of hot stones, with butter-soaked biscuits on the side. We stopped at the Angelmo market on the way back into town to buy some of the superb close-woven bread salvers in which the biscuits had been served, but when I tried to photograph the vendor she protested loudly and covered her face. When Jorge asked her why she objected, she replied: "I would lose prestige!"

Petrohue Falls, a couple of hours' drive inland from Puerto Montt, is an awesome conglomerate of white cascades with more than enough power to run all of Chile if industry ever challenges natural beauty in this wilderness of a thousand lakes. It is a favorite vacation area for the Argentines, we were told, though why—with Bariloche [5] and all the superior hotels an hour away—we didn't discover until we crossed

[5] See Chapter 1.

the border and I had a reprise of Swiss prices and authoritarian bland-ness among the rucksackers.

There is nothing bland about Punta Areñas, the world's southernmost city, to which Edwards and I flew. Yugoslav immigrants settled here after World War I with their sheep, cheeses, fishing, lumber, and (later) petroleum enterprises. But the three pioneer families that really made the big fortunes in this wasteland that Chile had assumed to be worthless were the Montes', the Menendez', and the Brauns. They intermarried, spurning the nouveau riches from Zagreb. The original Menendez was an Uruguayan married to a Hungarian, and his castle, a bizarre contraption with thirty-eight bedrooms topped by square cupolas on little campaniles, is presently boarded up while the family dallies in Argentina and the European spas. Elias Braun was a Latvian Jew, and Sara Braun's mansion is now a restaurant, Club de la Unión, a showplace of Punta Areñas. The splendid dinners of *centoyas* (king crab) and *bejereyes* (sea urchins) are served in the greenhouse. But the foyer, with its grossly carved armoires, clusters of gaslights, and huge "real oil" Munich landscapes in one-thou-sand-pound gilded frames, sets the tone.

Near the Menendez' Victorian dream of grandeur, and across from the Ford Agency in the Esso Building at the exact center of the city, is the swingingest night spot in Punta Areñas, with a jazz combo and nineteen lovely *putas*.

Edwards and I were bound to see a penguin before we left Punta Areñas. But flights to Penguin Island, and even across the glaciers of Tierra del Fuego over the Strait, revealed not a one. Finally a sympathetic citizen directed us to the local zoo. There was a scrawny condor in one pen, a family of pigs in another, and the cage labelled PINGUINO contained a dachshund. The only other exhibit was an armadillo, a nervous crea-ture built like a small tank that trotted back and forth incessantly and refused to look at us. "Very medieval and sinister," said Jorge as we gave up our search and walked away. "I'll have bad dreams for a week. Or until I get back home where penguins in my childhood were a dime a dozen on every offshore rock from Zapallár to Pablo's Isla Negra. I won-der whatever happened to them?"

Neruda in His Element: Isla Negra

Isla Negra (Black Island), which is not an island at all, is an hour's drive south of Valparaiso on a rocky Pacific headland. When Neruda acquired the property on the bluff for thirty-five dollars after returning to Chile from his years abroad, his only (then) neighbor, hoping to at-tract tourists, put up a sign renaming it Mar de las Golondrinas (Seaside of the Swallows). "Every night," Neruda told me, "I went out and laid that sign flat on its face. After the fourth night my neighbor came to me and held out his hand: 'O.K., you win. Isla Negra it shall remain.'"

Isla Negra, Chile
House of Pablo Neruda, 1969

The whole Neruda personality could be described in terms of this house, how it grew, where it is going. But Matilde Neruda, who came out to welcome me at the time of my first visit, is best described as the presiding genius by the poet himself:

> *Your house has the sound of a train in the afternoon:*
> *a buzzing of wasps, a singing of casseroles . . .*
> *while you move upward or down on the stairs, walking or running,*
> *singing or planting, sewing or cooking or nailing things down,*
> *writing, returning; or gone: when all the world says: It is winter.*[6]

My room was in the round tower. Nothing startling there except that the balcony railing had fallen the night I arrived, and I almost walked off into space. Perhaps I was a little startled too (and grateful, for the night was cold) when a maid knocked at my door and came in holding a hot water bottle wrapped in flannel: *"Un balsita, señor?"*

Under this room, and connected to it by a booklined balcony, is the famous living room with its open fireplace and monumental wooden ships' figureheads looming from the shadowy corners. Jorge Edwards was with Neruda in Paris when the poet saw one of these beauties for the first time at an expensive dealer's, and he remembers how upset Neruda was when he brought with him to the negotiations for its purchase the following day a friend who happened to be a member of the French Communist Party. Edwards remembers also a many-coursed

---

[6] Translated by Ben Belitt from "Cien Sonetos de Amor," *op. cit.*

luncheon with Ilya Ehrenburg at the Dôme, which Neruda topped off with a plate of several dozen oysters he happened to see passing on a tray. The Russian writer looked at the Chilean poet with amazement and murmured: *"Pablo, tu es bar-bare!"* to which Neruda quipped back good-naturedly: "Ehrenburg, you are a victim of Western corruption."

About being a bon vivant, a gourmet, a collector, a lover of handmade things, Neruda has no reason to be apologetic. It is part of his persona, and the communists will be well advised to go on taking him as he is in return for his prestigious support, which he gives without reservations. Ever since his surrealist days in Paris he has collected bizarre objects as well as works of art, and at Isla Negra the oddities are concentrated in the bar. I had a good chance to catalog them one afternoon when a family of autograph seekers barged in and the poet was graciously obliging a girl who wanted hers inside a Swedish matchbox.

Antechamber: both walls glassed, with shelves containing bottles in the shapes of dogs, politicians, babies, violins, Eiffel Towers, dice, etc. One shelf has bottles with painted wooden crucifixions inside them. The carpet is one of those wooden-trellis deck mats.

Other furnishings: a bidet, painted with roses; outsize insulators and shoes; a small icebox decorated with tarot cards; a poster issued recently by the Peking faction of Chile's communists: NERUDA GO HOME! On the ceiling beams: autographs of poets burnt into the wood: Federico, Paul Eluard, Alberto Rojas Jiménez. On the bar itself: an ancient horned gramophone, a thirty-eight-inch bottle of cognac, a painted carving of a vaudeville type Negro in a wicker chair. (Half the catalog.)

Neruda's library and writing room are in a separate building a few feet from the main house which angles around the sand dune with fine views of the surf breaking on the black rocks below. There is another monumental mermaid hanging here, with bare breasts and erect crimson nipples; on a later visit I overheard the last two words (in English) of Neruda's comments while showing it off to Bill Negron: ". . . ve-ry jui-cy." The library doubles as a picture gallery, prints of favorite poets include: Whitman on a mountain peak in a loincloth (New York, 1870), Poe, Verlaine, Essenin, Keats, Baudelaire, Mayakovsky, and Rimbaud, so alike with their sullen mouths. At the end of the gallery is a rotunda. A door to the left leads to a half-enclosed courtyard in which stands a stuffed horse, the nose of which Neruda loved to pat as a child when it graced a livery stable in Temuco (the people of that city presented it to him when the stable burned down some years ago). A door to the right leads to the little room in which Neruda writes his poems. The only object on the writing table, besides pen and paper, is a small daguerreo-type of Whitman. Whitman who wrote those edifying poems . . .

It displeases the esthete to edify: the poem with a moral
that went out of fashion when the poem taught the man

251

how to live like a man, leaving behind its violet
cachet in the soul. I speak of the whithers and wherefores
as I choose, from the throne to the oil slick
that bloodies the world, asking
How much? while the grains of my anger grow greater
with my How many? syllables speaking all the world's languages:
yes, I speak, I speak on; and will be, if need be, a cracked violin
or a troubadour wracked by the truth and the doubts of the world.[7]

A Day with Nicanor Parra

Since the death of Gabriela Mistral in New York twelve years ago, Neruda has so completely dominated Chilean poetry that there have seemed only two ways for other poets to survive: to hate him or to join him. Pablo de Rokha, a poet of considerable ambition and sonority, tried hating Neruda. Unfortunately their politics coincided, so de Rokha wrote a whole book, *Neruda and I*, to explain the fine points of their difference, ranting and raving, and calling Neruda everything from "an enemy of the workers" to a "bourgeois imperialist." Nobody took this seriously, so finally de Rokha committed suicide. The joiners haven't fared much better. Their imitative noises are lost in the Nerudian torrent. Only Nicanor Parra devised a strategy to maintain his identity. He defined it as "a wrestling match with the elements; the anti-poet concedes himself the right to say everything without caring about the practical consequences . . ." When I met him he was amusing a dinner party in Santiago by drawing for the guests little Thurberish pictures with one-line poems attached, for instance, the Statue of Liberty under

USA
where
liberty is a

Or, when I told him about the cemetery in Guayaquil

LOS POBRES
que
son
realmente pobre
no
tienen
ni

✝ ✝ ✝

[7] Translated by Ben Belitt, *ibid.*

"For five years, between the ages of twenty-five and thirty," he told me, "I was so bemused by Whitman I couldn't write poetry at all. I snapped out of it when I realized he was a bag of potatoes. Poetry is a funny thing. It's only a convention that we poets do it better than other people. The only really essential ingredient is madness. The case studies in Krafft-Ebbing are pure poetry." And then he quoted Vicente Huidobro's

> *Don't sing the rose—*
> *make it open in the poem.*

I talked to Parra about the suffocating influence of Neruda on the way to Isla Negra, my last day in Chile. He had offered to drive me from Santiago to say goodbye to Neruda, whom I hadn't seen in several months. "By his very presence," Parra said, as we proceeded to get lost in his Volkswagen, "Neruda forced Pablo de Rokha to be a windbag, straining for effect. He compelled me to be a buffoon. I'm only beginning to get over that now. For the first time I'm beginning to write naturally, about what really moves me. So now I'm going to start a new revolution —perhaps religion is the better word. I will no longer be the prostitute I had become in my desperation to achieve purity. In order to be pure you have to fight dirty. Fidel wanted so much to be pure—and now he has to trade with Franco. No principles are worth dying for. Life is the only absolute value. To enhance life one must improvise and solve problems little by little."

"Were you speaking ironically," I said, "when you remarked in *Discursos* that Neruda's life had been completely dedicated to the cause of humanity?"

"No," he answered. "Pablo has been the only Chilean faithful to his political credo, right or wrong."

"Then you agree with the sentiment he expresses in the poem 'To My Party'—'You have made me see the brightness of the world and the possibility of happiness'?"

"In those days," Parra replied, " I was close to the party myself. But my own spiritual development turned me toward skepticism, toward solitude, toward individuals who are actually there when you talk to them, not ghosts who are not permitted to invent. You could call me a sniper from the trees. Political poetry tends to become preaching. It ceases to be mad, and if poetry is no longer mad it is no longer poetry. It's a metaphysical impossibility to write a political poem. Pantomime is the supreme artistic form—"

"Pantomime?"

"Gesture—with meaning, and humor—farce. It probably comes from my childhood fascination with the circus clowns in Chillán. True seriousness is comic. It is Whitman's limitation, like Milton's, that he had no sense of humor."

"Pablo has a great sense of humor," I said, "as in the 'Ode to the Socks.'"

"Yes. His humor saves him from that metaphysical impossibility. He writes political poems and then forgets them. He returns to writing poems. He thinks about himself. He thinks about Chile, not as it ought to be but as it is—"

"And you, Nicanor—?"

"I'm beginning to come out of my defensive position. I want to make people laugh and think and even cry. I'm even writing poems about Chile. Here's the start of an unwritten one:

> They're always fat before they're forty.
> They go around hawking at the sky.
> They don't recognize the merits of anyone.
> They claim they're sick but they're malingering.
> And worst of all
> They leave dirty paper in the park.

I laughed. "That's going to get you in trouble with some of your teen-age idolators."

He laughed. "I get in trouble with everybody. I shocked your friend the critic Alfred Kazin once at Stonybrook by saying 'The more we read, the less we write.' Critics need to be shocked, don't you think? I remember Robert Lowell once at a conference in Caracas turning to Kazin and saying quite deadpan: 'Alfred, do you really like literature?'"

It was late in the afternoon by the time we got on the right road again. We were approaching Neruda's driveway when Parra pointed to a house right above it and said: "I almost bought that one."

"You mean," I said, surprised, "you could actually live that close to him?"

"I'm so sure of myself now," he said with a smile, "I could live under Pablo's bed!"

Neruda, who tends to romanticize Chile more than Parra does, and to see the enemy outside rather than under the skin, had just gotten back from a long day inspecting nearby school sites with the Minister of Education. He greeted us cordially, but his eyes were heavy with sleep. "Wait!" he said, lumbering up the stairs for his irreversible siesta, "Matilde will give you tea. I'll be down in an hour and then we can have dinner."

As we walked up and down the beach talking, Parra suggested we sneak out.

"Why?" I said.

"Because I know you want to keep our date for dinner with Jorge Edwards and Enrique Lihn—you are an American, no? And I know

Pablo well enough to know what he'll say when he wakes up. He'll say 'Jorge is a young man. I am an old man. If you don't have dinner with me you may never see me again.' He's lonely and quite demanding, you know."

I asked him whether he thought Pablo supported himself in his lavish style entirely from the royalties of his poetry.

"Impossible," he said. "Even though he's the best-selling poet in the Spanish language by far—impossible."

"Then how?"

"It's a mystery. Of course he writes for papers, including that regular column in *Ercilla,* and these pay better than poetry. Perhaps the University gives him a stipend. Perhaps the party helps him—"

"And what will happen to this house and the grounds when he dies? Will he leave them to Matilde?"

"What would Matilde do here? He's bought her an apartment in Santiago, I'm sure. The house and grounds will be left to the party, I suppose."

I left him walking on the beach, and on the way up to the house I thought of two things Neruda had said. The first helps explain why his individualism survived his Marxism. "My people, friends, neighbors, uncles and parents in Temuco," he said, "scarcely expressed themselves. My poetry had to remain secret, strongly separated from its origins." The second testified to Chile's sway over his emotions: "My heart is still touched by those wooden houses, those huddled streets that start in Victoria and end in Puerto Montt, and which sound like guitars when the wind blows through them." I got down the *Collected Works* from the shelf in his library and reread the conclusion to the "Ode to the Socks":

> *. . . Notwithstanding, I resisted*
> *the sharp temptation of keeping them*
> *as schoolboys collect fireflies*
> *or scholars texts.*
> *I resisted the impulse*
> *of putting them in a cage*
> *of gold, of giving them*
> *birdseed and rosy melon chunks.*
> *As discoverers in the forest*
> *deliver green venison*
> *to the spit*
> *and eat it*
> *with remorse, I stretched my feet*
> *and put on those beautiful*
> *socks, and then my shoes.*
> *So this is the moral*
> *of my ode:*

twice can beauty
be beautiful,
and that which is good
is doubly good
when it concerns
two socks
in winter.

Goodbye and Goodbye and Goodbye

Through the window I watched Nicanor striding up the beach, a half smile on that rugged, handsome face that makes me think of a successful executive, or the tweedy, retired outdoorsman in the ad, or Lee J. Cobb; but never a professor of physics, or a poet. Or is that the way an anti-poet should look?

Every real poet, Neruda included, is an anti-poet part of the time, of course. But Neruda—like the compassionate internationalist Whitman, who was an outspoken hawk during our imperialist rape of Mexico—doesn't attempt to be consistent. The single-minded South American youth, that revolutionary who despises compromise above all else, hates Neruda for his party-line orthodoxy which makes him countenance the Soviet rape of Czechoslovakia, mistakenly assuming from this that the poet has no principles and that the poems are tainted. But like Shakespeare, whose amorality is notorious and who has been accused of justifying everything from race prejudice to imperialism, Neruda goes right on writing universal poems.

Parra, on the other hand, may be the victim of his consistency. By taking greater risks, by destroying the idea of poetry as an exceptional language, he may come closer to the truth, sociologically speaking, but he sacrifices any chance of modifying it through incantation or a vision beyond reality. Paradise lost and regained (or at least regainable) is Neruda's theme, but Parra's world is all gray, always was, and always will be. And he falls back inescapably on the Francophile vogue that has plagued South American verse since Rubén Darío, the vogue of avoiding homely or idealizing clichés via the negative romanticism of noncommittal obscurantism. Gonzálo Rojas, a Concepción poet who had been in Havana with Parra attending one of Fidel Castro's cultural *kaffeeklatches*, told me about a journalist who had asked Parra whether he recommended anti-poetry for the young.

"People have the right to it," Parra had answered, "and the old wouldn't lose anything by participating in it either."

"But what is the point of it?" the journalist had insisted.

"To remove the masks."

"From whom?"

"From the politician, the priest, the policeman, the taxi driver, the father of an ordinary family."

Jorge Edwards had been in Cuba with Parra too, perhaps at the same writers' conference, and one night in Santiago when we were walking home past Santa Lucia he turned to me with that characteristically wise, amused expression and said: "Nicanor is not a political animal. Neither am I, as you know; yet I was moderately impressed with the progress the Cuban workers seemed to be making. So I was amazed at how strongly Nicanor reacted to the regimentation and hardships. Instead of talking like a leftist as he usually does, he was talking like an extreme conservative! In other words, he was vulnerable to what he saw, as Pablo from his fixed political position would not have been."

Parra came in and said he had another poem about Chile in his head, if I wanted to take it down. It went like this:

> *It makes you laugh to see the peasants of Santiago*
> *with that studied frown*
> *going up and down the streets of the Center*
> *or the streets of the outskirts,*
> *worried, pale, frightened to death,*
> *because they have no money,*
> *because they can't pay interest on a loan,*
> *because they are too poor to publish a book;*
> *taking for granted the city and its inhabitants,*
> *ignoring the fact that the inhabitants have yet to be born,*
> *and will not be born before they die,*
> *and that Santiago de Chile is a desert.*
> *We think we are a country*
> *and the truth is we are hardly a landscape.*

Neruda came downstairs at last, and after trying unsuccessfully, just as Parra had predicted, to talk me out of being a good American and keeping our dinner date with Jorge and Pilár Edwards, he suggested we have one more cup of tea.

He was disturbed when I told him that Borges resented his not having included Perón in his inferno of villainous *caudillos.*

"That is ridiculous, Selden. I have held many mass meetings here against Perón, and I have written against him too. Perón disturbs Borges because Borges is part of the upper class Perón disturbed. Perón was a special kind of politician, you know, like our Alessandri—the old Alessandri. He did many things that had to be done, good things; and of course many bad things, too, because he was a dictator. But Borges despises and dislikes him for the wrong reasons—for the good things he did against the landowners and oligarchs."

I told him I'd be off to Easter Island tomorrow, and he regretted that he and Matilde wouldn't be able to make it as they had planned. I told him I'd heard that Yevgeny Yevtushenko had flown there from Santiago last year, and I asked him what his impression of the Russian poet had been.

"It's difficult for me to judge how good a poet he really is since I don't read Russian," he said. "Some Russians say that Voznesensky is a better poet."

"But as a man—?"

"Yevtushenko seemed very nervous when he was here," Neruda replied. "Very worried that he wouldn't have a big enough audience. I was talking and reading poetry with him in the same hall but he was still worried. He kept counting the heads and taking pills—tranquilizers, I suppose. There was no need. We had a bigger audience than the hall would hold. When he began to read he forgot his nervousness."

It was in Easter Island, two days later, that I heard the story of a similar poetry reading in Santiago, a story that threw a good deal of light on Neruda himself. It seems that he had just returned from the Soviet Union, some years ago, and the overflow audience that came to hear him speak that night was expecting sensational political revelations and pronouncements. But he opened up by saying that it would bore them, and him, to say the usual things; he preferred to talk about the way they catch fish in the Volga River—and proceeded to talk about nothing else for the whole two hours, holding them spellbound.

"That's Neruda's genius," said Edmundo Edwards, Jorge's young cousin who told me the story, and who had been there, "—to talk about the simplest things with the greatest penetration." A pretty good definition of poetry . . . to which Neruda, in one of his poems, adds:

And I sing because I sing because I sing.

INDEX

INDEX